ONE LIFE -
ONE CENTURY

Dorothy V. Wilson

One Life - One Century

ISBN: 1987439759
ISBN-13: 978-1987439755

This book is dedicated to
Albertine Roseline (Bertie) Clawiter Courtnage Moore,
without whom there would be no story—and no author.

Dorothy V. Courtnage Wilson

Other books by Dorothy V. Wilson

THE GREEN TUNNEL, a serial killer mystery

ACKNOWLEDGMENTS

A special thanks to the Great Falls Tribune for details about the fair airplane collision, Charlie Russell's funeral, and other historical details from the past. And huge thanks to the Big Sandy residents who wrote A GATHERING OF MEMORIES: A HISTORY OF THE BIG SANDY COMMUNITY where I gleaned many details of life during those homesteading years. Also, my thanks to the Smithsonian Magazine for their detailed description of a strychnine death.

I wish to thank the Emerald Coast Writers' critique members for their fine tuning and polishing of my manuscript.

And, a particular thanks and appreciation to my gifted editor, Laurie Allen. She patiently worked with my narrative from start to finish and assimilated our ideas to craft the cover for ONE LIFE - ONE CENTURY.

Our Bertie inspired Ellaraine Lockie, a broadly published author of poetry and nonfiction books, to write a poem about her aunt's life. Lockie is the author of seventeen books, Poetry Editor for *Lilipoh Magazine* and has won sixty-some poetry competitions. Aunt Bertie became her role model as a child and they remained close. After visiting Bertie in the nursing home near the end of her aunt's life, Lockie wrote the award winning "Wellspring" that has won two competitions.

Wellspring

She collected waterfalls
Circulated them from the ground
to river to ocean to sky inside her
Five hundred six at final count
Her Blue Ribbon cascading 1450 feet
down Hi'ilawe Falls

The hydro-electric power supplying fuel
for ninety-four years of farm working
square dance calling, accordion playing, art creation
And car tripping with the mannequin Sylvester
napping in the backseat in her dead husband's suit
Hat tilted over imposter eyes

Until she couldn't travel anymore
And the waterfalls plunged
under fingertips on photographs
She scratched off the honey rhubarb
scent of wild calendula
The used litter box fetor of French marigolds
rendered faint by disinfectant of cypress
and ponderosa pines
All of it better than the attic smell of old skin
or urined air in an Alzheimer's ward

Until she couldn't see or smell anymore
But some days the splash and roar of water
still play like old movies
across the cracked walls in her mind
Launching her up and out of the wheelchair
To show her friends in the TV room
how she can still hula
If she holds on tight to the handles
and listens hard for the music

Ellaraine Lockie

My mother told me tales of her remarkable life all my childhood. As an adult, I recorded her stories once again to write this book. Other than detailed scene descriptions, the sagas are much the way she told them to me—her thoughts, her words. The cover photograph is the actual homestead.

CHAPTER 1

A fiery orb broke the horizon, illuminating an earth that little cared about the special event taking place on May 28, 1906—the country still reeled from the April mega earthquake that destroyed San Francisco. No one cared about an amazing child's birth except her parents. The baby's first cry burst forth from a powerful set of lungs announcing she would one day entertain thousands. Dark hair, the typical baby-button nose, and sparkling hazel eyes completed the adorable bundle. Albertine Roseline Clawiter (CLA-viter) came to life on the family farm near the small town of Amenia about twenty miles west of Fargo, North Dakota. Max and Adelia (Della) Clawiter had married fourteen months earlier. The proud parents were thankful to have Della's mother there to assist with the birth. They were not happy about what happened next.

No one knew if family tradition or parental domination ruled, but Della, the mother, who carried the baby for nine months and labored fifteen-hours, seemed to have little say in the matter. Della's parents chose the infant's poetic name. One wanted to name the baby Albertine; the other insisted on Roseline. The dispute raged on, neither grandparent giving in, and the arguments grew louder and more abrasive. For a week the infant was known as "Baby." A weary and glassy-eyed Della didn't want to hurt either parent's feelings; to solve the impossible situation, she suggested using both names. Surprised to meet no resistance as to which came first, she chose Albertine and the matter was settled—for a while. Della and Max soon found Albertine too long for conversation and nicknamed her Albertha. Afterward they shortened it still further to Bertha. Later another problem would arise—she detested all four names.

Bertha's earliest memory was the day Della clad her in a Sunday-best dress and took her to Amenia. She was three. They visited a man with a box on stilts, which did magic tricks, with a blinding flash. Like most first-time parents captivated by their daughter's birth, Adelia and Max wanted a professional photograph. The photographer encased the picture in an elegantly carved, gilded wooden frame. A diminutive Bertha posed in a white, handmade dress with lace trim, one arm draped over the back of a plump, overstuffed chair. Her dark hair, parted in the middle, sported a gigantic white bow; black bows adorned each shoe. She was the picture of stylish-cute.

These framed photographs were an extravagant but well-loved fashion of the times. Every home had at least one and four hung on Max and Della's walls: one wedding photograph each of their parents, another of their own nuptials and that of young Bertha. All six adults, on the happiest day of their lives, are somber, not a hint of smile cracks their lips. Bertha wore an impish grin.

In the early days of photography, people needed to hold the pose a long time for the exposure to be effective, so no one smiled. When photographic equipment improved, it appeared hard to break the habit because sober faces lasted into the 1940s. Then photographers began urging their clients to "say cheese."

A few hand-painted plates—a fad of the times—and those framed photographs encircled the family dining room, providing the sole *décor,* as it did in most homes. One afternoon, four-year-old Bertha sat staring at her parents' wedding portrait. The gold shadowbox held her mother's wedding headpiece above their photograph with the sheer veil tucked around it.

"Why is your veil in the picture, Mama?"

"I wanted to save it."

"Where did you meet Papa?"

"I met him right here."

Bertha wrinkled her forehead. "But Papa said he was born in Minnesota."

"For heaven's sake, let's put an end to all these questions. Your papa's full name is Max William Frederick Clawiter. Born in *Schneidermill*, Germany, in 1877, his family immigrated to the United States when he was five. They landed at Castle Clinton and all their seven trunks were lost. They had nothing but the clothes on their back, so your papa doesn't have a birth certificate or know how old he is. He grew up in Minnesota, but couldn't find work so he came to North Dakota and my papa hired him.

"I was born on August 26, 1884. I was seventeen when I first saw your papa, and I thought he was good looking with his dark brown hair and eyes. We were the same height, five-and-a-half-feet. I was slender and your papa said I had a pretty face.

"I never met many boys other than farmers, but I saw your papa every day. We fell in love and married on March 29, 1905, in the Lutheran Church.

"Your papa was so handsome in his dark suit buttoned high on the chest. He wore a boutonniere that matched my headpiece—the one in the picture frame. His thick mustache was waxed at the tip ends, hiding his upper lip. His hair was slicked back with oil and parted in the middle. He looked very stylish."

"Yes, Mama, but tell me about the veil in the picture."

"Everyone thought my dress was beautiful. I designed it myself. The lace insets in the yoke ended under my chin. Making the hem lace took me hours, but my headpiece was what everyone raved about. It had white imitation flower buds entwined on a net-like cap in front of a crowned ruffled back. Long tendrils of the same flower buds trickled down in front of my ears.

"After the wedding, the animals needed care and we went home to the farm we rented from my folks. Now you know everything about your family—let's get back to work."

Della had been a happy newlywed until gruesome news arrived. Her bridesmaid died mere days after the wedding. When the family later exhumed the body to relocate it, they discovered she'd been buried alive. Della was horrified realizing how her friend suffered in those last agonizing moments. That night and every night thereafter, a horrific nightmare haunted her: white mask—gaping, with hollow eyes—floating in a dark box, crashing from side to side, the screaming mask streaked long, blood-red hair behind. Then Della would awaken shrieking, her blue-flannel nightgown clammy from sweat. She struggled to erase the horror from her mind. But the fear that it could happen to her plagued her existence.

Otherwise, life on the farm was good, and Della had her mother's help to become adjusted to married life. She was happy. But Max felt deep discontentment renting property. He dreamed the impossible dream: owning a farm. He had no money.

In due course, Della gave birth to eight children: Scharlotte Minnie in 1908; Mamie Sarah in 1909 and Ella Dorthea in 1912. About two years separated the birth of all Della's children except a four-year lapse due to a miscarriage. Large families were a trend of the times, and many women died young from bearing children too close together. Like most farm mothers, Della gave birth to all her children at home. Sometimes a doctor delivered her child, but often the baby arrived with the assistance of a neighboring woman.

Either times became too hard or the thrill wore off when Della's second child arrived, because neither she nor any of the other children had a framed portrait. A group picture of Bertha, Charlotte, and baby Mamie went unframed. All three girls wore elegant dresses with embroidered flowers, satin stitching, and lace. The oldest girls still wore huge bows in their hair. The baby wore an elegant christening gown with a yoke of lace and a petticoat with three rows of hemline lace. The dresses required many hours of stitching and crocheting, and one has to wonder how Della found time to do fancy work for herself and three daughters with all her other chores.

Max cared for the farm livestock, but Della had livestock of her own to contend with—houseflies. They were horrendous. Every time someone entered the house, Della yelled, "Quick, shut the door, you're letting in the flies." In self-defense, she mounted a brigade of children swinging towels to shoo the filthy pests out the open door. It was an exercise in futility because more flies came inside than were shooed outside. Later, Max brought home flypaper. Della opened the sticky strip and tacked it to the ceiling. Curling downward, dead flies soon filled the strip, ending the towel war.

When she wasn't fighting flies, Bertha often walked to

her grandparents' farm and played in the small creek flowing through the property. Grandmother Scharlotte's flower bed enchanted Bertha. She loved pretty flowers. One day, the sun burned bright in a cloudless sky, and she sat on the porch shaded by a giant maple tree. Bertha watched the twittering birds dart from limb to limb. Loud chatter drew her attention and she laughed at two squirrels playing tag around the maple; they scrambled up, down and around, bushy tails flying. Pansies grew beside the porch, and she began counting happy pansy faces when she caught a whiff of rose scent. She wanted to pick a rose for her mama. She didn't dare. Grandma grew the best roses in the county. Pesticides didn't exist, but her bushes were pest free and she would be furious if Bertha, or anyone else, picked one. Grandpa joked— when Grandma wasn't around—that even the bugs were afraid to touch those damn roses. The roses were hale and hearty because whenever Scharlotte finished washing dishes, she drenched the bushes with soapy Fels-Naptha dishwater. The rose bushes thrived—the bugs found less dangerous lodging.

Sometimes, Grandpa took Bertha home in his convertible horse-drawn buggy, the latest craze. The buggy's collapsible canvas roof could be pulled over the passengers if it rained, and she always pestered Grandpa to "make the top work," raining or not.

When Bertha visited one afternoon, Grandma, whom Bertha thought as "bossy and mean," became enraged with her husband. She launched a heavy cast-iron frying pan straight at his head. Her aim was off and the pan struck him in the shoulder. He retreated to the barn. Bertha idolized her grandpa and rushed out to console him. She crawled upon his lap, put her arms around his neck and whispered, "I'm sorry, Grandpa." A soothing hug followed.

Bertha walked home. "Mama, why is Grandma always so mean to Grandpa?"

Della sighed. "You don't know anything about your grandparents, do you?"

"No, but why is Grandma so mean to him?"

"Sit down and I'll tell you about them. Your grandfather, John Wahowske, was born in 1841 and your grandmother thirteen years later, both in Poland.

"Your grandmother spoke five languages and translated for the marine dock authorities. Few females worked in those days, so she probably was worldlier than other women. Her life is a love story—of sorts. She'd loved a man named Charlie Bishop. Her parents forbade her to marry him, so she decided—daring for the times— if she became pregnant, they must let her marry him. She was wrong. Her parents then forced her to marry John Wahowske, who adored her. She loathed him as much as he loved her. Her parents told him about the coming blessed event, and he agreed to accept the baby, but he refused to give the child his name. So her first born was a Bishop.

"Your grandfather fought in two wars and didn't want to fight in another." He and Scharlotte immigrated to America—in a way. They were stowaways. Cleverly masquerading as cooks, they sneaked aboard a passenger and cattle boat sailing for the U.S.A. in 1875. It's not known if they made use of their culinary skills, but their adventure was successful. They were never caught. The stowaways landed in Galveston, Texas. Their story, passed down through the family, created a mystery. Today, no one knows if baby Bishop was left behind in the interim or if they found a way to stow away him too.

"Your grandparents stayed in Galveston a year to learn English and save money. Then they traveled north by an oxen wagon and eventually landed near Amenia in

1880. All new homesteaders lived in anything cheap they could build fast: warm in winter and cool in summer sod houses, tar-paper shacks, tent-like log huts, and in your grandparents' case, a root cellar until he completed their home.

"Your grandmother never learned to love her husband during their entire marriage. Her temper was legendary and, considering the life forced on her, she'd good reason for her rage. Whenever she became angry with your grandfather, she hurled pots, pans—whatever was at hand—as he ran for the door. Her often-erupting fury didn't seem to dampen his enthusiasm—they had twelve children.

"Now maybe you can understand. Your grandmother's life was not one of her choosing. Her life has been hard in many ways."

Della buzzed about the kitchen one morning preparing breakfast and Bertha helped. "Watch the sausage, Bertha; don't let it burn. I'm going down to the cellar." Della flipped back the small braided throw rug, opened the trapdoor, descended the ladder and Bertha heard a horrific scream followed by a loud thud. She ran to the opening and gasped. A broken rung dangled near the ladder's top and her mother lay on the floor shrieking, "Bertha, run. Fetch Papa."

Terrified, Bertha bolted out the door screaming, "Papa! Papa! Mama fell down the cellar." Frantic, Max raced for the house; he knew something Bertha didn't. Della was pregnant. Max couldn't carry his wife up the ladder for fear of breaking another rung. After great effort, he managed to push her up. Bertha stood nearby paralyzed in fear. Her mama must be dying because Papa was so upset. "Oh, please God," she pleaded, "don't let Mama die." No one told her anything and she cried as

Max ran to the barn to harness the treasured Flora and Dora to fetch the doctor.

It was an age when a good team of horses almost equaled their weight in gold, and that day Flora and Dora were golden as they thundered down the road, almost a blur. The team didn't look special; they weren't even the same size. But their synchronized gait blessed them with stupendous speed. Bertha would later say, "The horses understood an amazing number of verbal commands. If they needed to run fast, Papa stroked their heads and talked to them first, and then they ran like the wind. He never tied the reins when he stopped; he only ordered the horses to stay. They never budged from the spot."

The team made an astonishing run for the doctor, but Della miscarried. Any miscarriage was a heartbreaking ordeal. Max was devastated. He'd lost the long-awaited son to join his family of four females.

Della's sister came to care for the family while Della recuperated. Bertha's little pink ear was "accidentally" pressed against the door, when she overheard her mother tell her sister about the miscarriage. Surprised, Bertha rushed out to tell her sisters. Della hadn't told the children, but that wasn't unusual. Things of a sexual nature were never spoken of. Primness, religion, or both, forbade it.

CHAPTER 2

All the children were baptized in the Box Elder Lutheran Church. Della, more religious than Max, insisted the children kneel at their bedside each night for prayers. German was the family's first language, so conversation, prayers and songs were in German. One prayer began, "I am small, my heart is clean; Nobody can live in it, but Jesus alone." Another started "Tired am I going to rest, close my eyes tight," but telling this story at age ninety-six, Bertha couldn't remember the rest of the English translation. However, she could still recite the entire prayer in German after not speaking the language for eighty-five years.

Naturally, Christmas was the children's favorite holiday. The family gathered around the fir tree in 1912 for baby Ella's first Christmas. Kerosene lamps were dimmed to emphasize the candle-lit tree. The room glowed with soft yellow light that flickered shadows on the walls, weaving magical patterns. Mesmerized kids stood in awed silence. Suddenly, the tree burst into crackling orange flames. Three-year-old Mamie ran to the tree and picked up a tiny fallen angel. Her hair caught fire. Grabbing a towel, Della threw it over her screaming daughter's head, to smother the flames. Max, in utter panic, made a dreadful decision. Grabbing the burning tree by the trunk, he ran to the door, flung the tree on the floor, snatched the door open, reached into the tree again, and threw it outside. Della shrieked. And, Max did a bit of bellowing himself.

Della placed a washtub on two chairs and poured in a pail of cold milk, the home cure for burns in those days. "Bertha, you must be a big girl now and take care of Papa. You make him keep his hand in that milk." The family didn't have a phone and Della ran a half mile to her parents' house to call the doctor.

Bertha tried to follow her mother's orders. But Max, delirious with pain, flailed his burnt hand in the air with skin flying off in all directions. In his frenzy, he appeared to be shooting at ducks and howling, "I'll get them sons-a-bitches."

When Della returned, Bertha burst into tears. "Oh, Mama, I tried. I tried, but Papa wouldn't listen to me; he just kept cussing." The event was a traumatic memory for all, and a recollection *burned* into Max's brain as well. His hand healed, but Della still lived with her harrowing dreams.

Her nightmares of being buried alive had haunted her for years, screams rousing her with pounding heart and shortened breath. Della could not erase the image of her friend waking in her coffin, only to suffocate. She needed to lay her fears to rest, but how? After one horrific night, she extracted a solemn vow from Bertha. With one hand on the Bible and the other over her heart, a very serious Bertha swore if her mother died, she would open Della's vein herself to be sure no blood flowed before burial. Finally, Della slept without nightmares and exciting news soon entered her waking world.

Max's brother Will had acquired a homestead three miles from Big Sandy in 1911. He and his wife Sophy ran a chicken and egg business, delivering to town every day. The next year, Will telephoned his parents and asked to have Max call him. Expensive long-distance calls were rare and used only for emergencies. Realizing it must be important, Max called at once.

"Oh, Max," Will said, "You gotta get out here quick. My neighbor is giving up his homestead. No one knows about it yet. You can buy it if you get here fast."

"Has he worked it long enough to own it?"

"No, but he can sell it as a relinquishment."

The U.S. Congress passed the Homestead Act in 1862. Any U.S. citizen who lived on the land for six months of the year for three years could receive a deed to the land. If he or she wanted to quit before then, the homesteader could sell the property as a relinquishment. The new owner would then finish the required time and acquire the land title. If a homesteader didn't fulfill the residency requirement, "standby watchers" contested the filing and legally took over someone's property. Acquiring a homestead by this method took less time—and less work. Montana became a state in 1889 and by 1912, little free land remained. A relinquishment sounded like the best and perhaps only chance for Max to acquire a farm. He was aboard the next train.

CHAPTER 3

Max arrived in Big Sandy after a heavy snowfall. Will met him at the railway station in his sleigh and they left immediately. Arriving at the homestead, the horses fell up to their bellies in a snow-filled coulee. The horses jumped out, but the men struggled thirty minutes to free the sleigh. Then Will asked, "Do you want to look around some more?"

Still pale and shaken, Max said, "No, no, I've seen enough." Despite their misadventure, Max was eager to become a Big Sandy resident.

When Montana opened to homesteading in 1910, the prairie disappeared overnight. Big Sandy was supported only by small farms and the population was around 700 people. Because of its proximity to Fort Assiniboine, it soon sprouted new enterprises: churches, two livery stables, two bars, an opera house, a hotel, a blacksmith, and two "mysterious houses" with red lights in the windows. Big Sandy became so successful that some homesteaders sold their relinquishment and opened a business in town to make a better living supplying the hard-working farmers.

Signing the relinquishment papers, Max's hand shook. He laid down the pen and a jolt of joy shot through his body. For the sum of 200 dollars, he became a proud property owner.

Descending from his state of euphoria, Max departed at once for North Dakota. He was excited to tell Della, but she would have to hear it from him—he wasn't about to make another long-distance phone call. Della was as excited as Max about the news. They needed to decide what to do with everything they'd acquired in seven years of marriage. Electing to take only the essentials and sell everything else, the kids received a limit and choice as to which toys they could take. They opted to keep their doll dresser and cupboard, sacrificing the toy bed and table. It broke the children's hearts and the younger ones cried. To console them, Della said, "Don't worry, Uncle Will is a carpenter and he'll make you a new bed and table."

For a long time after they reached Montana, Bertha asked her mother, "When is Uncle Will going to make the table and bed?" As so often happens with hasty promises made to children, it never happened.

Auction day arrived all too soon. Patches of lacy clouds clustered the brilliant blue sky. A chilly nip sliced the air as Della and neighboring women made sandwiches and pots of hot coffee to soothe the bidders' chilled bones. A stiff breeze floated the aroma of fresh brew across the barnyard, and Della darted to and fro handing out hot steaming mugs. People came from miles around. The event was a "big do," nearly party atmosphere. Neighbors who knew Flora and Dora, the renowned family buggy team, asked Max, "Are you selling the buggy team?"

Hands on his hips, Max said, "There isn't enough money to buy them," and he turned down some lucrative offers. It was the right decision because the horses would be called on for some dire emergencies in Montana.

At the auction, bittersweet emotions washed over Della and Max, as they watched their possessions sell for far less than anticipated. Still, they looked forward to their new life. Max decided to take only necessary farm machinery and animals. Della added basic furniture and packed dishes and other breakables in barrels filled with oats intended for future seed and horse feed. They loaded everything into half a boxcar Max rented from the Great Northern Railway. Many families utilized these "immigrant cars" to move west. Then it became time to say good-bye to parents and friends. Tears flowed amid hugs and promises of future visits.

The high adventure began on a blustery March day in 1913. No amount of gloomy skies could dampen Max's spirit. Saying goo-bye to his family, he rolled west toward the Treasure State; Della would follow later with the children.

Max rode in the caboose to care for his stock in the last car. By law the train stopped every so many hours, and Max took the animals off to muck out the railcar. The railway provided pens, food and water. As they neared the small town of Havre, Max's excitement grew—he was almost home.

Because of the Army's lengthy pursuit of Chief Joseph and the Nez Perce and the recent defeat of Custer by the Sioux and Cheyenne at the Battle of the Little Big Horn, the government created Fort Assiniboine to protect the settlers. No Indian problem occurred. The fort was abandoned, and various homeless Indians established a community on the land. Later, with the help of Paris Gibson, Charlie Russell and others, the land would become the Rocky Boy Reservation in 1916. Max's homestead lay only a few miles away.

CHAPTER 4

When Della and the four girls boarded the train a few days after Max's departure, tearful good-byes were repeated. The ride—the first of Bertha's life—was an awesome adventure. Her eyes never left the window as she watched astonishing panoramas hurtle by. As they crossed mile after mile of Montana prairie, neither mountain nor trees intruded on the horizon, and the brilliant blue sky stretched on forever broken only by low rolling plains.

Della and the girls arrived in Big Sandy on a brisk day. The wind whipped their skirts about their legs as they stood on the station platform. A strange man ran toward them. He approached so fast he frightened the girls, and they hid behind their mother. Max had shaved off his mustache and none of his daughters recognized their father.

Max couldn't wait to show the family their new home. The distant mountains were snowcapped, the plains bare for the buggy. Della knew about the property from Max's description, but when she saw the original homesteader's lone little hut, she gasped. "Oh, Max, it's gonna be a lotta work."

"I know, but we'll be working our own place. We can do it. Will promised to help."

Six-year-old Bertha couldn't keep silent any longer. She tugged on Della's sleeve and whispered, "Mama, I don't like this place."

Della slapped her on the shoulder. "Well, I like it, and you just better learn to like it too." Bertha never would.

The rickety homesteader's hut wouldn't keep a mouse dry on a foggy day, so the family stayed with Will and his wife, Sophy. Their house measured twenty-two by sixteen feet. Will and Max retired to the attic, Mamie and Ella slept with Della in Will and Sophy's bed and Bertha and Charlotte on the floor. No one remembers where their poor hostess slept.

The words "Clawiter farm" sounded so incredible that Max repeated them over and over; he couldn't believe he owned property. His relinquishment was six-and-a-half-miles from both Big Sandy and Box Elder between the highway and the Bears Paw Mountains. Centennial Mountain loomed in front of their property a few miles away. Will lived three miles from Max's place by road, but only a mile and a half as the crow flies. Except for a coulee and a small seasonal pond, the land was flat and barren, typical of the surrounding acreage.

The Big Sandy area was known as Lonesome Prairie. Buffalo, cheat, salt, and wheat grasses covered the plains. Pale grayish-blue sagebrush grew in abundance and dotted the prairie with muted color. In dry years the plant died, broke off at the stem and rolled across the prairie, adding to the annual wind-blown migration of tumbleweeds that existed everywhere.

Other than the plethora of mosquitoes, the prairie was home to skunk, badger, gopher, jackrabbit, and coyote. Occasionally, a lone wolf wandered down from the mountains, a rare sight. Gold-breasted Meadowlarks, the future state bird, were plentiful and robins and sparrows common. Hawks, owls, and other raptors were plentiful and plump because of the prolific field mouse.

Max and Della were determined to make this land their home. Bertha felt the one redeeming feature was the view of the Bears Paw. Every spring a tiny creek flowed down from the mountains, forming a small pool in a shallow hollow before meandering off the property. The pond supported three willow trees. Della planted chokecherry bushes to provide berries and trees to form a windbreak, improving the ambiance. A few years later, a heavy wet snow froze on the branches, breaking them, and killing the trees. Eventually, the creek stopped flowing, and the pond dried up never to be seen again. Sometime around the mid-1930s, the last willow tree died and the land looked dreary, good for cattle but not scenic.

Still, Max and Della were eager to start their new life and the barn became the first order of business. In those years, brutal cold temperatures dominated March weather. While the men worked on the barn, Della brought their meals by horse and buggy. When finished, the red barn would have a big sliding door for animal access with stalls for horses on one side and cows on the other. When the barn was completed, Della would cook their dinner on a small stove in the barn by putting the stovepipe out a tiny window.

While Max and Will wielded hammer and saw, Della wrote her sister in Amenia asking for cuttings of roots for her garden. Max went to town for supplies one day and the cuttings had arrived. While the men created the farm, Della prepared soil for a spring garden.

She mailed a postcard thanking her sister and telling her how nice the cuttings grew. Somehow, that card dated May 26, 1913, found its way back to Della: "The frame of the house is done, the space is small." The front of the postcard was a picture of Will's house. Sending friends and relatives postcards with pictures of their home and property was all the rage at the time and helped provide a living for traveling peddlers. This postcard treasure would surface in Bertha's memorabilia boxes eighty-nine years later.

After the barn, water became the next most pressing business. Buying the relinquishment was risky because there was no water on the property. The original homesteader hauled his water, but that wasn't practical for farmers with animals. Max needed to dig a well and a windmill would have been the easiest way to draw water. They were also expensive. Max saw no need to spend that kind of money. He had a cheaper kind of power—children.

One word described Lonesome Prairie's water situation—scarce. When his second well went dry, Max sliced the air with a few well-chosen German words that almost made the kids run for cover. Another attempt produced good water, but the well went dry. When he complained to Della, she spotted an anthill. "Dig there; the ants know where there's water." The ants were right—the twenty-eight foot well produced drinkable water flowing at three gallons per minute. Max was lucky. Most farmers had to haul their water.

A rusty wire hook hung on the new pump for the communal tin-drinking cup. No one seemed to mind sharing the same utensil. It's doubtful it was ever washed with soap, only rinsed under water. If anyone felt persnickety, they put their lips right next to the handle assuming no one else would use such an awkward grasp on the cup—everyone else thought the same thing.

With the barn and water problem solved, the house was next. Farmers constructed their own homes in those days, a simpler job before indoor plumbing and electrical wiring. Max also had Will's carpentry help. They built the house without discussing the floor plan with Della. The house measured twenty-four by twenty-eight feet, large for the day, but it utilized a steep roof. A different roof would have allowed for rooms upstairs. Three or four of Will's houses still exist in Big Sandy and Havre. All have the same roof—perhaps it was the only kind "that carpenter" knew how to build.

When Della saw the completed house, she exploded. Bertha was stunned by her mother's outburst because Della was quite placid as a rule. But her anger did little good; it was too late. The house contained a parlor, combination kitchen and dining room, and one long bedroom. The dining room included a tiny narrow alcove where Della cooked the meals on a small wood-burning stove. The undersized recess held only the stove, cupboards atop a narrow shelf and room for one person to turn around.

The house provided for their current family, but Della was still a young woman. Child planning didn't exist and it was almost certain she would have more children. She would—four more. The single bedroom held two beds. The baby slept with Max and Della; the three girls slept in the other bed. As the family grew, Max put a folding bed in the parlor for children. One has to wonder *how* the family was created further with the kids sleeping in the same room as their parents.

Later, Bertha would say, "I saw them doing it many times. I knew *what* they were doing—I just didn't know why."

The dining room potbelly stove and the small alcove one provided the home's only heat. A large chunk of coal in the black-iron stove lasted the night, and the alcove stove was left to burn out. The parlor and bedroom received only what little warmth drifted through the open doors, so beds required many blankets in the winter. It wasn't unusual to awake and find ice in the water bucket and teakettle. On frosty mornings the children huddled around the dining room stove to dress. Lollygagging wasn't allowed, chores waited.

By late April, Max and Will were still creating additional buildings. No snow had fallen for days; the ground remained bare, but the pair worked up rivulets of sweat in spite of the cold. Looking up from work one day, Max saw a cloud of dust toward the mountains but thought little of it. Then he recognized Indians riding down from what would soon be the Rocky Boy Indian Reservation. The Indians were supposedly friendly, but Max felt edgy—he hadn't yet met any.

Few fences existed and the Indians had a short ride. They stopped a distance away, looked a moment, whirled their mounts around and left. Three days later, the Indians repeated the performance and came every few days, but never coming close or speaking. They only looked. With each visit, they grew bolder and came closer. At last five Indians reined in their mounts right in front of Max and Will. The Indians were lined up in a cavalry-style row, and like clockwork, all five horses turned their heads in unison to look at the Clawiter family. Bertha never forgot the mesmerizing sight and spoke of it often.

Della came outside. "I'll go talk to them."

"No," Max said. "They'll scalp you. You better go back inside."

"They won't do any such thing. You go back to work; I can take care of myself."

Approaching the lineup, she asked, "Does anybody speak English?"

One Indian grinned, displaying a gap in his teeth. "Me Roasting Stick—me talk." Apparently, he was the only one who spoke a little Pidgin English.

Della smiled. "Are there any berries in the mountains?"

"Many, many chokecherries."

"How do I get there?"

"Me bring um to you."

Speaking in the same abbreviated English, Della said, "How much you charge?"

"Not much—you look—you no like, we take back."

It was almost noon and Della invited the Indians to have a sandwich. After Roasting Stick interpreted, the invitation was met with toothy grins and nods. She went inside, brought out a washbowl with lye soap and returned to the house.

The sight of real Indians mesmerized Bertha who watched from a discreet distance. She loved the pretty pinto pony one Indian buck rode. But where were the war paint and feather bonnets she'd seen in pictures? She was disappointed; they were dressed like her father. The Indians grew excited and were jabbering among themselves when they saw all the sudsy foam from Della's soap.

When Della came out, Roasting Stick said, "Where you buy soap?"

"I make it myself."

"We trade berries for soap."

Della agreed.

A few days later, Roasting Stick and the same silent partners brought the berries. There were no leaves, stems or bad fruit, and Della said she'd take the entire pail full. With that transaction, Della and Roasting Stick sealed their bartering partnership. She never knew when they were coming—they just arrived. During one visit, she asked Roasting Stick if he could bring her firewood for the stove. He was a man of few words. "How big you want um?"

"About this big," she said demonstrating the size with

her hands. The next week he came by horse and wagon, the bed full of the right sized wood. From then on, Della's foamy, lye soap and later her home-canned meat brought her all the berries and firewood she needed. Whenever Roasting Stick visited, his little band consisted of only men. During one bartering session, Della asked, "Why doesn't your wife ever come with you?"

He replied, "Me wife, me squaw," whatever that meant, and Della forgot about it. The next visit, Roasting Stick came in a wagon with his squaw and young son. As dictated by custom, the more important boy child sat on the seat with his father; the squaw sat in the hard wagon bed. Whenever the Indians came to trade, Della fed them if they arrived around mealtime. Not surprisingly, they always came to barter just before lunch.

Store-bought soap was available, but Della made it for barely any cost. Saving the fat from their butchered animals, she cut it into pieces, boiled it down and stored it in the cellar until needed. Adding fat to lye, which she bought in Big Sandy, causes a chemical reaction producing soap, but stirring them together creates caustic steam so she worked outside. The task took two or three days so she made huge batches.

Della showed Bertha each step but wouldn't allow her to stir the bubbling cauldron, afraid she might splash the toxic liquid on her skin. So Bertha watched.

"How do you know how much lye to use?"

Della explained each step. The secret of her impressive soap was because she knew too much fat made the soap greasy, and too much lye made one's skin turn to sandpaper—and subtracted years off the life of garments as well.

Della was delighted the Indian's liked her soap; it would be needed often.

CHAPTER 5

After the important buildings were finished, Max planted forty-two acres in corn for income. When the neighbors heard Max planted corn, they snickered. "This is wheat country; you'll never grow corn worth anything." Max had the last laugh. Farmers came from miles around to see corn stalks towering over their heads, producing bushels of corn.

Max bought a hoe for each kid and two others, which puzzled Bertha. Her parents never weeded. It was the children's job. Max planted corn every year thereafter and the crop did well. Later, he planted wheat, and most of the family's income came from wheat and corn. He planted oats for the horses that also provided oatmeal for the family.

The Clawiter's livestock included cattle, pigs, chickens, turkeys, geese and ducks. Loud squawking filled the air among the ducks and geese. Like jockeys, they jostled for position on the miniature pond where they liked to spend the day. Della raised ducks and geese one year and turkeys the next. The free-roaming rafter of turkeys often numbered 100 birds, an amazing sight as they strutted across the barnyard like band majorettes. Most were sold, but the family ate some, and Della canned a few birds. They were a big hit with Roasting Stick.

In addition to six horses, Max kept an average of twelve head of cattle. The cows provided milk and intermittently meat. The family kept a sow and boar, so there were piglets every year. The number of pigs on the farm depended on the size of the sow's litter, always at least six or seven. Della kept a kitchen slop bucket, a permanent fixture for farmers raising pigs. Extra milk, peelings, table scraps and boiled vegetable liquid all went into the pail to supplement their feed.

Buckets also carried a free source of food for the family. After heavy rains, the Clawiter's pasture blossomed with mushrooms. One morning their field was spattered with the delectable fungus, and Bertha grabbed her pail. Later, removing her muddy boots, she showed her bounty to her mother to inspect to be sure they were the right kind. Della cleaned and sliced them and what they didn't eat, she sun-dried on screens put high up on the roof to avoid the flies.

Like all farmers, Max branded his livestock to prevent theft. Ancient brands were simple markings, but soon became a bewildering alphabet of letters, numbers, and geometric symbols. Still, clever rustlers changed poorly designed brands with a running iron.

Max registered his brand as the M bar C. Most farmers combined the branding letters, so they used the iron only once. Max used two branding irons, perhaps to save money. A straight iron bar used five times made the "M" and the bar between the letters; the second iron was the letter "C." That meant the pitiful animal was stuck with the red-hot branding iron a horrifying six times.

Bertha loathed branding. She didn't believe the adults

when they said it didn't hurt the animal. The creature's wild kicking and bawling wasn't because it 'didn't hurt.' The pungent odor of burning hair and hide sickened her. She felt relief her assistance wasn't required often.

All farmers' crops required machinery. The equipment, made of wood and iron, was big and bulky. No one bought obsolete machinery, so in a few years farmers had dozens of outdated and rusty implements rotting in their fields.

A buggy, wagon or sleigh provided family transportation. Hayracks and grain wagons were made to use wheels or runners. The wooden body wasn't heavy and a few people could lift it off the wheels onto four runners to be used in deep snow. Later, Max bought a real sleigh. Hayrack or sleigh, it didn't matter, Bertha loved zooming across the deep crusty snow. It was her favorite part of winter. In later years, when horses were no longer a part of the animal population, the sleigh disintegrated in the field, leaving only the rusty metal runners laying in the quintessential 'farmer's junkyard' as a reminder of once glorious sleigh rides.

The last building Max constructed was a smokehouse that looked something like an outhouse. Inside, meat hung from wall-to-wall rods near the ceiling. He used various kinds of wood from the mountains for smoking, but chokecherry was always the base wood. Max butchered four or five pigs every year, and neighbors came to help. He smoked hams, and Della canned some meat, but he used most of the pork to make time-consuming sausage links using the pig intestines for casings. Using a dull knife, Della scraped the insides clean, turning them inside out and scraping again. She repeated the process washing the casings after each step. The intestines were fragile and if torn, irreplaceable. After Max ground the meat and added salt and seasoning, he smoked a sample to taste. During that time Bertha tried to keep track of her papa's whereabouts. If she saw him heading toward the smokehouse, she tagged along and pleaded for a taste. Max couldn't put much stock in her opinion. She loved it all.

When Max liked the sample, the sausage-stuffing machine was next. He eased the casing over a greased nozzle, and the ground meat was forced into it when Bertha turned the crank. Max tied off each ring with string and hung them in the smokehouse. If he produced more than they needed, Max gave some to friends, and he acquired quite a reputation as a sausage maker.

Every year following the smoking, Max and Della would throw a potluck party and invite all the neighbors who helped with the butchering. They provided the sausage. After feasting, everyone moved the bedroom furniture into the dining room and shoved Della's parlor organ over by the bedroom door. The men rolled up the rug—music and dancing began. Bertha loved these social gatherings and wondered why no one else ever gave parties like it.

When finished, the farm included a house with no running water, a barn, pig shed, chicken coop, smoke house, granary and, of course, the obligatory two-seater outhouse complete with the ever-present Sears Roebuck and Company catalog. The outhouse had one large hole for adults and a small one for children. Creating the homestead took a long time. Luckily, the family made friends faster.

O.K. Olsen and his wife lived a quarter-mile to the south, the family's nearest neighbor. The rugged looking Norwegian had a jolly personality, and was always willing to help anyone. The Clawiters adored him.

O.K. and his brother were perfect examples of how U.S. Immigration Authorities took a liberal attitude about changing an immigrant's name. If they found the name difficult to spell or pronounce, they often changed it, and Lewandowski became Lewis or Smith or Jones. The hapless immigrant had no say in the matter. O.K. Olsen's brother was Jonus Nigard. Both men had the same father, but they immigrated in different years.

One spring afternoon, O.K. stopped at the Clawiter farm on his way home from visiting Roasting Stick. Typical of Montana's swirling currents, a stiff wind gusted across the yard, and everyone sat in front of the house watching the tumbleweeds dance across the prairie. Overhead, a huge V-formation of Canada Geese headed south for the summer.

"Max," O.K. said, "do you remember that puppy I had on the place?"

"Remember seeing one. Why?"

"Well, Roasting Stick admired him so much that I gave him the little dog. I was visiting him today, and his squaw insisted I stay for dinner. I was spooning out a second helping of tasty stew when Roasting Stick nudged me."

"Dig down deep, puppy in bottom."

Merely repeating those words, O.K. turn a little green. "Max, I gotta admit, I had a helluva time trying to swallow that half-chewed piece in my mouth."

Max laughed. The kids were near tears. They wished O.K. had given them the puppy. They would have loved him. But they didn't love all animals.

That first spring brought a shocking new danger none of the family had experienced before, rattlesnakes. They slithered everywhere. Because rattlesnakes offer a warning to something approaching, none of the children had been bitten.

Picnics were popular social events held once or twice a year when townspeople and nearby farmers gathered in the Bears Paw Mountains. One warm Sunday, the adults were resting quietly after a hearty lunch, and the children were busy at what they do best—having fun. A peaceful calm overshadowed even the screeching of the children. Then a piercing scream shattered the tranquility.

"Damn! A rattler got me," a neighbor bellowed grabbing his leg.

Max ran over and crosscutting the fang punctures, he sucked out the blood and spit it on the ground. He did it several times because that was the only known remedy for snakebites.

As musicians, Max and Della were popular as soon as they moved to Big Sandy. He played the fiddle and she, the pump organ, so they were in demand for country dances. Like most old-time musicians, neither read music. He listened to a new tune and picked it out on the fiddle. Della played by combining chords on her "automatic" organ—the kids took turns pushing the foot pedals with their hands. The music they played had been passed down ear-by-ear for generations. No sheet music existed for these songs and many that came from the old country would later be lost forever.

Country dances and home concerts were the family's only entertainment and a joyful way to offset their laborious lives. Dance halls didn't exist, so schools and barns filled the need. School floors were sprinkled with cornmeal for easier gliding. In barns lacking floors, you did the best you could. Whenever Max and Della played for a dance, they removed the organ's beautiful top section, loaded the keyboard box into the wagon and took it with them, along with all the children.

Six-year-old Bertha sat on the sidelines one night watching the dancers whirl around the floor. Her toe tapped a steady beat, and she wished she knew how to dance. Max came over and held out his hand. "C'mon, it's about time you learned to dance." She'd waited so long, and now her feet felt like cement refusing to do what she wanted. She was afraid her papa would get disgusted with her clumsy effort and quit. But he pulled her around the floor two or three times until she got the idea. Those few brief blunders were all it took—she was addicted.

Everyone brought food to the dances for a midnight supper, and none of the kids wanted to sleep until they ate. Afterward Della laid her coat on the floor behind the organ and the youngest child slept there. The other kids bunked down in the cloakroom, on benches, in a box or anywhere they wouldn't get stepped on. There were usually several fiddlers at dances, and if her papa wasn't playing, she begged to dance with him. Unfortunately, life with Papa had fearful times too.

Without a fence, Max's cattle wandered. "We gotta get a fence up," he complained, "but buying posts is expensive." Della got out her soap-making pot. A week later, Roasting Stick brought the needed tree wood stakes.

An iridescent black crow glided down from the cloudless sky. The big bird landed on a fencepost, near the raucous commotion taking place. Squawking, it stayed only a moment before flapping its wings in agitation and flying to the next stake.

The loud crack of a belt striking bare skin almost drowned out the screams of seven-year-old Bertha. Time and again the leather belt whistled through the air before striking her bare bottom. In between blows she cried, "But, Papa, I didn't break it—the horses stepped on it."

Max's wrath consumed him—he wasn't listening. In the turmoil, the horses began dancing about, and he whirled around. Cursing in German, he struck them across their backs before returning to Bertha. Finally, out of breath, Max leaned against the wagon running his belt back through his pant loops. Without glancing back, he stepped into the wagon and drove off, leaving Bertha on the ground.

She lay still, not moving because every motion surged pain across her buttocks. After a while, she reached back with her fingertips and felt rows of blisters crisscrossing her skin. *I don't feel any blood—Papa didn't break the skin.*

Still lying on the ground, Bertha became angry—she hadn't used the post-hole digger, her father had. At last she stirred, and ever so carefully dressed. She looked at the crow still perched on the fencepost and yearned to be free of this life. The now peaceful calm didn't appear as interesting to the bird; it cawed, flapped its wings and flew off toward the clouds crowning the horizon. Bertha watched the bird soar into the unknown world. *Someday I am going to fly away too.*

CHAPTER 6

If the children did something requiring punishment, Della shook them or slapped them on the shoulder. If the offense warranted it, the children went without dessert for a week. Max's punishments were more severe—the razor strap. He had a split personality. Not in the scientific sense, but in that he was a different person in public than with his children. In the company of others, Max was a jovial man who could liven up any party with his happy-go-lucky personality. Everyone liked him because he was such a good friend and neighbor. No one would have believed he could be abusive. But Max had a vile, hair-trigger temper, and he usually grabbed the nearest child without learning who actually committed the offense. Often one kid was whipped for something another had done. As senior citizens, all the siblings denounced their father for his terrible punishments—all except Erna and Charlotte. Erna said her father was good to her as a child, but she was a 'favorite child' too. Floyd and Little Max remembered being punished frequently for something Erna did.

All the kids lived in constant fear of making their

father angry. The animals suffered abuse too. He often took the harness strap to the horses when they didn't behave as he wanted. Hearing the horses pitiful screams made Bertha cry, and all the horses were whipped except the pampered Flora and Dora. Many families whipped their children in those times, and abusive behavior can be passed down from generation to generation. Perhaps Max was whipped as a child too.

Della knew Max prayed for a son, but she gave birth to their fifth daughter, Evelyn Hazel, in 1914. The new baby was again cause for a trip to the photographer where Ella and baby Evelyn posed for a portrait. By now, caring for a home and five girls put a damper on the children's fancy clothes. Only Evelyn had an elaborate christening gown. However, the hair bow was still in vogue and Ella's huge white bow sat atop her head like a fluttering seagull taking flight. All professional portraits ceased to exist after that, as did the fancy stitched dresses.

After church one Sunday, the family waited to enjoy a special dinner treat, canned salmon. Della asked Max, "Do you think we should give any to Evelyn? She's so young."

Max shrugged. "Surely a tiny bite of salmon won't hurt her."

Evelyn loved her few bites, and Della served the salmon to everyone else to be sure of equal portions. Everyone took lip-smacking pleasure in the seldom eaten delicacy. An hour later, one at a time, the entire family became violently ill. The baby's immune system wasn't developed enough to fight off the toxicosis. She died. Evelyn was eight months old.

The entire family was distraught—Della was desolate. She blamed herself. Guilt consumed her. The can looked dark when she opened it, but next to nothing was known about food safety in those days. Evelyn lies in the Box Elder Lutheran Church Cemetery.

O.K. visited one evening and was talking with Della and the kids. Max poked his head in the door. "Hey kids, get out here." Everyone rushed outside. Max pointed to the sky. Huge swirls of green and blue swished across the night sky creating a colossal display of flowing wonder.

Bertha stared. "Papa, what is it?"

Max had seen the phenomena before. "It's the sun reflecting off the icebergs," which was the theory for the Northern Lights at the time. Bertha stood mesmerized and she wanted to watch the wispy images waltz on. Two minutes later her reverie was shattered—now only doom and gloom loomed on the horizon. Max had uttered that dreaded phrase, "Let's play Pinochle." He'd taught Bertha the game so they could play whenever O.K. visited. She liked their neighbor but dreaded his evening calls knowing what was coming. Bertha detested the card game because she always was partnered with her father. Whenever she made what he considered a mistake, he would bellow and scold her. Thankfully, life sometimes had tasty moments.

If Della wanted to treat the kids, she whipped up her version of soda pop. Buying bottled soda wasn't a good reason to spend money, so Della put a bit of sugar and a dab of vinegar in a glass of water and stirred in a spoonful of soda. The drink was only as cool as the water from the well. The kids thought it delicious.

Bertha loved to draw and make anything creative. Whenever time allowed, she drew the barnyard animals, sketching on thin, beige paper. She used a board as an easel and hid it after each use. The hobby wasn't unusual as many children enjoyed drawing, but even at ninety-five, she still had some of her artistic efforts. And her drawings had once created a special treat.

Occasionally, Bertha was allowed to spend a few days with her Uncle Henry, the supervisor of the Milwaukee Railroad in Great Falls. Seeing the "big city" with her favorite uncle was always a thrill.

On one of Bertha's visits, he drove her to Volta Dam. The Great Falls of the Missouri that Lewis and Clark had heard seven miles away. Even dam tamed, the falls were impressive. Standing on an observation rock, mist enveloped her body as she gazed awestruck at the thundering white water. The sight left an indelible impression and a lifelong obsession with waterfalls.

On another visit, when she was eight, Bertha told her uncle a story about Roasting Stick.

Henry laughed. "Oh, we must go tell Charlie that story; he'd want to hear it." So off they went to see Henry's good friend Charlie Russell.

Charlie was already a famous self-taught western artist who would create 4,000 paintings and sculptures during his lifetime. He'd already done one-man showings in New York City, Chicago, Washington DC, Winnipeg, Rome and London. Born in St. Louis in 1864, Charlie drifted to Montana at sixteen to become a cowboy. Herding sheep and wrangling came first, but in his spare time he painted everything he saw, often trading a painting for a free drink. The image sometimes wound up in the Mint Bar spittoon. After eleven years of being a cowboy, he decided art was an easier way to make a living.

A log-cabin studio stood next to his home. It was to this studio on Fourth Avenue North that Henry and Bertha traveled. Henry introduced Bertha and told Charlie she'd some Indian stories to tell him. Bertha had no idea who Charlie was. Her uncle only said he was a painter—

she thought he painted houses. One look at his studio and she knew he didn't paint houses.

Bertha thought Charlie resembled her father in looks and stature, but he dressed funny, wearing that long dangling ribbon around his waist. Fascinated, Bertha gawked. A work in progress rested on the easel. She couldn't help being envious of the art supplies scattered about the room. His collection of exotic Indian clothing, fancy horse bridles, blankets and weapons intrigued her. They covered every wall and available surface. After a few minutes talking to Henry, Charlie turned to Bertha and smiled. "Now, young lady, tell me your story about the Indians."

Bertha was shy, but Charlie's easy manner made her comfortable. As she began her tale about Roasting Stick, Charlie picked up a sketchpad. While she talked, he sketched. When she finished her story, he handed her a drawing of a horse.

"Thank you. That's a pretty good horse."

Charlie laughed.

The next time she visited, Bertha took a picture of a horse she'd drawn. "I can draw too," she announced, brazenly presenting it to him.

Charlie looked at her drawing. He smiled. "That's a pretty good horse."

They both laughed—they were a mutual admiration society.

Henry took Bertha to Charlie's studio several times after that and Charlie was always eager to hear more stories about the Indians. He would chat with her and ask how the MacNamara and Marlo store and ranch were doing. She was surprised at the number of people he seemed to know in Big Sandy. Every time they visited, Charlie made her a drawing. Whatever happened to the drawings? Bertha sure wishes she knew.

If only...

Later, Henry moved to Portland and Charlie died in a plane crash in 1926, so Bertha never obtained more drawings. Her future husband received several letters from Charlie. Each had an exquisite miniature-watercolor scene painted across the top as Charlie so often did with his correspondence.

If only...

CHAPTER 7

At last, Della gave birth to the long-awaited son, Max Henry, in 1915. Everyone called him Little Max to distinguish him from his father. Technically, he wasn't a junior because they didn't share their middle names. No one ever knew why his parents didn't give him a less confusing name or make him an official junior. Later, there would be three Maxes in the family, but the confusion wasn't only with first names.

Max's father, Eugene, had a Deed of Record for his Minnesota property and they spelled Clawiter with two "t's." Most people of the day were uneducated and couldn't read or write, which made it difficult to keep accurate records. A prime example of this occurred in the family tree of Bertha's future husband. One man had three children baptized in the same church—each child's last name had a different spelling.

Mail of any kind was a treat. Letters from back home were rare, because only two out of ten adults could read and write, and the two-cent postage was problematic for some. The biggest treat of all was the Sears Roebuck or

Montgomery Ward catalogs. The family rarely ordered anything, but the catalogs were multipurpose wonders.

Mail lay in the post office until Max went to town for some other reason. One day he came home wearing a broad grin. He carried a Sears and Roebuck catalog. Bertha couldn't wait to finish her chores.

The book's first duty was to provide an evening's entertainment. That night, the family crowded around the table to look at the awesome "wish book," and everyone was admiring a small wagon.

"Oh, Mama," Bertha said, "Can we buy that wagon for Little Max?"

"No. It costs three dollars"

"Oh please, Mama, if you get the wagon, you don't have to buy me a present."

Her sisters chimed in with the same sentiment, so Little Max received his miniature hay wagon with side racks and a buckboard seat. He was thrilled, but he never knew the sacrifices his sisters volunteered in order to buy it.

After everyone admired the new catalog, Bertha pounced on the old one. Her paper dolls were in pathetic condition. Catalog paper dolls were flimsy and didn't last long, and she always needed new ones for the pretty Valentine cards she made. After the girls snipped out their paper dolls, the rest of the old catalog went straight to the privy for its final duty.

Most German people of that era were parsimonious and Max and Della were no exception; they didn't spend money on nonessentials. The family was consistently cash poor, so Little Max's wagon and Bertha's ornate framed portrait were among the few extravagances. A more typical gift would be the powder puff Bertha received for her sixteenth birthday. Since the children were never spoiled with expensive gifts, she loved the puff and patted and dabbed at her nose and then rushed to the mirror to see if she looked more grown up.

After arriving in Montana, Bertha had been kept from school for two years. Creating a homestead required even the labor of a six-year-old child. Despite the two-year age difference, Bertha and Charlotte started first grade the same year, and Mrs. CLA-viter took them.

Small one-room schoolhouses were scattered across the Great Plains to accommodate farm children, who walked or rode horseback to school. The Clawiter children walked three and a half miles, but Max took them in the sleigh during severe winter weather. Teachers boarded with nearby farming families and also walked to school. All of Bertha's teachers were daughters of nearby farming families—a college degree wasn't required. Until daughters married, teaching was the only available job while living at home.

The one-room, square framed school had an entrance and cloakroom, but no bell tower. Children were summoned to class when the teacher swung a big brass bell. The fenced property had no playground equipment; the children entertained themselves. Ubiquitous outhouses were the same at all schools, located far in the back. Because there was only one privy with several multiple sized holes, it often became a social occasion.

Because the property had no well, kids carried their own drinking water as well as their lunch, and there wasn't enough water to wash. Daily routine included studying, recess, lunch, and using the outhouse all without ever washing their hands. Diarrhea was common—'social occasions' frequent.

Miss Mack, Bertha's first teacher, was the daughter of farmer and mine owner, Cecil Mack, who lived a half mile from the schoolhouse. A lanky, young woman with a warm personality, she twisted her hair in a fashionable bun at the back of her head. Bertha adored her—most of the time.

Bertha, a born southpaw, did everything with her left hand. But society of the time dictated only the right one should be used for penmanship. Della corrected her daughter at home and told the teacher to slap Bertha's hand if she wrote using the left one. It's a wonder she'd any feeling left in her hand by the time she grew up and decided she could use either hand she wanted. Forcing her to use her right hand in childhood made her quite ambidextrous, but may also have contributed to the extreme nervousness that plagued her life.

Country schools taught children of all ages, from first to eighth grade in the same room. Like a battle-clad samurai standing guard, the potbellied stove filled the center of the classroom. On cold winter days the children clustered around the stove to keep warm while they read their books. Once comfortable, they sat down at their desks until they began turning blue; then returned to the stove. On bitter freezing days, feet shuffled back and forth in a minuet of survival.

Pump, Pump, Pull Away, May I, and Kick the Can were hotly contested recess games. Tug-of-War and Shinny were loud and exuberant. Shinny was similar to hockey. A tin can sufficed as the puck, and any old stick became a club. The much used can soon turned into a hard metal ball with sharp edges, and players' shins took a beating, thus the name.

Miss Mack often held spelling bees. Because of multiple grades in one classroom, she selected words appropriate for each child. At one such session, Miss Mack said, "Ella, please spell sit."

Without hesitation Ella replied, "s-a-t."

"No, that is not quite right. Try again."

Still confident Ella came back with "s-e-t."

All the younger children got three chances, and Bertha hoped Ella wouldn't miss again. Miss Mack smiled. "You get one more chance Ella."

Now frustrated, Ella sat dejected and squirming in her seat. After a moment, a glint of recognition flashed in her eye and she shouted, "I know: S-h-i-t."

For a moment the silence was deafening; then raucous laughter almost vibrated the windows. Bertha said the teacher appeared to be biting her tongue, but she was giggling so hard she couldn't be sure.

As the oldest child, Bertha made school sandwiches for her siblings. She hated the task, finding it difficult to avoid monotonous sandwiches every day. Cold meat or cheese didn't exist in their home; she'd little to work with. But her creative mind blossomed. A paste made of cocoa, sugar and cream was one creation. Another, melted butter mixed with rock-hard peanut butter bought in wooden pails. Fried onions in butter were another specialty. Sometimes Bertha and a school friend decided the day before to both bring hard-boiled eggs the next day. Bertha liked yolks and the other girl the whites, so they swapped and Bertha ate egg yolks for lunch. Cholesterol—what was that? No one ever heard of it. Max told the children, "Eat the meat fat, it's good for you."

The three and a half mile walk to school was only one and a half miles if the children cut across a neighbor's field. Feeling lazy one day, Bertha, Charlotte, Mamie and Ella decided to cut across the pasture. The field held cattle and, as they soon discovered, a large and angry bull that didn't take kindly to their intrusion in his bullring. He charged as if they'd waved a red cape in his face. Four little matadors raced to the fence as fast as their legs could carry them, scrambling under the barbwire in record time. From then on, they agreed three and a half miles wasn't so far.

Della wanted Bertha to learn the piano, so she sent her to live with Will and Sophy for a week. Bertha practiced the scales that Sophy taught her, and when she returned home, Della said, "Sit down and play me a tune." Bertha was talented, but not quite that talented. Della decided losing her daughter's help for an entire week wasn't worth it if she couldn't play one song. Bertha never had another lesson. But she enjoyed visiting Uncle Will anyway. He raised white chickens and Bertha thought they were beautiful. Oddly, the cacophonous squawks and cackling were music to her ears, and she developed a lifelong love of chickens—chickens and horses.

The economics of Della's world were different than today's throwaway society. No one discarded anything that could be mended or repaired. If an item couldn't be fixed, it landed in the attic. After all, "We might find a use for it later." Pants were mended, often with patches on top of patches; shirt collars turned, so the frayed side was underneath, and socks were darned—a lot of socks for a family of seven. But shoes couldn't be repaired. One day, Max learned the cobbler shop in Big Sandy was closing. He rushed to town and bought the shop's sewing machine. From then on, shoes, like clothes, were repaired again and again.

Della utilized an overworked treadle sewing machine. Making undergarments and dresses for six females was a monumental task. She made the boys' attire only when they were young; later, they wore store-bought clothes. Della's and Max's sisters often gave the family unwanted dresses, and Della altered them to fit herself or Bertha. When Bertha outgrew hers, they passed them down to the other girls. That was the only time being the oldest child in the family had a perk, sometimes Bertha received a new dress—at least new to her.

As the oldest child, Bertha had worked the farm from the beginning. Two years later, Charlotte joined the crew when she turned six. Later, Della told Max she needed one girl in the house to help her, so Bertha worked in the house until Mamie was old enough to help Della. Mamie was not a candidate for farm labor being a sickly youngster, and Bertha then went back to the fields.

Della and Max tasked the children with specific chores. Their biggest responsibility was fetching water from the well, an enormous job for a big family. Bertha manned the pump that squeaked in rhythmic protest with every down stroke. The younger children toted half-gallon buckets, and the older kids used gallon-syrup pails. All the kids dreaded washday.

Della's washing machine was a round, wooden tub that housed a spindle inside attached to a long handle on the outside. Pushing the handle back and forth turned the spindle and was kid powered. After washing, they drained the water into a pail from a plug in the bottom of the machine and carted it away—to the garden in summer—to avoid leaving the machine in a sea of mud for the next load. And more water was pumped for rinsing. Other chores proved even more demanding.

Extra-large throw rugs in the parlor and bedroom covered the home's wood floors. Carpet sweepers didn't pick up dust or dirt particles that settled between the fibers, so the heavy rugs were rolled, carried outside and draped across the clothesline for beating. That was Bertha's job. She applied the carpet beater with mighty swings that brought forth thick, clouds of dust. She sneezed, choked and gasped for breath in the prolonged effort. Later, she shared the chore with her siblings, who took turns venting their frustrations on the helpless carpet. Moving the furniture and getting the rugs out to the line was a massive undertaking, so Della only orchestrated the chore once or twice a year.

Bertha's everyday chore was to clean the chimneys and refill the kerosene lamps that provided lighting. Other tasks included feeding chickens and milking cows. The chickens were "free-range" before the term came into being. The birds wandered the farm but slept and laid their eggs in nesting boxes in the chicken coop. Bertha loved feeding the chickens and found the fluffy bundles of peeping, yellow baby chicks irresistible. She enjoyed gathering eggs and listening to the hens' proud cackling with the delivery of each future chick. If eggs were expensive—sixteen cents a dozen—the family sold them. If eggs were not paying much, the family ate 'future chicks' for breakfast.

The children learned to milk when young. A lantern, hung on a high peg, filled the barn with a soft glow as the contented cows munched on sweet-smelling hay that Max pitched into the feeding trough. Pale yellow light silhouetted a line of cats waiting for their tin of warm milk. When everyone finished the chore, Bertha poured milk in the cat dishes and the kids carried the pails to the house where Bertha turned the crank on the iron monster that towered over her.

The family cream separator was a floor model, with a large steel bowl to hold the milk. The bowl rotated at tremendous speed when Bertha turned the crank. Heavy cream stayed in the center while lighter skim milk clung to the outside before both drained into two smaller bowls.

Della removed whatever milk and cream she needed for cooking and making butter. The rest went to the hogs. The farm was too far from town to sell the milk. Most farmers delegated butter churning to the children, but Della always made it herself—pumping the dasher up and down gave her a chance to sit down. Forming the butter into small blocks, she finished each with a swirling design on top. She sold the surplus to the MacNamara and Marlo store in Big Sandy. Obviously, she perfected her technique, because the store kept a waiting list of customers for Mrs. Clawiter's butter. Whenever Della sold eggs and butter at the store, she received credit against their annual bill.

CHAPTER 8

Anton Horcika and his brother Rudolph were neighbors and good friends. The family was closer to Anton and they missed him when he was later drafted for World War I. Everyone was relieved when he came home with the same number of body parts he left with.

Rudolph was unlucky getting his homestead, and he had great difficulty making a living because the property was rock filled and hilly. Often, he survived on potatoes and was sick one year because of malnutrition. He ran a barley mill, and Max felt sorry for him, always taking his barley to Rudolph for milling. But even good friends didn't see each other often—they lived miles apart.

Farming was isolating work. Most folks used one of the new, wood-box inventions with a hand crank that hung on the wall and allowed a dozen people to talk to a neighbor miles away. Each telephone had a different set of long and short rings, but soon everyone knew the recipient of every call. Listening in became entertainment for many and eavesdroppers often butted in. Aside from personal calls, the telephone system had one important function. If there was a fire, death or news that the operator deemed important, all telephones emitted six short rings that meant *everyone* should listen. The Clawiters never heard the important news flashes—they didn't have a telephone.

Once there was another source of entertainment for the family. Small circus companies toured the country stopping in small towns on their way to large cities. In 1916, Big Sandy hosted the spectacular event. This was a huge treat in farmers' lives. Bertha was delighted because she rarely went to town, being Little Mother while Della shopped. The burden was unfair but necessary—the life of the first born in big families was hard. When the day came, Max said, "C'mon kids, we're goin' to town." They jumped in joy. Then Della broke the bad news. "We can't afford the show, but we can see the parade." Bertha and her siblings' joy were fragmented, but they knew it useless to plead for reconsideration. Max hitched the buggy and they were off. A bright sunny day provided the setting as Flora and Dora trotted down the dirt road raising a cloud of dust. The ride was noisy, filled with merriment and anticipation. By the time they reached town, Bertha was wound up like a two-dollar watch about to pop its main spring. Everyone for miles around came to see the Ringling Brothers Circus and parade. People stood shoulder to shoulder in the street and could barely move—cars and buggies couldn't budge at all. The circus would parade down the main street before setting up for its show near the stockyard.

When the parade started, Bertha couldn't believe the dazzling sights. Huge horses—a breed she never saw before—pulled large, lavishly carved bright-colored circus wagons that sparkled like gold nuggets in a clear creek. Mysterious calliope music resounded from one wagon while magic puffs of steam escaped into the air like smoke rings. In other wagons, caged lions and tigers paced and roared in bored agitation. Clowns dressed in gaudy costumes complete with red-ball noses skipped and did cartwheels down the street, prancing up to children making them laugh or cry, while strutting young ladies in scandalous costumes blew kisses to the crowd. Bertha squealed in delight when a giant elephant passed by flipping his pie-plate feet in slow motion. A tall man in a black silk hat and funny coat waved and beckoned all to come see the greatest show on earth.

The amazing wonder passed in minutes. Everyone piled back in the wagon and went home. Bertha's heart ached. Max had raised good crops for several years, and not being able to 'afford the show' might have been German frugality more than lack of funds. The circus came to town only once in Bertha's youth. At least another form of entertainment came more often.

Bertha spirits were low after a grueling workday, but she forgot her discontent when a joyous event occurred. It happened on a cold, crisp winter night when the family went to a dance at the Flatness School. Anton came over to help lift the hayrack onto the sleigh runners before filling it with sweet-smelling hay. Max hitched up four horses and away they went, sending snow spraying in their wake. There was room for the entire family with space to spare for friends they picked up along the way. Everyone huddled under blankets and a horsehide throw.

An orange harvest moon hung low in the sky, lighting their way. Deep, fluffy snow blanketed the ground and billions of twinkling stars gemmed the cloudless, black night. Sleigh bells tinkled as they zoomed over the glistening crystals. Anton played his accordion and everyone sang, accompanied by the muffled clippety-clop of horse hooves. After dancing until almost dawn, they repeated the marvelous experience returning home. It wasn't a historical making event, only a simple evening, magical to nine-year-old Bertha. She talked about the joyful memory the rest of her life.

Country dances weren't held often, so they lasted until the wee hours of the morning. When they got home, the kids wanted to go to bed, but animals dictate farmers' routines and Max stipulated a rule: "Feed the chickens and milk the cows; then you can sleep."

When they weren't working, the children played made-up games to offset their lack of toys. The older girls played "house," turning the dining room chairs on their side and covering them with blankets. Sometimes when Max and Della went to town, leaving Little Mother in charge, Bertha and Charlotte were naughty. Both put on Della's dresses to play "grownup." Using their mother's powder and rouge didn't seem adequate, so they used red food coloring on their lips. Della didn't wear lipstick, but the girls saw it on catalog models and they loved pretending to be one of those pretty, fancy ladies. They kept a close eye on the road and when they saw the buggy turn the corner, they scampered helter-skelter to put the clothes back and wash their faces. They knew Della wouldn't be happy if she caught them. The girls were extra watchful; they were never caught.

On Bertha's tenth birthday, she received a date book from an aunt. Each page had a Psalm, poem or saying with room for a name. Her birthday, May 28, read:

A Psalm of Life.
Let us, then, be up and doing,
With a heart for any fate;
Still achieving, still pursuing,
Learn to labor and to wait.

She didn't know what an apropos prophesy of her life it would be.

Awaking, Bertha rushed to the window. She hoped for a nice day because she had a routine chore. The sun beamed with nary a cloud in the sky, and she smiled. Today, she would walk the 160 acre fence line carrying a hammer and staples to repair any downed barbed wire. Cattle seemed to have a sixth sense and zeroed in on the tiniest clump of grass on the other side of the wire; they also honed in on the smallest fence opening, often with bloody results. The task was a big responsibility for a ten-year-old child and needed to be repeated often.

After a breakfast of fried pork and potatoes, Bertha gathered her tools for the long trek. When the weather was good, she enjoyed the walk and easy work. Heading for the pasture, her stomach began playing leapfrog with her backbone. Some cows never seemed to learn. If an animal went through the fence, it had wounds. If a barb only cut the hide, the slash healed, but if the teat were cut, it might require stitching and her papa would be furious. He would blame her for not doing a good job the last time. That meant a whipping. Until she counted the cows, she was always uneasy. That day she smiled.

By 1916, Max and his daughters' labor had resulted in tremendous prosperity. One year, his wheat crop was phenomenal. Commercial fertilizer didn't exist, but he had an abundance of manure that he plowed under on seven acres. The synchronized rains produced a crop with wheat stalks twice as long as usual. Before hauling his wheat to town to sell, Max withheld enough to take to the Mundy Mill in Gilford. For every 200 pounds of wheat he received 100 pounds of flour.

With unexpected money, Max bought a 1916 Overland automobile for 535 dollars. Only 8,000 cars and 184 miles of paved road existed in the entire country, and

Montana with little population didn't have an equal share. The family was ecstatic with their first car. Flora and Dora became semi-retired.

To celebrate, Max announced the family was driving to Great Falls to visit Della's brother Henry and his wife, Mary.

Compared to Big Sandy and Amenia, the city was a metropolis, and Bertha loved going to Great Falls. She bounced like a jack-in-the-box, her exhilaration infectious. Everyone was excited and didn't mind the ninety-mile trip on a rutted, dirt road. When they arrived, Max drove down Central Avenue so everyone could see the city. Bertha's eyes sparkled at the panorama spread before her.

"Oh, Mama, look at the stores. Can we see some?"

"No, we don't have time."

The enjoyable visit was brief, and soon Max said, "We gotta get home to milk the cows." The 'big city' had worked its magic—no one complained. But the good times were about to end.

CHAPTER 9

One spring day, Max and Della went to Big Sandy leaving Little Mother in charge. While shopping in MacNamara and Marlo's, Della grew uncomfortable. People were standing back, staring and appeared to be talking about them.

She shifted from foot to foot, clutching Max's arm. "Why is everyone glaring at us?"

"We'll talk later." Outside, the situation was the same. It was April 1917. The United States had entered World War I. When alone, Max said, "It's because we're German. Everyone hates Germans now."

"But we're the same people we were last month, and we're U.S. citizens."

"It doesn't matter, they hate anything German."

"Well, we'll quit speaking German."

They began pronouncing their name CLAY-witer because it sounded less German. Nothing worked. They still received menacing looks and malicious remarks in town, so they went only when necessary.

The intimidating stares weren't unusual for German immigrants; they had good reason to worry. Montana's sedition law was one of the harshest in the country. One man was threatened with hanging because he refused to buy Liberty Bonds, German books were burned in Lewistown, and one man jailed thirty-four months for saying, "This is a rich man's war and we have no business in it." Other immigrants weren't bothered, only Germans, so times were unpleasant when the Clawiters were among people other than their friends. Still, selective isolation wasn't possible. They needed supplies.

Coal was discovered in the southern slope of the Bears Paw Mountains, and farmers found it cheaper to go straight to one of the four mines and haul their coal.

About twice a year, Max hitched up the wagon and went three miles to buy coal. One day, after the war began, he pulled into the waiting line at the mine. The man in front glared. "You're a damn German. We don't need your kind here."

Max defended himself. "I'm a United States citizen."

The harassing continued and Max looked around to see if he could escape quickly if needed, but the lineup was tight. The atmosphere bristled with tension and he felt anxious. After several worrisome minutes, another man walked up behind Max causing him to almost jump out of his skin. His quickened breath slowed when the man said, "He has as much right to be here as any of you." That ended the situation.

When Max returned home, he told Della about the incident. Her face paled. When they needed coal the next time, she insisted Max take Bertha along, thinking a child's presence might prevent another incident. Bertha was ecstatic to ride along, but she didn't know why she'd been invited. Her going anyplace other than school was a rarity.

The cloudless day was warm as the empty wagon bounced along the rutted dirt road. Carefree as the hawk gliding overhead, Bertha prattled on about some nonsense or other, and didn't notice her papa's strange silence. At the mine, they no sooner pulled into the lineup than the same man in the wagon ahead said, "You're that damn German again," and the tormenting started. Bertha jumped off the wagon, startling Max. Running over, she kicked the man's shin. Dancing on one foot, he yowled in pain. She turned as if to leave; then she whirled around and "kicked him again for good measure." The agitator made no more comment. Going home, Max didn't say a word, neither scolding nor praising. Bertha's self-satisfied grin spread across her face and she couldn't wait to get home to tell her siblings about her adventure.

Life was complicated. And it got worse. No one would believe existence could change so radically in one year, but it did. Severe drought in 1917 left farmers with poor to nonexistent crops. The dry cycle continued and the farmers' seed blew away in the wind, dried on the ground, or was eaten by birds. If sprouts did appear, grasshoppers and gophers ate them.

Desperate farmers rigged up homemade devices made of wire, high voltage coil and a battery. They mounted the strange apparatus to the front end of a Ford Model T to electrocute the grasshoppers in the fields. The clever, but futile gesture did little to eliminate the hoppers. But the farmers received meager benefit for their efforts; they scooped up the dead insects and fed them to the chickens. The chickens thrived—the crops died.

Once the family quit speaking German, Bertha forgot the language over time. The only German spoken in the family in later years was slang; such as, *Han-yaw-ker* and *Frutzen*. Max sometimes cut loose with German curse words, but just as often he spit out his favorite English expression: "Shit and molasses."

Bertha was cautious when she became angry, because

Della didn't allow profanity. At times, the urge to spew out strong curse words was more than Bertha could bear. One day, her anger became explosive. She felt the words creeping up the ridges of her throat, alive and pulsating. She couldn't hold them back, and they spewed forth like a wildcat struggling for freedom. Bertha split the air with a piercing, "Dammit to hell!" The words no sooner left her lips than her heart began pounding, and she shrank back trying to make herself invisible. *Did Mama hear me?* Della had gone inside. Bertha heaved a sigh of relief. Next time might be different. *There can't be a next time.* She thought about the problem all day.

The next time her anger overwhelmed her, she shrieked, *"Ach der einer stechenflugel."* She exhaled and dropped her shoulders, *Oh, that felt good.* What did it mean? Absolutely nothing! She'd made it up.

Thereafter, she spit out the phrase often and one afternoon Della overheard her. "What did you say?"

"Oh, nothing, Mama, it's only some words I made up."

Della arched her eyebrows and went back to work. A Cheshire grin crept across Bertha's face, and she snickered. *Mama doesn't know I'm cussing.*

Some of Della's other rules weren't sidestepped. Whenever someone gave one of the kids money, or if they won it at a picnic or earned it working for someone else, it all went into the children's community-share bank. Bertha detested it.

If someone brought the kids candy, Della took it and put it away to dole out later, one piece at a time. Bertha didn't have a sweet tooth—she had thirty-two. When one particular uncle visited, Bertha became excited. He always brought a bag of candy for the children. He had experienced Della's habit of rationing before, and this time he refused to give her the sack. He held the bag out.

"Here, kids, eat your fill."

Della frowned but didn't speak. Bertha looked at her mother and shyly munched away on a piece of candy. After she finished the treat, he still held the bag and she snatched another piece. After the kids ate a few pieces each, Della couldn't stand it. "Now that's enough," she said and took the rest of the candy and put it away to distribute later. Sometimes, the kids got candy and Della didn't know.

Everyone in the family adored their neighbor Erick Leding. No one ever used his first name; they just called him Leding. His farm bordered the Clawiter farm a quarter-mile away. He was a warm and sociable fellow who loved children; Bertha visited him often because he always gave her treats of candy, and Mama wasn't there to ration it.

Leding was a bachelor. He was a homesteader, not a farmer. The law didn't require anyone to "farm the land," only to live on it, so he didn't need to buy expensive farm machinery. Max planted and harvested Leding's land for three-fourths of the profit. Leding was not only a good neighbor but also a helper in a special way.

At the turn of the century, Montana winters were far more severe. Blizzards blew in and forty degrees below zero was common. Country families could be snowbound for days, but the rapid weather changes were also astonishing. After a powerful storm, sometimes chinooks flowed down from the eastern slope of the Rocky Mountains, raising temperatures as much as thirty degrees in two hours, creating deep mud and making roads impassable.

The Clawiters experienced one of these vicious storms shortly after arriving in Montana. Della needed groceries, but the snow was too deep for the horses and Max couldn't get to town. A bitter frosty morning greeted the day as the sun glistened off a world blanketed in deep fluffy powder. Crackling dry air produced a brilliant blue sky almost surreal in its radiance. Inside the kitchen, sweat trickled down Della's brow. She dabbed at her eyes and mopped trickles of sweat flowing toward her chin. Regardless of the weather, she always baked bread in the morning, because later in the day the kitchen would boil like the fires of hell. However, the rewards were sweet, and now a delightful aroma permeated the house. Fresh baked bread, hot from the oven and slathered with homemade butter, was one of Bertha's favorite foods.

"Can I have a slice, Mama?"

"You have to wait until it's cool enough to cut." As Della removed the last loaf from the oven, she heard a knock at the door. Startled, she almost dropped the pan. "Who on earth could that be? No one could get here in this snow."

Wiping her hands on her faded apron, Della opened the door to discover Leding holding skis. "I'm skiing to town. Do you need anything? I can get your mail and groceries because I'm taking my backpack."

Della was delighted. She gave him her shopping list. "Now bring only what you can easily carry. It's a long list."

On his return, he brought their mail and everything on her list, all added to the Clawiter's tab at the store. From then on, Leding checked with her whenever he skied to town. Technically, he was cross-country skiing because there were no hills. That sport didn't yet exist, but Norwegians learned it as children.

O.K. Olsen and another neighbor came to visit one Sunday afternoon. Everyone except Della sat outside enjoying the sunshine, entertained by a jackrabbit popping out near the barn. Spotting people, the hare almost somersaulted in its frantic hopping to escape.

Bertha laughed at its antics as a mouthwatering aroma drifted outside the open window—Della removing sour-cream pies from the oven. Bertha's sweet tooth tingled in anticipation; sour-cream pie was her absolute favorite.

In her typical tomboy fashion, Bertha began "showing off" for the neighbors by throwing rocks over the house. Several times the rocks sailed over the rooftop, and she enjoyed her accomplishment in front of the admiring audience. Then her aim was off; the rock hit an attic window, producing a small crack in the corner. Max shot off the chair like a human cannonball. He grabbed Bertha, pulled her panties down and spanked her as hard as he could, until his reddened hand pained him too much to continue. Her buttocks burned, but even worse, she felt mortified because he took down her panties in front of the male visitors. Della later glued a small piece of glass on each side of the crack. They never needed a new window.

CHAPTER 10

Della gave birth to her sixth daughter, Erna Adelia, in 1918. She loved her children, but prayed she wouldn't become pregnant again. She was tired. Soon, a fun day arrived. On the Fourth of July, the family went to a potluck picnic the locals held every year. Everyone wanted to see the new baby, so Della and Erna made the rounds. A cloudless sky promised an ideal day as the men set up long tables soon laden with fried chicken, potato salad and more. Footraces were popular at these picnics, with the winner receiving a dollar. Max often won the men's race, and Bertha nearly always won the girl's event. As the men pitched a hearty game of horseshoes, the children broke into tug-of-war lines. Bertha waited for the races. She loved to run. And she loved winning that dollar, even if it did go into the community-share bank.

Max stood near the race starting post, and a small group of girls talked nearby. He couldn't help but hear their heated conversation.

A tall skinny girl with pimples was loud and intense. "I'm not gonna enter the race if Bertha Clawiter is in it."

A smaller girl chimed in, "Me neither."

Another nodded. "Ya, she thinks she such a high muckety-muck just because she always wins."

Max ran over to Bertha. "You can't race."

"Why?"

"The other girls don't want to run with you."

Bertha cringed. Not only was she losing the thrill of victory, she was losing a whole dollar. Bertha's budding practicality sprang into motion and she solved the problem. "Okay, I'll race with the boys."

"No, you can't do that either."

"But, Papa, it's not fair."

"You can't enter the race."

Sitting on the sidelines, Bertha sulked. Her antagonist, who overheard the conversation, gloated at the starting line. Bertha promised herself she wouldn't cry, but her eyes filled with tears. She turned her head so no one would see and brushed away the flow sprinting down her cheeks. Silently, she wished—she hoped—she prayed her opponent would fall. But she had to watch as smug Miss Pimple Face took home Bertha's dollar. Her racing days were over. Until the day she outran her father.

That day came a few months later. Max had released the pigs from their pen to eat the green clumps of grass edging the barn. He ordered Bertha and Charlotte to keep the animals away from a nearby haystack, but when the hogs spotted the luscious feed, they streaked toward it. Bertha couldn't herd the hungry pigs away.

"C'mon, Charlotte. I can't do it alone, get over here."

"I'm busy. I'll help later." She was playing in the sand.

Bertha dashed to and fro. "Dang it," she yelled seething in frustration, "get over here."

Charlotte didn't move.

One child couldn't do the job because the pigs spurted in all directions and were munching the haystack when Max appeared. Livid with rage, he exploded like Mount

Etna. Snatching a two-by-four plank lying on the ground, he lunged toward Bertha, his eyes bulging in a reddened face. She recognized his furor and the routine. He intended to whip her with the heavy, three-foot-long board that had a nail in one end. Utter panic surged through her veins. *He'll kill me with that big board.* Bertha "lit out and ran." Max chased her, board in hand. She outran him.

A half mile from the house, two crossed fences trapped a high pile of thistles. Reaching the brush— gasping in deep gulps—she stopped, her fragmented thoughts exploding in all directions. *What can I do? He'll kill me! I have to run away. How? I don't have any money.* Not knowing what to do, she sat there trembling in fear.

Finally, Della shouted, "Bertha, come home. It's getting dark." For the first time Bertha disobeyed her mother. From the window, Della had seen where her daughter sought refuge and went to fetch her. It took her some time to convince Bertha that her father wouldn't whip her. When she went home, Max, still furious, didn't speak to her for days. Even more unjust, Charlotte, his favorite child, didn't get disciplined. Max never punished Charlotte as much as the other children, even when she deserved it. Della didn't seem to have a favorite child and punished them all the same.

Being the two oldest, Bertha and Charlotte did many chores together. A chilly winter day enfolded the world, but the kitchen was warm and cozy. Bright orange stove coals radiated warmth throughout the room. The aroma of peppery sausage lingered in the air, but only Bertha and Charlotte remained at the table. Bertha pushed the meat around with her fork, delaying the last bite as long as possible. They were in no hurry; a detested chore awaited them.

At last Bertha stirred. "C'mon. We gotta feed the animals."

Charlotte groaned. "My back hurts."

"Well, ya know we gotta do it—c'mon."

"Okay, I'm comin'. Keep your shirt on."

Reluctantly, they donned winter coats and pulled on their boots. Snow had fallen most of the night, and giant flakes still drifted down from a dull-gray sky. Max had broken a trail to the barn earlier, but not to the granary. Bertha loved new-fallen snow; it was like a fresh new canvas awaiting design. The unblemished snow issued a challenge to her artistic soul and she couldn't resist. Sprinting forward, she flopped down in the snow, swinging arms and legs back and forth in frivolous joy. "Look at my angel." Huge flakes drifted onto her face and she laughed trying to catch them in her mouth.

Giggling, Charlotte joined her and soon two angels beamed skyward. Thinking of no way to delay the detested job any longer, they trudged through the snow to the granary. Lifting a heavy sack of oats, Charlotte moaned, "Oh, if Papa would just buy us a wheelbarrow."

"Papa's not gonna buy one when we can carry the bags, so forget it."

Struggling with their backbreaking load, they slogged through the falling snow toward the barn. The girls had already acquired strong hands from milking, so maybe Max wanted to strengthen their backs as well. If so, the ploy failed with Charlotte, who suffered lifelong back problems; but it worked wonders for Bertha, whose back was strong as a mule's. A wheelbarrow would have simplified the job, but like the windmill, kid power was cheaper.

After feeding the animals, they mucked out the stalls. As if thanking Bertha for breakfast, a cow lowed and dropped a steaming pungent cow paddy in the newly cleaned stall. Bertha groaned, attacking the putrid pile. Feeding the animals, like most farm chores, was hard sweaty work, even in winter. Baths weren't yet considered a daily necessity in spite of the intense body odor farmers acquired after daylong work. Bathing required dragging in the big, round washtub and hand filling it with water from the reservoir. If the stove was used recently, the water felt warm. If not, bathwater was barely tepid because Della wouldn't use firewood to heat bathwater. Everyone used only two or three inches of water because otherwise the tub was too heavy to drag outside to drain. The washtub was big enough for young children to sit inside, but adults combined various methods of washing body parts while striking peculiar poses. Between the real thing, spit baths were routine.

Their wonderful neighbor, Erick Leding, retired and sold his land to Max before moving to Minnesota. Bertha would miss his candy treats, and there would be no more skiing trips to town for her mother if they ever became snowbound. Max moved Leding's house—a squat building with a low-rounded roof—next to the family home to use as a guesthouse. During the early years in Montana, relatives from North Dakota and Minnesota came to visit every summer. Eventually, the annual visits ceased and the bunkhouse became a storage area. Frugal Clawiters never threw anything away. "It might come in handy someday." The bunkhouse soon filled to overflowing. As adults, half of the Clawiter siblings would maintain that parsimonious philosophy forever and half escaped the brainwashing. Bertha was frugal of necessity most of her life. In her nineties she could spend freer after inheriting money from two childless sisters. Then she had little to spend it on.

CHAPTER 11

When Max's sister wed a dairy farmer, the event was anticipated for weeks. After the wedding, dancing began. These events always lasted hours, and everyone outdid themselves on this occasion, dancing until six o'clock in the morning. By the time the family said good-bye, the post office was open, so Max stopped to get the mail. After milking the cows and feeding the chickens, everyone went to bed, the sun high in the sky. Such was country living.

The lifestyle, however, posed a serious problem should anyone get injured or became seriously ill. Rural doctors only attended substandard medical schools. But they were deeply admired by a grateful community who would be in serious trouble without them.

Country doctors didn't make appointments. If his services were needed and the family didn't have a phone, they "fetched him" or the doctor harnessed his own horse or buggy team, and regardless of blizzard, snow or rain, transported himself and his little black bag to some distant farm to offer his services to ailing patients day or night. Often his patient barely spoke English making diagnosis difficult. He rarely received cash payment; chickens, eggs, milk and other farm products were offered instead. Sometimes payment was never received at all.

Box Elder's Doctor McKinzie was the family's doctor. In 1918, Max challenged Flora and Dora to make one of their amazing runs for the doctor—Della was gravely ill.

At the doctor's house, Max dropped the reins in the buggy—his regular practice—and the horses stayed right there. On the return trip, the doctor rode in the rear seat. Max never reined in the horses. The buggy tilted around corners almost on two wheels for six miles. When they arrived, Bertha thought the doctor looked pale and white knuckled.

Della suffered fever and chills. Ugly red lesions covered her entire body. Though Doctor McKinzie examined her at great length, he was mystified. No wonder, his final diagnosis was erysipelas. The prognosis was grim. No one had ever survived the bacterial infection. The news shattered the family, and twelve-year-old Bertha ran from the room crying.

The doctor said, "I'll do everything I can." He coated Della's entire body with some kind of "black gunk" and didn't leave the farm for three nights. The double boiler bubbled on the stove twenty-four hours a day because everything leaving her room had to be boiled or burned. The process was the same *failed procedure* used in attempting to contain the bubonic plague, the Black Death pandemic that killed seventy-five-million people in the 1300s. Erysipelas was extremely contagious and the doctor wouldn't let anyone near Della. Whenever he left the room, he called out, "Get away from the door, I don't want you within breathing distance."

The family floated in exhausted limbo, eating and

sleeping little. After three days of unimaginable stress, they erupted in pure joy. Their prayers had brought a miracle—Della would live. Doctor McKinzie said, "Della is the thirteenth case of erysipelas in the entire country, and she is the first patient to survive." The case was written up in medical journals around the country. No one ever learned where or how Della contracted the disease, and strangely Erna, who was still nursing, didn't catch it. The doctor switched her to canned milk immediately but later said that he'd felt sure the baby would get sick too.

Whenever Max fetched Doctor McKinzie, he tried to pay him in cash. Instead of asking the cost, he usually said, "Is five dollars enough?" It always was. Frequently the family didn't have any money, and Della took the doctor a baked chicken. Anytime he visited a patient beyond the Clawiter farm, he stopped on the return trip to chat. While there, he asked how everyone felt, and had the kids line up and stick out their tongues for inspection. Della always fixed him something to eat, and Bertha suspected the doctor enjoyed Della's cooking far more than he was interested in the children's tongues.

During Della's illness, Max had taught Bertha to make bread. She already did much of the cooking because Della suffered from severe asthma and was often bedridden. Little Mother developed a profound responsibility to her family not only as a child, but during her adulthood as well. Unfortunately, Little Mother couldn't do anything about her father's temper.

After finishing a repair job one day, Max handed the hammer to three-year-old Little Max for a toy. Happy with his new plaything, he toddled around pounding on everything in sight. He stumbled across one of Della's pickling crocks—one good clout shattered the crock. Max exploded. He grabbed the razor strap, pulled down the little boy's pants and whipped him. That evening Little Max stood to eat.

"Why don't you sit down?" Della asked.

"I can't. It hurts too bad."

Della took down his pants. Tiny blisters and welts—row after row—crisscrossed his buttocks. Infuriated, she whirled around and walloped a startled husband on the shoulder. "Don't you ever touch my kids again," she shrieked. "I'll handle any punishment from now on."

Max, in a state of shock, never uttered a word. Della had never hit him before. Bertha didn't remembered Max using the razor strap any more, but the harsh punishments continued.

Della should have objected to the ghastly chastisements sooner. But in those days, the man ruled the house. Even though Della and Max got along well, he did as he wanted, and like most wives of the time, she allowed him to make the decisions—until Little Max's whipping.

Whenever Max had razor strapped a sibling, Bertha cringed; tears filling her eyes. The victim's screams sent shivers surging down her spine, and she hated her father more with each snap of the strap.

Bertha was envious of O.K.'s children who were never whipped. Instead, their mother sat them down and talked to them when they did something wrong. When they told Bertha, she couldn't believe it.

"You mean you've never been whipped?"

"Never," they chorused.

The news shocked Bertha. At that moment, she vowed, "If I ever have children, I will never whip them. I'll talk to them instead." Until then, she still faced more punishments at home— and her family's struggle intensified.

When the war ended in 1918, grain supports ceased.

The price of wheat plummeted and the area still suffered severe drought. By 1919, there were no crops at all. A hailstorm wiped out Max's entire yield in 1921; he didn't have insurance. Money was scarce. Farmland used as collateral was worthless and banks collapsed along with the farms. Every farm in the immediate area was mortgaged except one—the Clawiter farm. Max gathered the family around the table. "I know it's bad, but we must hang on. We could never repay a mortgage. We'd lose the farm."

And 'hang on' they did, through incredibly hard times. Even when crops were good, a family of nine struggled, and farmers and ranchers were always in debt to the banks. Times were far harder for the family in the late teens and early twenties than they would be during the Great Depression—farmers couldn't be laid off from work. Though the family was cash poor, as hard-working farmers, their bellies were never empty.

During such terrible struggles, an occasional joyous event took place. Max had taught Bertha to call square dances when she was eight, allowing the family to dance at home. If not exhausted, some evenings Max and Della played music and the kids would square dance, while Bertha called. If she made a mistake, Max corrected her. She loved calling. "Oh, Papa, teach me everything."

"It takes a long time to learn all the steps."

"That's okay, Papa, teach me." Later, she learned her father didn't call correctly and his calls were difficult to dance to. A caller must identify the steps two beats ahead of time, so the dancers know what to expect next. He didn't do it—she picked it up naturally.

Billy Williamson lived in the Bears Paw Mountains, and his stone barn was built beside a hill with the upper floor at ground level. One day before filling the barn with new hay, he decided it was the perfect time to hold a "shindig."

Both the Box Elder and Big Sandy papers advertised the dance. The affair was a "big to-do" and as always the Clawiter family attended. Musicians and callers weren't hired for dances. Everyone assumed—and hoped—they would appear, and they usually did. This particular affair brought many musicians, but neither of the two callers in the area came. Dancing only the waltz, two-step and polka, the people complained. They wanted to square dance and some talked about leaving.

Aware of the discontent, thirteen-year-old Bertha sauntered over to Billy, and with an air of certainty she announced, "I can call."

Billy looked at her suspiciously. She was a child. He didn't want to hurt her feelings and asked, "What do ya call?"

His interest spiked when she named the most popular calls. Taking her aside, he said, "Call me a few lines?" Those few were all he needed.

"That's enough. C'mon." He walked to the front of the musicians and announced: "Form yer squares folks—we gotta caller. Max start ur up."

Max looked around, he hadn't seen a caller arrive. He assumed Billy planned to call, and he received quite a shock when his little Bertha stepped forward. Billy picked her up by her tiny waist and put her on a big box so the people could see her. Bertha broke loose.

"Honor your partners now and swing em a while,

Step right back and watch em grin,

Step right up and swing em again."

Everyone heard Bertha—she had a mighty set of lungs.

Afterward, everyone told her what a good job she'd done. Bertha strutted around the floor like a just-mated rooster. She'd called for a real dance. They liked her. A shiver of euphoria swept through her body. "I'm going to be a square dance caller." She didn't know what a journey it would be.

The next day Bertha couldn't speak, and her throat burned. Not knowing how to use her voice properly was worrisome. She was determined to call again.

Bertha called at home for the family and visiting kids who "played square dance" in the yard while she sang out her best singing call. She called for other public events, like the Fourth of July dance, and with each performance she learned to use her voice more correctly. Never receiving training, she was a natural.

CHAPTER 12

Della and Max were good parents in that they worked hard to provide for their family, but neither was demonstrative. They never told their children they loved them, kissed, hugged or praised them, and Bertha developed a tremendous guilt complex. As an adult she would become an avid perfectionist, constantly seeking the approval she never received from her parents. Like other insecure people, she hid it well by being the life of the party. Maybe that was why Max was the 'life of the party' too. Insecurity, like abuse, can pass from generation to generation when the same childhood parenting is repeated. Bertha hated her father. Her childhood was an unhappy one. She was also stubborn, refusing to surrender to self-pity.

After church one Sunday, the family visited Bertha's Aunt Mary on the dairy farm. When they arrived, Bertha's cousin grabbed her visitor's hand. "C'mon, I want to show you something." She almost dragged Bertha across the yard toward the privy.

Bertha yelled, "For cryin' out loud, I don't have to go to the bathroom."

"No, I wanna show you something—you ain't gonna believe it." Bertha couldn't imagine what was so special about the privy. Her cousin opened the door and took out a small roll of white tissue paper with perforated lines separating the paper into small sheets. "You're supposed to take off six little sheets and do a thorough job of cleaning yourself," she said. Obviously, she'd received specific instructions so as not to waste toilet paper. Amazed at the wondrous new discovery—softer paper than catalogs—Bertha rushed to the house to take the other kids out to see the fabulous never-before-seen item.

Later, Aunt Mary went to the outhouse and came back frowning. "I just put a new roll of toilet paper out there and it's almost gone." She held the nearly depleted roll, in her hand. The toilet paper wasn't replaced, and the visitors went back to using catalog pages. The kids apparently didn't drink much after that because they made fewer visits to the outhouse.

O.K.'s wife sat by the bed to act as midwife for Della, who, at thirty-seven, was in labor with her eighth child. With the doctor out of town, no one expected this birth to be any different than the previous seven. This baby nearly killed Della. Her labor went on and on; water boiled relentlessly on the range but never used. By the end of the second day, the family existed in frozen numbness. Deathly stillness permeated the home, interrupted only by Della's shrieks of agony that shattered the silence like breaking glass. The screams penetrated to Bertha's soul and she ran from the house unable to stand her mother's pain. At long last, Floyd Clifford came into the world in 1921. He was anything but a little bundle from heaven— he weighed more than fourteen pounds. Della survived, but the family's difficulties still lingered on.

Like all farmers in those eight drought-stricken years, Max suffered repeated crop failure. The situation became so severe in 1924, he sold the Overland car and brought Flora and Dora out of retirement. Little Max often herded the cattle along the county road to eat the free grass, the family trapped coyotes for the small fee paid for pelts, and other austere measures were taken, to no avail. The day arrived. No longer were they cash poor—there was no money at all. Max had no choice but to sell cattle even though the price was a mere pittance of their value. Little Max drove them eight miles round-trip to the buyer's farm on foot because they didn't have a saddle horse. The family was penniless, yet still had some blessings.

They had wonderful neighbors like Anton. He had acquired a retired racehorse named Girlie, but lacked a stable. He rode her to visit Max one day and asked if he would like to have the horse.

"I don't have any use for a saddle horse."

Standing nearby, Bertha interjected, "Ya, we do. When I check for downed fence lines, it takes a long time. I could do the job faster on horseback." Girlie was then stabled and became their horse because Anton never rode her again. Bertha adored Girlie and now the fence line was checked more often.

To provide food during winter, Della canned everything from the garden, meat from butchered animals and chokecherries. Gleaming jars of golden corn, red tomatoes and bright green pickles rested on floor to ceiling shelves lining the root cellar.

Breakfast usually consisted of pork sausage. Occasionally, they ate chicken, duck, or turkey if neighbors visited on Sunday. Their diet laden with pork and cream didn't seem to bother the five sisters in later life, but both brothers would require bypass surgery. Jejune meals were common, but they never went hungry.

Farm living guaranteed the children were around animals, but even the barn cats were working animals—not pets. A neighboring farmer gave Max a young, golden retriever mix. The kids loved Carlo, and the tail-wagging canine returned their affection. Bertha felt sorry for Carlo because he never had much to eat other than bread, milk and table scraps, but that was the life of a farm dog in those days. Carlo pursued the kids everywhere, often appearing torn about which child to follow. There was one particular kid chore, which he never hesitated; he followed whichever child fetched the cows in the evening.

Exceptionally aware of his surroundings, Carlo missed nothing. He lay on the doorstep one late afternoon when Max headed to the barn carrying milk pails. Suddenly, Carlo leaped up, looked at Max, whirled and raced off. Mystified at the dog's behavior, Max wondered what the canine was doing. When Carlo returned, he had every single cow. From then on, the children had one less chore, which suited them fine. It suited Carlo too. He brought in the cows every time he saw Max head to the barn carrying milk pails.

The children's favorite holiday was Christmas. The candle-lit tree held only decorations the children made. Della taught Bertha how to cut paper snowflakes. Fascinated with the surprising design when she opened the decoration, she experimented folding the paper different ways. Unlike the other kids, she didn't rush, delighted in seeing how delicate and fragile she could cut them. It was an amusement she would continue into her nineties when the top of her coffee table would be covered with snowflakes under glass. Candles were hazardous so Max only allowed them lit for thirty minutes on Christmas Eve and Christmas morning. Max and Della were cautious, but they didn't have water buckets standing by like many folks, which seemed odd since they had already experienced one appalling incident with a burning Christmas tree.

After the children spent weeks making gifts and decorations, Bertha detested taking the tree down the next day. "Mama, why can't we leave the tree up longer if we don't light the candles?" Her query fell on ears that didn't want to hear the question. Subsequently, Bertha vowed the tree would go up early and stay up late when she acquired a home of her own.

One special Christmas treat Bertha and her siblings looked forward to was the traditional nut cracking. After evening chores, the family sat around the table in the soft glow of the wick lamp. All eyes focused on Della as she brought out the holiday nuts kept on a top shelf out of the children's reach. The kids were excited; Christmas was the only time they ate nuts. The family's one nutcracker then passed from hand-to-hand so each person could crack one nut; then each waited for eight others to do the same before the utensil returned to them. Intentional or not, the nuts were strictly rationed.

For holidays, Bertha's teacher, Miss Mack, had the children move their desks to one side of the room, and she hung up a sheet for the pretend stage. Excited to be relieved of their studies, the kids put on little plays. The children's families attended; even childless farmers came, it being the only amusement other than dances. Bertha's creative talents had surfaced early in life. Starting in the fifth grade, the teacher asked her to write the plays. Bertha was not only the author but also the set designer, making decorations and drawing appropriate pictures on the blackboard, like Santa's sleigh with the reindeer swooping down from the sky. She was ecstatic to be called on for these chores—they weren't work, they were fun.

Much of the children's entertainment was making things. Bertha loved creating dainty wonders with her hands. She made decorations for Halloween, Easter, and Christmas, but valentines were her specialty. Minuscule vines of painted flowers on delicate arches and hand-cut filigree paper lace decorated her cards. Tiny human figures cut from catalogs folded out on tissue paper hinges when opened. Creating fragile things was great fun and easy for her nimble fingers. The cards were gorgeous, and she kept some of them all her days.

Bertha often missed school because of her mother's asthma, a serious illness at the time. The only treatment available wasn't much help. When Della suffered an attack, Bertha stayed home to cook and care for the children. And if her mother shopped in Big Sandy or did time-consuming work, Bertha tended the younger children. She didn't mind the motherly duty, but she hated missing school. If the children's grades were poor, Della helped with their homework. Bertha didn't have time for homework—she still worked at household chores. Eighty years later, Charlotte would write in her sister's memory book: "I always felt so sorry for you because you had so many chores to do when we were kids."

Little Max was the only child to go to high school, but only for three months because Della couldn't find someone to board him. High school attendance was rare for farm children; their labor was needed at home. Max and Della had completed only third grade. Max's father told him he didn't need an education to take care of himself, which was the prevailing attitude of the day. This changed drastically in the future when farmers needed to study chemistry, accounting, government regulations, and animal husbandry—apparently, farmers no longer thought the animals knew how to "do it" properly.

Neighboring kids often visited and played games they invented. One game required two upright sticks in the ground with another tied across limbo style, but they jumped over the stick instead of going under. Then they raised the horizontal stick and tried again. All-American tomboy Bertha loved the game. One day, Della saw her jumping over the stick and she ran outside. "Stop that right now. You might hurt yourself."

"But, Mama, I'm just jumping over the stick."

"Quit it now." Her tone was such that Bertha knew better than to argue.

She sat on the sidelines and watched the other kids have fun. She felt confused. *Why doesn't Mama think the other kids might get hurt?*

Like most families of the day, the word sex was never mentioned in front of the children. If one of the girls asked a question, Della said, "Never mind about that." The words were her standard reply if she didn't want to answer an inquiry—the kids heard a lot of 'never minds.'

The morning after the jumping incident, Bertha went to the privy and discovered blood on her panties. She was horrified. "Oh no, Mama was right. I hurt myself jumping." She was afraid to tell her mother. *It's only a few drops; it'll be better tomorrow.* She consoled herself with that thought as she rushed back to the house to wash out her panties with hot water, setting the stain. She didn't sleep much that night and the next morning, she hurried to the outhouse and let out a cry—it was worse. All composure deserted her as she sat in the privy crying. *I'm bleeding to death! The doctor can't help me. The hurt is inside.*

That afternoon while they were washing clothes, Della saw the stains in Bertha's panties. "Bertha, what are these stains in your panties?"

The dam burst and Bertha sobbed, "Oh, Mama, I did hurt myself jumping over the stick. I'm dying. I'm bleeding to death."

"You're not bleeding to death. That's what happens so women can have babies." She didn't say another word.

Still shaking, Bertha felt bewildered. Asking questions was useless. Later, calmer and thinking more logically, she became angry. She'd lived in utter terror for two days for no reason. *If this is what happens so women can have babies, why didn't Mama tell me?*

The more she thought about it, the angrier she became. *My sisters aren't going to suffer the fear I did.* One at a time she took each sister aside and told them of her experience. She didn't know much to tell, but at least they wouldn't go through the same anguish she had. "Now this is our secret," Bertha said. "You mustn't tell Mama I told you because she would be mad." Her sisters kept the secret.

Like most parents of the day, Max and Della's view of teaching their children about life was unrealistic. Whenever a farm animal neared giving birth, Max sent the kids to the house. Bertha wanted to watch. Instead, she lived on the farm for two decades and never saw an animal being born. She learned to wring the neck of a chicken and witnessed death and butchering, but never the miracle of birth.

CHAPTER 13

Riding Girlie to school one day, Bertha met her neighbor Earl Hall on Silver. He always bragged Silver could outrun any other horse, and he could. Earl had never seen Girlie before, so he challenged Bertha and the newcomer. "I'll race you."

Bertha said, "Okay" and they were off. Whenever Silver took the lead, Girlie ran faster to get in front. Then she slowed only enough to stay ahead. Girlie and a smug Bertha won the race. Earl never asked her to race again. He didn't know Girlie was a racehorse. She wasn't about to tell him.

Bertha was spending more and more time being Little Mother. She couldn't keep pace with the other students. Her report cards confirmed that she missed two months of school in each nine-month term of both sixth and seventh grades. How she managed to make mostly "B's" remains a mystery. Three months into the eighth grade, she told her teacher she needed to drop out. The teacher didn't want her to quit; Bertha was her most enthusiastic student. "Isn't there any way you could at least finish this year?"

"No, Mama needs me. I'm already so far behind that sometimes I don't know what the other kids are talking about." Tears filled her eyes; she fled before the teacher protested further.

Bertha had been a major player in creating the homestead and Charlotte had joined the team at six. Now that they were older, they did the same heavy field work as the men. They wore men's long-sleeved shirts, denim-bib overalls, and men's hats. With their makeup-free faces and bobbed hair, they almost looked like men. Their sweat-soaked days were rewarded with dirty bodies and aching muscles.

Planting was hard work, but harvesting was more labor intensive and required a bigger crew. Neighbors took turns helping one another. Bertha and Charlotte joined the crew. After harvesting the Clawiter's wheat, the team moved on to Cecil Mack's farm and then back to Max's to harvest the barley. The work was hot and dusty, pure misery for anyone with hay fever. Like Bertha.

Max, Bertha and Charlotte often hired themselves out to other farmers. Max usually worked on top of the haystack while Charlotte and Bertha pitched hay into the wagon and drove the stacker team. Both girls were hired, but *together* they received the pay of only one man. The girls felt it unfair—they did the same work as two men. Even worse, when it came time to "settle up," the farmer gave all the money to Max. He kept it. Bertha simmered. If he'd let her keep one dollar she would have felt satisfied. But that wouldn't have worked either, because Della would have brought out the dreaded community-share bank.

The 'male lookalikes' were working a harvest with Charlotte driving a somewhat wild team. Max warned her to hold the reins tight, because the horses were apt to act up. They did—with Bertha's help. She'd accidentally pitched a rattlesnake on top of the hay. The horses heard the snake, snorted and reared several times threatening to race off.

Bertha screamed, "Hold onto the reins—hold on!"

"I'm trying," Charlotte yelled. The horses won the struggle. They bolted just as Anton grabbed the reins in mid-leap avoiding a potentially dangerous mishap. It was an accident, but with Bertha's gigantic guilt complex, she suffered far more than Charlotte did.

Earl Hall visited seventeen-year-old Bertha and wanted to take her for a ride in his new car. Obviously, he'd forgiven her and Girlie for winning the horse race.

"Mama, can I go?"

"No."

Bertha accepted her answer. Earl didn't give in so easily.

"I only want to take her for a short ride. I won't go over the hill. You'll be able to see us the whole time."

"She can't go."

Bertha felt the reason Della held her down was because she acted so wild, the term not being used in the sense it is today. She was boisterous and always a tomboy.

Aunt Mary visited the family once and, seeing Bertha's rambunctious behavior, put her arm around Charlotte. "What a nice little lady you are." The subtle hint fell on deaf ears. Bertha remained a tomboy and Charlotte remained a 'nice little lady.' But 'nice little lady' Charlotte wasn't allowed to date either. Anton, a family friend for many years, sometimes took both the girls to dances; he always needed to take 'both girls.' Soon Bertha's life began to change.

In her late teens, Bertha went by herself to help

harvest a neighbor's crop. Some of the men began to tease her and yelled, "Hey, Bert."

"What did you call me?"

"Bert," they all chorused, laughing.

Startled, and then thrilled, she loved the nickname. For the first time in her life, she had a name she liked. She couldn't wait to get home. "Mama, I don't like the name Bertha. From now on, I wanna be called Bert."

Della cocked an eyebrow. "Why, I think Bertha is a lovely name."

"Well, I don't. I want to be called Bert."

From then on, Albertine Roseline, Albertha, Bertha became Bert, when the family remembered—and she reminded them when they didn't.

With a new name and feeling quite grownup, Bert began to hire out frequently for harvests without waiting for her father. A day's work earned her a dollar. When she came home, Della brought out the community-share bank for her mandatory contribution. Bert's stomach would churn as she surrendered her hard-earned money. She resented the practice more each time. *It isn't right I have to surrender the money I earned.* One day she came home after earning three dollars, and Della brought out the detested bank. "How much did you make?"

"No," Bert spat out. "I don't wanna put my money in there. I wanna buy Christmas presents for everyone." Bert paled, her mouth gaping and recoiling in shock at her spontaneous outburst. She hadn't meant to say that. Her anger had simmered on the back burner too long and now that it spewed forth, she was determined to stand her ground. Della, shocked and hurt by her daughter's defiance, allowed Bert to keep the money. No more was said and Bert kept her money from then on. Her rebellion brought a close to the detested community-share bank. Her siblings were overjoyed.

At Christmas, she gave her mother a pickle dish and various small items to the rest of the family. She loved giving presents and remained a generous giver throughout her life, always saying, "It gives *me* pleasure."

The family's church acquired a young minister in 1924. He always managed to initiate conversation with Bert after church. He took "quite a shine" to the seventeen-year-old who had recently been confirmed. Soon, Bert received a letter. Stunned, she showed it to her mother. The preacher wanted a date; he'd enclosed a stamped, self-addressed envelope for her reply. Apparently, Della would have allowed Bert dating their minister, but Bert didn't want to go.

"Why don't you want to go?"

"I'm afraid. I don't know what a date is, what you do, or what you talk about. I don't want to go." She didn't want to answer the letter, so Della drafted a reply and made her daughter copy it. There went her first chance for a date.

In 1925, Max bought a nearby bankrupted farmer's granary. He and neighbors put the building on skids and workhorses moved it a mile and a half to the farm; when attached to the house, it became the kitchen. The original dining room and alcove was now just the dining room. After twelve years, Della finally had a real kitchen.

Max bought a big, black-iron range with a side reservoir. Della could now slide the pans around to vary the temperature that she couldn't do on her small stove. A shelf had room for her three clothes irons and one detachable handle. Della loved the stove—Bert saw only the huge water tank. Her arms ached already.

Soon after Della's new kitchen arrived, a what-on-earth-will-they-think-of-next appliance made its appearance. The miraculous wonder: a small, hand pump used *inside* the house. Max mounted it to a kitchen counter and built a cistern outside to catch rainwater in drain fields. The water couldn't be consumed, but was fine for washing clothes and summer baths. Bert was happy visualizing less outside pumping in nasty weather, but she was also troubled.

She often heard her parents' depressing conversations about needing things for the kids or the farm and not having any money. The situation hurt her deeply. She was now quite headstrong and longed to leave the drudgery of farm life. Her 'dream' of becoming a square dance caller was alive and well. "I'll go to Great Falls, Mama, and get a job calling square dances. Then I can send money home."

Della was able to talk her daughter out of going only because Bert loved her mother; she wanted to leave the farm, but not her mother. Things worsened and finally Bert insisted on going. She had no experience with men or experiences of any other kind; she was ill equipped to be in the city alone. Realizing this, Della wrote her brother Henry. He invited Bert to stay with them while she looked for work. Now that she had a place to live, Della agreed to let her go.

Two months shy of twenty, Bert prepared to leave home. Della helped her daughter pack her belongings in a cardboard box and tie it with string. Tearfully, she brought out the 'community-share bank' that no longer received deposits. Della divided the contents into seven piles. Bert's lifetime share of mandatory contributions came to thirteen dollars.

Ironically, at the train station, Bert's ticket was exactly thirteen dollars. Della gave her daughter three dollars the family couldn't afford. Bert was a poor, young woman when she left home for Great Falls in March 1926.

As if taking notice of Della's sorrow, the murky sky

matched her mood. Great dark clouds swirled across the heavens, escorted by reverberating thunder threatening a deluge at any moment. A sharp wind howled across the plain and even the birds ceased their twittering. Tears rolled down Della's cheeks as Bert mounted the train steps, clad in a daisy-yellow gingham dress. In her arms she carried the pitiful little cardboard box holding her worldly possessions.

Looking out the train window at her tearful mother, bittersweet thoughts swept through Bert's mind. She hated leaving her mother, but not the laborious and poverty-stricken life she'd lived for fourteen years. She wondered what exciting experiences lay ahead. Whatever they were, she vowed her new life would be better than the one she was leaving. Visions of becoming a square dance caller flitted in and out of her mind, blocking any serious concerns, demonstrating her vast inexperience. A sudden jolt shook her from her reverie. As she waved good-bye, a hiss of steam shrouded her mother from view as Bert's childhood faded into the past.

Too immature to realize the enormous journey she embarked on, she wasn't frightened in the least. Instead, she grew more excited as each clack of the train wheels carried her to a new life. And what a life it was to be.

Bert gazed out of the train window, not seeing the wheat fields, cattle or passing panorama. The glass reflected only visions of square dancers sashaying across her mind. After the train left Fort Benton, the storm clouds lifted, and as they pulled into Great Falls the sun came out welcoming Bert to a bright new future.

At the station, a highly immature—ignorant in the ways of society—young girl masquerading in an adult body, stepped off the train into an unknown world. Bert's willowy slim figure stood five-feet, five-inches tall, and dark brown bobbed hair with straight bangs framed her face, a style all the rage with "flappers." She didn't know what a flapper was.

She never saw a movie or fashion magazine to learn the chic style of the day; but her costume, copied from the Sears and Roebuck's catalog, was surprisingly smart. Her yellow dress had a long tunic with a belt riding on the hips, the hemline above the knee. The frock gave the appearance she'd neither bosom nor waist, though Bert had a good figure. Years of laborious farm work had made her strong, in spite of her thin frame.

Uncle Henry met her with a welcoming hug.

Bert beamed—at last, *I'm living in a real city.*

In 1926, the 'big city' consisted of 24,000 people. Great Falls was built in a deep depression, straddling the Missouri River and the smaller Sun River. Open prairie still surrounds the city with the Highwood Mountains thirty-miles east providing the only scenic view other than its rivers and waterfalls.

Bert knew none of this, but Great Falls captivated her. She found everything fascinating. She'd lived almost twenty years on two farms near a tiny town neither of which she saw often. Walking down Central Avenue the first time, she felt dazed at the activity. Her family still used horse and buggy, but here the streets were full of cars belching smoke and chugging down the avenue, horns blaring. Fancy-dressed ladies bustled in and out of stores, arms full of packages and shopping bags. A little boy bumped her as he chased his dog down the street, and new mothers pushed baby carriages holding sweet little bundles from heaven. To a lifelong farm girl, the city was exciting, inviting exploration. Every time she went out, she discovered something new, especially window shopping, which was cheap. Life was good.

CHAPTER 14

As soon as possible, Bert sought a job calling square dances. All the dance halls already had long-established callers. Devastation washed through her mind, but she knew there would be an opening one day. In the meantime she satisfied another craving—candy. She bought three candy bars and consumed them all at once, putting a small dent in her finances.

Bert enjoyed staying with Uncle Henry, but she wanted a job so she could send money home. She wore her yellow dress when Aunt Mary took her to Woolworth's Dime Store to apply for work. Counters—row after row, each with a cash register and clerk to assist the customer—filled the store. Bert told the interviewer, "I hain't got no job right now." She didn't get the job, which wasn't surprising considering her poor vocabulary. She had other interviews, but no success. She couldn't believe it would be so difficult to find work in the city.

Desperate, Bert searched and found employment as a domestic—for that work she had experience. Aunt Mary wanted her to refuse the job. Bert said, "I can't. I already accepted it." She didn't know she'd hired herself out to the town's well-known slave driver who never kept domestic help more than a week or two. Her employer demanded Bert wash windows every week, change the sheets daily and other tasks to assure she kept busy every moment. Two weeks later Aunt Mary found her another job. Bert hadn't complained. Mary did.

Mr. and Mrs. R. M. Graham were Bert's new employers. They lived at 1027 Fourth Avenue North with their three children. The large two-story house had a big veranda with a porch swing. Mrs. Graham's easy-going manner made her a joy to work for. The Grahams already had another girl for cleaning. Labor was cheap and many households had domestic employees.

Aunt Mary had informed Mrs. Graham about Bert's sheltered life. Her employer promised to look out for her, and she took to Bert right away. Bert did the cooking, earning room and board and a dollar a day, the going rate for a house girl with Thursdays off. All domestic help seemed to have Thursday off. Bert told Mrs. Graham she didn't have any money, so her employer agreed to pay her twice a month instead of the usual once. Bert almost bounced in glee when she received her first fifteen dollar wage; she'd never seen that kind of money, much less held it in her hand. She sent five dollars home, thrilled to help her family even in such a modest way, but five dollars was a tidy sum in 1926.

Bert had never seen a picture show and went at the first opportunity. As a senior, she still remembered the plot of a depraved man trying to break into a young girl's room. The unsavory storyline did not prevent her from going to films. She adored them, and they became her favorite pastime—after dancing.

The city's first Charleston contest took place that year. Bert didn't attend. That type of dancing was foreign to her—a flapper she was not.

Bert loved Gibson Park and often went to see the ducks and swans and walk around the man-made lake. She loved visiting when the goslings hatched; they reminded her of home. In the summer, people fed bread to the ducks, geese, and swans until they were too stuffed to eat more.

Bert needed dental work, but for once, her fierce practicality weakened in favor of a long-held dream. She bought a pair of shiny black patent shoes. In another store window, she saw a red dress, her favorite color. The sheer material had painted white polka dots and she marveled at the unusual fabric. She went in.

Hesitating, she asked the saleslady, "Can I buy that dress?"

The clerk arched her ultra-thin pencil-drawn eyebrows, having shaved off the real ones. "That's what it's here for." Bert wasn't yet accustomed to shopping. The outfit was available in her size, and she purchased her first store-bought dress. Carrying her precious cargo home, she almost skipped down the street in pure joy. *City life is wonderful.*

When she returned to the Graham's house, she still bubbled in excitement about her new shoes. She put them on and walked around the block twice to see if anyone noticed. No one did. That didn't diminish her excitement—she wore them all day. Mrs. Graham saw Bert return with the packages and gave her some unsolicited motherly advice. "Now you mustn't run out and spend all your money. You need to save some." It was unlikely Bert had embarked on a lengthy spending spree. Her practicality was too strong for that, but she knew Mrs. Graham was right. The next day, her substitute mother took Bert to the First National Bank. Leaving the establishment, Bert felt very grown up; she possessed a bank account.

After a short time on the job, Mrs. Graham asked Bert, "Do you always work like that?" Bert's guilt complex erupted and her knees trembled thinking she was about to be fired. Her employer was only astonished at the speed Bert worked. Mrs. Graham didn't know Bert did everything at a trot-like pace. Her employer claimed she became tired merely watching Bert rush around like a whirling dervish. There weren't enough chores for two people, and Mrs. Graham let the other girl go. Each girl had earned thirty dollars a month before. Now Bert did the work of two, but her wage increased to only forty dollars, not sixty. It wasn't fair—still, Bert felt rich.

She couldn't wait to share her newfound wealth with her family. As soon as possible, Bert took the train to Big Sandy bearing gifts for everyone. When she moved seventy-five-years later, a small notebook surfaced. Listed were 183 gifts: safety pins, stamped envelopes, fifteen cent scissors, candy, stockings, needles, clothes and toys for the kids and ten dollar curtains that were quite an extravagance for her wage. She also took food items her mouth had hungered for when she lived at home: bananas, honey, pineapple, Wheatena, and cheese. During future visits, siblings surrounded her when she walked in the door eager to see what mouthwatering delicacies she'd brought. Every month or two she sent money home, and bought a few things for herself.

A camera ranked first place on Bert's wish list. She asked someone to take a picture with her shiny-new, folding Kodak camera. Standing in the Graham's yard, her uniform depicted a black long-sleeved dress with white cuffs. A large round collar, apron and lacy cap were white. The outfit and the pose of pouring tea seemed to suggest that in addition to the cooking and cleaning, she also served at dinner.

Bert soon acquired a new friend. She met Sally,

another domestic with Thursdays off, in Gibson Park. The cute blue-eyed redhead with turned up nose had freckles splattered across her pale face like raindrops. Sally and Bert became fast friends going to the park, movies and dances.

Various halls and lodges held dances open to the public charging a small fee to cover the musicians and hall rental. As soon as Bert learned of their existence, she attended. She carried a purse to shop or attend movies but she knew a pocketbook would be a nuisance when dancing. Still a girl might need a little "mad money for emergencies," and she solved the problem by knotting a few coins in a handkerchief and dropping the tiny packet into her brassiere, recently invented. She didn't wear lipstick and her bobbed hair required no combing so she didn't carry a purse to dances for several years.

She began attending dances at the Odium Hall. Not dating, she went alone. A live orchestra played the most requested music and men who came stag were plentiful as fleas on a hound. The men's ticket cost seventy-five cents, but as an incentive to attract men, single women paid only twenty-five cents. As soon as the men realized Bert could follow anyone—good dancer or not—she never missed a dance. And she began acquiring a suitable wardrobe for dances.

Bert took the opportunity to make a few dresses with Mrs. Graham's sewing machine. She felt proud of a new green figured dress with matching belt. She'd finished the belt with a fancy metal buckle from Woolworth's and planned to show off her creation when she and Sally went to the picture show that night. It was an age when people dressed up for the movies.

After the film *The Sheik,* Sally and Bert started home and were engaged in conversation about heartthrob Rudolph Valentino, the first male sex symbol. He had died at thirty-one and mass hysteria flooded American females. The studios cashed in on the publicity and were re-running his old films. Women around the country flocked to see his sensually dark and androgynous features one more time. As the girls walked home, Bert noticed the black clouds sheathing the moon and the strong breeze indicating an approaching storm. She hoped it wouldn't rain.

The young women were still talking about the handsome Valentino as they turned off Central Avenue onto a street with less activity and fewer streetlights. As they crossed an alley, two men appeared from out of nowhere. They grabbed Bert and Sally and dragged them toward multiple garbage cans in the dark alleyway. A man's hand clamped over Bert's mouth muffling her cry of fright. The stench from the garbage cans assaulted her nose; the burly assailant's breath reeked of alcohol. He reached under her dress and tried to rip off her panties, but her wild kicking foiled his attempt—for the moment.

No shrinking violet, she needed a weapon. She didn't have one. She couldn't reach her shoes that wouldn't have done much good anyway. In desperation she snatched the cloth belt from her dress and swung it at the man's head. Ordinarily, the belt would have been of little consequence. As a weapon it was laughable, but the belt had a sharp-edged, heavy-metal buckle that made it whip around the man's head. In a stroke of inconceivable luck, the buckle found the perfect target—his eye. He howled in pain, covering his face. When he took his hand away, blood streamed down his cheek. The surprise attack and sudden agony made the attacker forget every vile thing he had in mind. Both men ran. Bert and Sally fled in the opposite direction. When they realized they weren't being followed, they stopped. Bert had been too immersed in her own panic to know what was happening to Sally.

They stared wide-eyed at each other's quaking body, and not knowing what to say to comfort one another, they went home.

Still trembling, Bert told the Graham's about her ordeal. Mr. Graham jumped in his car and tried to find the men without success. Mrs. Graham said, "From now on you go to the early show even if you have to leave the dishes until you get home." Later, when she calmed down, Bert was still angry at the violation, but worried she might have put the man's eye out with the belt. It was typical thinking for her misplaced guilt complex. Unbelievably, she was still concerned about the man's eye and afraid she might have blinded him when she told the story again for this memoir seventy-seven years later.

Bert missed calling for square dances. Her dream of calling in Great Falls hadn't materialized. Then, one day, she learned a lodge hall needed a floor manager. She could hardly contain her excitement; the floor manager was also the caller. This was her chance—at last she would be a square dance caller.

Donning her red dress, Bert combed her hair, grabbed her pocketbook and set off full of confidence. She spoke to a short, fat man whose baldpate shone like a billiard ball. She bit her lip and stifled a giggle; she could almost see her reflection.

"Whatta ya want?" he growled.

His rudeness surprised her, but she rebounded swiftly. "I've come for the job. I'm a square dance caller."

He looked down his nose apparently unable to believe his ears. "It's a man's job. We don't hire women," he barked.

"But I'm a good caller."

Scraggly black eyebrows shot up crinkling his forehead. "I told ya, we don't hire women," he bellowed.

He stalked off leaving her standing in shocked disbelief. Her 'dream' exploded like a burst balloon. She couldn't understand it. Big Sandy folks loved her calling and didn't mind she was a female. Determined, she later tried other dance halls, but with the same results, though the rejections weren't delivered with such a nasty growl. Instead, some men acted as if they felt sorry for the poor demented creature standing in front of them. With each rebuff, she felt more dejected. *Is my dream going die before it's even been born? No! I will be a caller.* She continued her quest whenever she could. Each attempt failed.

Bert felt bitter disappointment at not landing a calling job, but in later years she told everyone, "Those early days in Great Falls were the most joyous period of my entire life. I was having so much fun it didn't seem real." She danced every weekend, was responsible to no one other than her boss, had the freedom to do what she wanted when she wanted, enjoyed spending money, and at only twenty-years of age, she had her first date. Life was sweet.

Bert met Frank, a good-looking man with dark hair, in the park. She went out with him, but one date was enough. He was a "masher," a word she'd learned since coming to Great Falls. He asked her out repeatedly—she said no. On one of her frequent visits home, she told her mother about an older man who also had asked her out. She'd declined. Della's first question concerned not how much older he was but, "What does he do for a living?"

"He owns a coal mine."

"Oh, that's wonderful."

That attitude commonly prevailed for mothers with daughters. Female employment was nearly nonexistent other than teaching. Marriage was the only answer for young ladies. Della knew Bert would be better off marrying an older, well-established man, rather than a younger one just getting started in life. Later, she encouraged both Ella and Mamie to marry older men. Since her mother thought it so 'wonderful,' Bert accepted a date the next time the gentleman asked her out. When he picked her up, Mrs. Graham saw them leaving. When Bert returned, her employer asked, "How old is that man?"

"He's thirty-nine."

Mrs. Graham gasped. "You cannot go out with him again. You need to date men nearer your own age." Bert, an adult, could do as she wanted, but she obeyed Mrs. Graham, as she would have her mother. That made a total of two dates in twenty-years of life.

CHAPTER 15

October 24, 1926, was a sad day for Great Falls and the entire art world. Charlie Russell died. As Bert read the paper, memories of her visits to his studio flooded back. She remembered how he loved children and what a tease he was.

Bert hadn't visited Charlie in several years, but she remembered him fondly and wanted to attend his funeral. Three days later, she put on her best dark dress accessorizing it with the new black cloche. Feeling chic in her new hat, she set out for the Episcopal Church of the Incarnation.

The funeral took place on a lovely Indian summer day. A light breeze rustled the few red and gold leaves resisting their eminent demise. Wispy gray clouds hung on the horizon, and she hoped it wouldn't rain. Nearing the sandstone gothic church, she stopped abruptly in stunned disbelief. She couldn't believe her eyes: hundreds and hundreds of people standing outside. The church was full. She opened the door, and a symphony of aromas nearly suffocated her senses. Hugh floral sprays covered the casket and filled the sanctuary. The Prince of Wales,

Douglas Fairbanks, and other movie stars all sent floral sprays along with those from the Mint Saloon and other local business establishments that Charlie frequented. One large spray with red and white flowers was fashioned into an artist's palette. With no room for all the flowers, someone strung up chicken wire along the south wall for smaller tributes.

The pretty, little church had a beautiful, seven-foot carving of the Last Supper—one of only two in the world—but that day banks of flowers outshone everything in the church. Bert joined the mourners outside.

Charlie detested cars and a fifteen-year-old hearse was brought out of storage. Viewers could see the casket through beveled glass windows edged with black curtains. The elevated coffin had ice placed underneath to preserve the body until burial. No modern-day coffin would have fit inside the short hearse—there was barely room for Charlie.

After the service, the longest procession ever seen in Great Falls formed outside the church. Two coal black horses trotted smartly in front of the hearse, and Monte, Charlie's saddled horse, trailed behind. As the hearse slowly made its way out Thirteenth Street North, a light shower fell and a brilliant rainbow appeared as if welcoming Charlie to the Pearly Gates. Charlie would have loved it.

The *Tribune* soon brought Bert thrilling news. Opening the newspaper one morning, exciting words leaped right off the page. A famous caller from California was scheduled to appear. She signed up, anticipation filling every waking moment. At the dance she was thrilled to observe his talent and technique. Her 'dream' was still alive but going nowhere. She knew she was good, but how could anyone hire her if no one ever heard her?

When the caller took a break, Bert approached the manager. "Can I fill in while he's on break? I'm a caller." The manager looked at her suspiciously but saw no harm in it most likely thinking she'd make a fool of herself. Bert broke loose with what she considered one of her best patter-calls. The crowd liked her and she beamed with joy. The professional caller returned, walked straight over to her, and put both his hands on her shoulders.

"Where did you ever learn to call like that?"

"My papa taught me." Her heart pounded until she felt it would burst. *He likes me. Is this the break I need?* Nothing came of it.

The *Tribune* announced a street dance to be held in front of the Strain Brother's Building. Bert went. Central Avenue was blocked off, and a small band of musicians and callers assembled on the sidewalk. Without a partner, she could only observe. She knew the trendy call in progress. When the caller finished the square, she told the woman next to her. "The caller is doing a pretty good job."

The women's mouth dropped. "Do you call?"

"Oh, ya, I've called for years."

The woman's eyes widened. "I've been trying to get a caller to come to the Wild Rose Dairy to call at my home in Manchester; we have several couples who join us to square dance." Callers didn't beat down her door because they were unpaid volunteers. Bert hadn't called since moving to Great Falls. She missed it.

"I'd love to call for you, but I've no way to get to Manchester."

"Most of our dancers live in Great Falls and someone will give you a ride." The woman introduced herself and the next day a man called Bert to arrange transportation.

Wearing her new green dress, Bert almost glowed in

anticipation. It wasn't a *real dance*, but there were four squares. Her great need to be accepted and liked was now a beneficial trait, and she gave an invigorating performance. The dancers loved her deep husky voice. Everyone could hear and understand her, important qualifications not all callers were blessed with. She called for the group every weekend. Attendance soon multiplied to six squares, and comments like, "Have you heard the new woman caller?" and "No, she's really good," were heard about the square dance circuit. Eventually, there wasn't enough room for all the people who came and the group rented a hall the *Leader Newspaper* owned. Still unpaid, Bert called for the pure joy. The assemblage used records and since she danced the polka, waltz, and schottische in between calling, she was delighted to call free of charge. And soon, she found a new kind of dance.

The first Halloween in Great Falls, Bert discovered masquerade dances at Riverside Garden. All the lodges and public dance halls held these costumed affairs. She adored dressing in disguise and had a marvelous time. No one knows what she wore the first two masquerades; the earliest picture of her in costume is a photograph taken in 1928 wearing a man's suit, tie and hat. She began collecting weird and wacky things for future costumes: wigs, fake glasses with attached big nose, phony protruding teeth, crazy hats, and more. She rarely wore a serious costume, preferring something comical and once in later years, a Big Bird outfit. Her collection grew larger every year, and she used the components in various combinations.

Occasionally, she dressed as a female, but her favorite costume throughout her life was that of a bum, a male bum. She had a good reason for this. As a man, she could ask the ladies to dance, and she could dance *all* the dances instead of waiting for a man to ask her. Bert's disguises were so complete that sometimes no one knew her identity until the unmasking. She attended her last masquerade at ninety-eight as a male bum—she won first prize.

After the poverty and abuse of her youth, Great Falls was an incredible tonic. Bert was having the time of her life. She didn't know it yet, but dramatic changes awaited her around the corner.

Mrs. Graham took the children to Gibson Park one Sunday, and Bert, wearing her new red dress with white polka dots, went along to watch the children. That day would give her outfit special meaning and she kept the dress the rest of her life. Arriving at the park, Bert settled on a bench to watch the children while reading the newspaper. Two men drove by and honked the horn. Looking up, Bert figured they were mashers and returned to reading. Arlo Courtnage and his friend, Jack Little, were cruising around town. Arlo drove around the lake and returned to park near Bert. She moved the children to another section of the playground, but the car found them, and once again parked. Arlo, who had never seen Bert before, stared at her for a long time. He turned to Jack and said, "I'm going to marry that girl."

"Are you nuts? You haven't even spoken to her." Jack told Bert the story later, and she could hardly believe it.

Mrs. Graham returned from her stroll and wanted to take the children home, but Sally had arrived and she and Bert wanted to see the ducks. Mrs. Graham told Bert she could stay, but gave her orders to be home before dusk. Bert and Sally ambled around the lake and then left for home. The mysterious car appeared again, the horn honking.

Arlo called out, "Tell us where you live and we'll take

you home." After their near rape, they were afraid and kept walking. Then a voice said, "Hey, Bert." For the first time she looked at the passenger, recognizing Jack.

Sally looked too. "Do you know him?"

"Ya, I dance with him at the Odium Hall."

"Well, it should be all right since you know one of them."

Jack started to help Bert into the car, but Arlo said, "Hold on. Switch places, I want this one," so Bert sat in the front with him. They all talked for a time and then Arlo drove Sally and Jack home first. Before Bert got out of the car, he asked for a date the next night.

"No, I'm gonna be busy." Somehow Arlo found out her phone number and called the next day to say he wanted to talk to her. He drove to the Graham house, parked in front, and honked the horn. Bert went outside.

"Let's go for a ride."

"Okay, but I can't stay long. Mrs. Graham doesn't allow me out at night." During their ride, Bert learned that he worked in the Great Northern Roundhouse maintaining the train wheels. Then as promised, he drove her home before nightfall. Bert liked him.

The next morning Mrs. Graham lectured Bert. "Gentlemen do not park out front and honk the horn; they come in to meet the family." Bert saw nothing wrong with his honking the horn; it was an etiquette lesson for both of them. She told Arlo and the next time he came to the door. They began a steady relationship, and on her next visit home, Bert told her mother about Arlo. She was shocked at Della's reaction.

"You're dating a Courtnage? You better be careful. Grant Courtnage is a drunkard and Arlo might be one too." Grant was Arlo's cousin. Once Della met Arlo, she liked him too.

Bert had grown up in a smoke and alcohol free world

and often heard about the terrible evil of drink. "If you drank, you were a drunk." One time after drinking a couple of beers, Arlo arrived for their date. Distressed, she refused to go out with him again unless he quit drinking. He never had another drink. Now that's love.

Born in Pierce, Nebraska, in 1903, Arlo Reimers Courtnage was the son of Frank and Ellenette from Geraldine. Considered good looking, he had dark brown eyes and a medium frame of five-feet, five-inches. At twenty-three, his straight brown hair was receding, a Courtnage trait. Everyone liked Arlo. A more generous and friendly man didn't exist. A member of the Eagles lodge, he didn't gamble or drink after he started dating Bert, but he did enjoy an occasional pipe—it isn't known why Bert didn't demand he quit that too. His concept of a good time was to visit family and friends or go for a drive. Unfortunately for Bert, he didn't like movies, and worse—he didn't dance.

When Arlo and Bert began dating, she asked him what his religion was. It didn't actually matter as long as it was not Catholic. Bert's Grandmother Scharlotte was Catholic but converted to Lutheran. She passed down terrible stories about Catholic priests having sex with nuns and lurid tales of nuns' pregnancies. From then on, Catholics weren't tolerated in the Clawiter family. Bert, demonstrating her practicality, told everyone, "If I never date a Catholic, I won't fall in love with one." She never outgrew her prejudice, although she was tolerant about anything else. Eighty years later, Scharlotte's stories didn't sound so farfetched when the pedophilia priest scandals made world headlines.

CHAPTER 16

For seven months, Bert and Arlo went on rides, visited family, and enjoyed picnics. Then one night while parked by the river, he pulled a ring from his pocket. "It's an engagement ring. Will you marry me?" Totally flustered, Bert stuttered, stammered, and was so bewildered she couldn't speak. She didn't answer for so long that Arlo worried she might refuse his offer. "You don't have to answer me right away," he said, slipping the ring on her finger anyway. She never did say yes. They just began planning a May wedding.

Two weeks before the wedding, Bert's Uncle Henry received transfer orders to Portland, Oregon. Bert was his favorite niece, and he recognized her special creative talent. Henry told her he wanted to take her to Portland, tutor her in English, and then send her to a designing school. He promised Arlo a job on the Great Northern in Portland. The move would be easy with a job waiting for Arlo and Bert's education paid for. Ecstatic at the incredible opportunity, her mind soared to a whole new world of fantasy. But there was a problem—Arlo didn't want to go.

"But you'll have a job waiting for you."

"It would be too hard moving away from our families."

"We can take the train back for visits." The conflict of wills collided for agonizing days. Unable to convince Arlo, Bert's emotions shredded into confetti. Like a clock pendulum, her decision swung back and forth. *I want to go to Portland. I love Arlo.* Finally: *I can't go. I'm wearing his ring. The date is set. If it wasn't, I'd go.*

When Uncle Henry and Aunt Mary moved, Bert grieved their departure, but mostly her lost world of opportunity. For the rest of her days she wondered how different her life might have been if she'd gone.

Arlo's parents wanted to visit family in Iowa, but they didn't have a car. So, Arlo applied for the new-fangled consumer credit recently established and bought a four-cylinder 1926 Star for his parents to use. When they returned, Arlo had a new car—almost.

He had a car, but he needed a home for his soon-to-be wife. He rented a small apartment and moved in. Bert moved over her meager possessions, a few things at a time. Eager to have a home of her own, she began shopping for household items. Then Arlo announced he had a hope chest—of sorts. She was shocked, she'd never heard of a man having a hope chest. He already had several household items, including a three-piece crockery bowl set. He brought out his items so they wouldn't duplicate anything. The next day, she showed him the silverware she'd bought at Woolworths. "They're pretty, but a set of six will never be enough," so he bought an additional set. The incident foretold the future; her family would grow by six new members.

Bert designed and made a knee-length, sheer aqua silk wedding dress with a round neck and a hint of sleeve. The stylish dress had no waistline; the hip-riding belt showed off a huge buckle with hand-stitched, rhinestone buttons. Everything including her slippers and the peach flower pinned to her shoulder came to twenty-two dollars, more than half her monthly wage. She kept that dress the rest of her life too.

They planned to wed in Fort Benton to make it easier for relatives coming from Big Sandy, Shonkin, and Geraldine. Unfortunately, that year it rained every single day in May, making the unpaved roads impassable. Arlo then suggested they wed in Choteau because that road was gravel. He had family living in town and Bert's surrogate mother lived there, so why they didn't marry in Great Falls was a mystery. Perhaps driving to another city was the romantic thing to do in those days if you didn't have a formal wedding.

On Bert's twenty-first birthday, Arlo arrived at the Graham house early. It was raining. He and Bert collected his cousin Frank and his wife to act as witnesses. Reverend Culbertson performed the ceremony. No immediate family on either side attended, a heartbreaking situation for two people who so loved their families.

After the wedding, the newlyweds returned to work, and Bert now gained a new family: Arlo's parents and siblings Winona, Harold, Grace and Chris.

Bert's wedding gift from her family was a pig cutting board her mother cut from an ordinary plank. Della burned in the eyes and tail with a hot nail. The gift proved the old adage: "It's the thought that counts." Bert treasured the pig. When she discovered the board wasn't made of hardwood, she never again used it for its intended purpose, but she displayed it in the kitchen of all her homes ever after.

Mrs. Graham so dreaded losing Bert that she pleaded for Arlo to live at their house and let Bert continue to work. He accepted the offer only after her winning argument that they could save some money. The newlyweds surrendered their tiny apartment, stored their things in the basement and lived in the Graham house. Arlo tolerated the situation for only two months before telling Bert, "We need to get our own place." She'd worked for her employer more than a year; when she gave notice, Mrs. Graham cried.

Arlo found a minuscule apartment opening into the alley. Their stay was brief and they moved to a one-room apartment at 717 Third Avenue North where Bert became pregnant. That didn't keep her from dancing.

Arlo worked the swing shift and knew Bert loved dancing. "There's no reason you should stop something you enjoy so much. You can go anytime you want, as long as you behave yourself." So Bert went alone and walked home or rode with friends. Arlo never raised a jealous word during the entire marriage.

Bert adored her new family, and they returned the affection. She often told people, "It's such a pleasure visiting with Arlo's relatives; they never bad-mouth other family members or squabble among themselves." The same couldn't be said for her family. She took as many pictures of the Courtnages as she did the Clawiters.

Only after marriage did Bert learn what an extraordinary man she'd married. Arlo was an absolute homebody. He enjoyed puttering around the house and being with his family more than any form of entertainment known to man. He was a rare husband who often put on an apron to do the dishes when Bert was busy. Everyone said his biggest fault was his extreme generosity. It is hard to imagine the extent of his generosity if Bert thought it a defect—she was more than generous herself. She loved her new family and kept in close contact with hers.

Bert wrote to her parents often. Max answered most of

Dorothy V. Wilson

her letters because he liked to write, but his lack of
education reflected in his poor spelling. Della wrote
phonetically because she didn't know how to spell the
words. Bert adopted the practice not because she didn't
know how to spell a word, but because "lite" made better
sense to her practical mind than "light." Letters to her
family were filled with "R U going 2 the dance, Cum C
us, I M going, B4 U go, Bo-k and ☐ dance." The system
was her personal form of shorthand, and she reverted to
proper English only for business letters. If her letters
looked strange, they were in no way difficult to read. Still
decades away, she would have been at home with
texting—she'd already invented it.

Arlo told Bert about an abandoned cat that had adopted
the Great Northern Roundhouse as home. The feline was
a nuisance because it was an affectionate animal. Arlo
stroked the cat a few times and tried to shoo it away—it
wouldn't 'shoo.' One day the cat was particularly
bothersome rubbing against Arlo's leg seeking affection.
He feared tripping over the feline, but he didn't want to
hurt the annoying animal—he only wanted it gone. The
train whistle sounded and its wheels began to roll.
Inspired, Arlo lifted the cat, put it on the departing train
and waved good-bye. When he went home, he told Bert,
"We won't be bothered with that pesky cat anymore. He's
living in Seattle now."

"Oh, swell, I didn't want him to go to the pound." A
week later the feline was back—someone in Seattle must
have had the same 'inspiration.'

Working for the railroad offered one phenomenal
perk. Arlo received unlimited free rail passes for his
immediate family. Bert missed her family and often took
the train to Big Sandy. She also visited Uncle Henry in
Portland and went to Seattle to see Uncle Will. Seattle

became her relaxation center, all courtesy of the Great Northern Railroad. Other than trips to visit family, they never used the perk for a *real vacation* during their entire marriage.

Whenever Bert went to Big Sandy, she looked forward to seeing her beloved grandfather, Eugene. A widower for twenty years, he had moved from Minnesota to Big Sandy to be with his two sons. As a little girl, she'd often crawled on his lap for affection while he regaled her with tales of his life. When she received the telegram about his death, she was devastated. She took the next train.

The gentle sway and rhythmic-clacking of the wheels seemed hypnotic and all Grandpa's stories came flooding back.

Born in Germany, Eugene went to school to be a Lutheran preacher. After graduation, he preached one sermon and quit, saying, "I can't believe that stuff." He studied law but didn't graduate. Maybe he didn't believe in law either.

Bert's favorite story was when he, his wife, and six children immigrated by sailing ship in 1880. Conditions on the three-month journey were atrocious. Many emigrants didn't survive. Those who paid the required duty at Castle Clinton stepped off the ship into America's prosperity. On the dock, the "Welcoming Committee" greeted them: swindlers, thieves, and prostitutes there to fleece the naive immigrants.

At Castle Clinton all seven of the Clawiters' trunks disappeared, leaving the family only the clothes on their backs—no birth certificates, important papers, or family treasures. No one knows how, when, or where their trunks vanished—perhaps they were lost to the "Welcoming Committee." Bert loved the tale as a child, but she never heard how they survived the event— probably a saga more appalling than the journey.

CHAPTER 17

As the train neared her destination, Bert relived the awful situation when her grandfather had moved to Big Sandy. He stayed for a week at Will's house and then at Max's for another week. Della loved him, but nine people already lived under her roof and an extra person made life almost unbearable in a one-bedroom house. Often, Bert had heard Della pleading, "Will, please take him back; it is so crowded here." Will's house was smaller, but he didn't have seven children.

When Bert arrived at her parents' house and heard the details of Eugene's death, she cried in great pity for her beloved grandfather—and she was furious with Sophy.

Eugene was too old for farm labor and being shifted from house to house made him feel utterly useless. One day he wet his bed, and Sophy scolded him. This was more than the shamed man could bear; he went out to the barn and hanged himself. Before his death, he was a healthy ninety-one-year-old man with a full head of hair, a lush, drooping mustache, and a six-inch beard—all snow white.

Bert couldn't understand how Sophy could scold him

for something he couldn't help. Later, she realized the rebuke most likely was the final straw added to feelings of futility he'd felt for years. She forgave Sophy.

Bert felt brokenhearted, but life goes on. She said good-bye to her beloved grandfather while bringing forth a new life—she was five months pregnant. Before Arlo and Bert had married, they discussed how many children they wanted. Arlo wanted four. Bert didn't want any. She loved babies; she also knew the struggle it took to raise them. They compromised on two, but her pregnancy was unplanned. Twins ran in the family and all through her pregnancy she prayed for twins to "have it all over and done with at one time." Her little *accident* arrived seventeen months after the wedding.

Calvin Coolidge was president, eggs were fifty cents a dozen, a letter cost two cents, Mickey Mouse's "Steamboat Willie" appeared in the first sound cartoon and the first television set with a three-inch screen sold for seventy-five dollars. It was a good time to be born.

Oscar winning "Wings" starring cupid-lipped Clara Bow played at the Liberty Theater, but Bert was too busy to attend. She was in labor. Arlo did the traditional pacing at the Deaconess Hospital. Dorothy Viola Courtnage came into the world on October 31, 1928.

The Germans had developed "Twilight Sleep" for birthing babies. Mothers in labor took scopolamine and morphine. The new procedure claimed to be pain free and to require fewer forceps deliveries. It didn't work for Bert. The doctor needed forceps for the difficult birth. The first time Bert saw her baby, she screamed. The nurse had not warned her about her daughter's lopsided head. Bert cried and cried. It took the nurse sometime to convince Bert the baby's head would be normal in a few days, and it was. However, it was lucky the baby wasn't a boy who might one day be bald because her daughter would always have a deep furrow on the side of her head from the forceps.

At eight pounds, fourteen ounces, Dorothy, a roly-poly cherub, measured twenty-inches long. Her brown cat eyes soon turned to mahogany like her father, and thick reddish-brown baby hair covered her head. It was a different age and the proud father wasn't allowed to hold his baby—he could only admire her through a large window. The mother didn't see her baby until it was cleansed and given a physical examination.

A bizarre episode happened at the hospital. A woman down the hall from Bert had given birth to twins two days prior. As soon as the mother awoke, she asked, "Are they girls or boys?"

The nurse smiled. "You have beautiful twin boys."

The woman burst into tears. "I don't want them!"

"Oh, you don't mean that. Let me show you how cute they are."

"I don't want to see them—I don't want them." Hysterical, she repeated her declaration for two days. She and her husband were already blessed with five boys, and they had agreed to try only once more for a girl. No one could get the woman to change her mind.

Bert heard the story and asked the nurse, "Would you like me to try?"

"Can't hurt. We haven't been able to get through to her."

Bert hoped to persuade the mother to look at her sons; she knew once she saw them, she couldn't help but love them. Bert introduced herself to the woman in bed. While they talked, Bert mentioned how she'd prayed for twins herself hoping to make the idea more acceptable to the woman. The distraught woman's eyes widened and she looked at Bert with new interest. "What is your baby?"

"I have a little girl."

The woman bolted upright. "You can have my twins if you'll give me your baby girl."

Bert couldn't believe what she'd heard. Still, she couldn't help thinking about it because she'd wanted twins so much, but she couldn't give up her daughter. Later, the woman did look at her twins and accepted them—but Dorothy had *almost* become twin boys.

Family and friends paraded in and out of Bert's room eager to see the new arrival. Bert wanted to name her baby girl Arloa. But her husband wouldn't even consider it. When Dorothy was older and heard the story, she regretted her mother didn't insist because she thought Arloa was a beautiful name.

New mothers were kept in the hospital a long time. Charlotte now worked in Great Falls, and she and Arlo took Bert and Dorothy home when she was eleven-days old. The baby buggy almost filled their already crowded apartment.

Bert took three-week-old Dorothy to the movies. The baby lay snug and cozy in a blanket, her eyes following the movement on the screen until she fell asleep. She never cried. When she became hungry, Bert wrapped a blanket around her shoulders and nursed Dorothy in the theater. She was almost raised at the movies and became as big a fan as her mother.

Eager to introduce Dorothy to her family, Bert and her one-month-old baby boarded the train for Big Sandy. Dorothy was the first grandchild and everyone wanted to hold her. They passed her round and round and Dorothy gurgled with each new pair of encircled arms. After a two day visit, they went home so Bert could prepare for Christmas.

Their apartment was too tiny for the six-foot Christmas tree Bert had promised herself as a child. She tucked a small fir in the corner, and loved it even if the height was disappointing. Christmas Day, the family took the train to Geraldine to spend the holiday with Arlo's family.

Dorothy reaped many gifts but was too young to know what it was all about. Arlo and Bert stayed a few days to visit and then took the train to Big Sandy to spend New Year's with the Clawiters. For the first time, Max and Della left their tree up and there were more gifts for the baby. Arlo returned to work after New Year's and Bert and Dorothy stayed for a week's visit. No wonder Dorothy would become addicted to traveling—she was initiated at a young age.

An active baby, Dorothy tried to sit up at six-weeks-old. Bert told everyone, "She isn't much trouble because she's such a good baby. She doesn't cry often and gurgles at everyone who comes near her." If Bert went to a dance, sometimes Arlo wrapped his daughter in a blanket and they went along to watch. Dorothy's eyes followed her mother around the room and when Bert danced by she waved, sending her daughter into spasms of laughter.

That Easter, Dorothy was one of five babies sprinkled in baptism at the Methodist Church. Charlotte held Dorothy—the only baby who didn't cry—while Bert glowed in pride.

Arlo belonged to the Methodist Church and Bert the Lutheran. They alternated church attendance each week. In a couple of months, Bert said, "This is ridiculous. One of us needs to change religion. Let's each write down the religion we liked best." When she unfolded both papers, each read Methodist. She changed.

A tiny apartment and a baby weren't enough to keep Bert busy; she was "fidgety from lack of work" and wanted to move. Arlo agreed. "We need to get started on our livelihood." The weather had produced a bountiful harvest on his property so they had extra money. "We can buy a house in town or build one and farm my property in Geraldine." Bert hated farming. Arlo said, "It doesn't make any difference to me," and the matter was settled.

Arlo's property bordered his parents' farm. Since he didn't work the land, he let his father, Frank, and later his brother, Harold, farm the property, and they split any profit fifty-fifty. An oil company looked at Arlo's property and other farms seeking the oil that "they knew was there." The prospectors drilled several times and Bert kept her fingers crossed. The supposed gusher never materialized. Seventy years later she sold the property to Frank's great grandson.

Arlo and Bert began looking at houses. One at 818 Third Avenue North drew their attention. The frame house, built about 1909, was two stories with a full attic, large basement and a porch across the front. The backyard was big enough for a garden, and two young apple trees caught Bert's eye. She could smell apple pies already.

Entering the foyer with its L-shaped staircase, Bert's eyes lit up. "What a perfect place for a Christmas tree." After exploring the premises, Bert said, "I like the house, but it's too big."

Arlo grinned. "No, it isn't. I've got a plan. We can make apartments or take in boarders, and their rent will pay the mortgage. When we get the house paid for, we will buy another and someday we'll own the entire block. Then I'll have something to keep me busy when I retire, and we'll have a good monthly income."

Boarding houses were popular but all included home-cooked meals. Bert wanted more work, but not that much. Apartments seemed more logical. After studying the layout, they agreed it could be done. On May 1, 1929, Arlo signed—not a mortgage, but contract papers—and bought the house for 9,500 dollars. Bert felt excited, but at the same time she trembled from anxiety. She'd never experienced debt before and couldn't help worrying. But soon she relaxed. "I don't need to worry. Arlo has reliable employment."

Bert had lived in only two homes for twenty years. After moving to Great Falls, she became a gypsy, moving five times in only two years. She'd not yet started her numerous collections and owned little to pack. Once they'd moved in their few possessions, both set to work. They worked together in the mornings. While Arlo was at work, she wielded hammer and paintbrush, moving Dorothy from room to room. Buying supplies for the house, their meager savings vanished. With no rent money coming in, Bert began to worry.

After modification, they had their one-room apartment at the back of the house where a small porch overlooked the backyard. The room's closet was fifteen feet long and four feet wide, a walk-in closet. Impractical for them, they converted it to a partial kitchen with a sink and cupboards. The stove was located in the main room, and meal preparations required many steps. They rented the other two-room dwelling. The upstairs had one apartment with a stove but no sink, and three sleeping rooms. The tiny basement room would be for a boarder; Bert could handle one. They were ready for business. Bert worried no renters would come when she placed the ad in the paper, but the apartments filled quickly.

Other than Bert and Arlo's apartment, the only running water in the house flowed from the upstairs bathroom. Bert was elated with her modern bathroom complete with toilet, large claw-foot tub and pedestal sink; tenants carried a pail to the bathroom for fresh water, and kept a second empty bucket in their apartment to hold the dirty water, later emptied down the drain in the community bathroom.

A furnace provided heat. The first time Bert heard the coal rumble down the narrow chute like distant thunder into a special basement bin, it triggered a memory: She and her father being harassed at the coal mine. Now it was simply a matter of a phone call.

In addition to the coal bin, the basement contained a tool room, a long workbench, and a larder for the canned goods Bert intended to make. In addition to the outside clothesline, Arlo installed lines in the basement for use during inclement weather.

Now that the rooms were rented, Dorothy once again became Bert's most time-consuming project. At first she was proud of Dorothy's early development, but when she began walking she seemed to be everywhere at once and into everything. Dorothy's first word was Mama, and Bert wondered if her colossal chatterbox would ever stop talking. Dorothy called herself Dor-Dor. Her first complete sentence was, "Dor-Dor be good girl now," a clue to her rambunctious activity.

CHAPTER 18

Vegetables in the city were available year round, so Bert didn't can as much as her mother. She only put up pickles, chow-chow, jelly, and fruit for the family. She planted a big vegetable garden but saved room for a few rows of flowers. Grandma Scharlotte would have thought her effort puny, but Bert loved her flowers. An avid gardener, she kept one into her mid-nineties, but by then she planted only flowers. One city convenience delighted Bert. She needed only step outside her door for fresh milk, easier than fetching and milking cows, then cranking away on the cream separator. Oh, how she loved city living. But sometimes there were unwelcome surprises.

Bert took eleven-month-old Dorothy to the movies on a beautiful day with gauzy-gray clouds hung low in the sky. On the way to the theater a few strong gusts developed. Vibrant red and gold leaves showered down. They crunched softly as Bert stepped on them, leaving a kaleidoscopic carpet behind her. Weather forecasts didn't exist, so Bert was shocked leaving the theater to find a raging blizzard enveloping the city. She wasn't wearing a coat. She'd taken a blanket for Dorothy, and she bundled her daughter and ran for home stopping three times to warm up at apartment buildings along the way.

In 1928 and 1929, one blizzard after another swept the state until Easter. The temperatures never rose above zero. Forty below wasn't unusual. Bert yearned for 1929 to end, but before it did, Grandmother Scharlotte died and Bert felt she should accompany Della to North Dakota for the funeral.

Scharlotte's husband, John, died in 1920 after forty years of lucrative farming, despite their illegal beginning as stowaways. He lies in the Amenia cemetery. Scharlotte couldn't get away from her husband even in death—she lies next to the man she detested in life.

As landlady of an apartment house, Bert lived the life of a radio soap-opera star. Not long after the apartments opened, a tenant knocked on her door.

"There's a baby crying somewhere. I'm worried because the crying is so constant."

"There aren't any babies living here."

"Well, there's one crying somewhere."

None of the apartments had a private outside door. Visitors rang the doorbell and were directed to the correct apartment. "I'll look into it," Bert said. She went upstairs and heard crying coming from a young, single woman's sleeping room. Bert knocked on the door. The only reply, crying. Trying the door, she found it open. She called out, "Hello" and went in. A pale, young woman lay on the bed, and on the closet floor, a baby already blue with the umbilical cord wrapped around its neck. Bert gasped and ran downstairs to call an ambulance. The baby died. The medics castigated Bert for not doing something about the cord.

"I was afraid you would blame me for doing something

wrong if the baby died, and it was awfully blue already."

The medics admitted that could have happened. Guilt wracked Bert's body. After everyone left, she burst into tears and began shaking. Still quite immature at twenty-three, she'd no knowledge of problems about birthing. Her mother never discussed sex. She never saw an animal born and was asleep for the birth of her daughter.

The woman moved out two days later. Bert never saw her again. Society of the day was unforgiving, and a baby born out of wedlock was an appalling stigma. The city had no home for unwed pregnant girls. Some parents shipped their daughters off to a distant relative where the baby was adopted and the girl later returned home from her "vacation." Many girls went to back-alley abortionists—often not surviving. Other families disowned their daughters.

After the incident, Bert rented that room only to single men. She didn't want to face that problem again. And there were other things she prayed never to see again.

Bert possessed many talents—one unwanted. She hated it, and she tried to rid herself of the gift. She was somewhat psychic and had mystical feelings of things about to happen that she couldn't explain. The intense episodes she called *feelings* frightened her, made her sick to her stomach, and left her extremely nervous. Sometimes she had a vague idea of what the problem was, but often the sensation was only a foreboding of doom. The incidents were never about anything good, only misfortune, which is why she hated the ability.

These experiences began at age eight and they terrified her. Frightened, she told her parents. They laughed, saying it was her imagination. Their laughter, of course, brought the expected results—she never told anyone again.

One such experience happened soon after their marriage. Unable to hide how much the premonition frightened her, she finally told Arlo. She explained as best she could and was so serious he didn't laugh, assuming it wouldn't happen again. But it did.

A new tenant asked Arlo to borrow his car on Saturday. A group of people from Great Falls and Vaughn wanted to picnic in Neihart, but they needed more transportation. Arlo loaned him the vehicle. He barely knew the tenant; an example of his generosity.

Late Saturday morning, Bert began pacing the floor like a caged tiger.

"What's the matter?" Arlo said.

"Nothing." She kept pacing. She still hated to say anything about her *feelings,* but Arlo insisted. She finally told him. "Those people don't have our car."

"Yes, they do, they took it to Neihart."

"No! The car is not in Neihart. It's west of town and the car is crooked."

"What do you mean it's crooked?"

"I don't know. It's just crooked."

At this point Arlo doubted her too. How could a car be *crooked?*

Unable to calm her down, Arlo borrowed his cousin's creamery truck because Bert insisted they find their vehicle. She knew only one thing for certain; their *crooked* car was west of town. Neihart lay east. At every fork in the road, Bert directed Arlo which way to turn. The nearer they got to Vaughn, the more she leaned forward as if searching. Keyed up and bouncing in her seat, she yelled, "Keep going, keep going—the car is out here."

Baffled, Arlo kept driving. A few miles later they arrived in Vaughn, and parked alongside the road, they saw their "crooked car." The vehicle was jacked up and the car leaned to one side with a tire missing. The tenant had only needed a tire, not the car.

The incident scared Bert because the episode was more detailed than past events, and the *feelings* were getting stronger and coming more often. She tried to suppress them—they came anyway. She might have learned to accept and encourage the ability if they were about happy events, but they never were. None were disasters, but the phenomenon plagued her life.

Bert loved their home's location, three blocks from Central Avenue, the eight-block-long business district. Less than a mile away were Bertsche's Food Market, the Methodist Church, Bailey's Ice Cream, and the Liberty Theater that played the first talking movie in 1928. The majority of the population never visited the Red Feather Bar with its "No Indians" sign and the houses of ill repute on First Avenue South. Arlo walked a mile to work. He had a car, but preferred walking to keep fit. Neighbors saw him every workday afternoon at 2:30, wearing navy blue bib overalls and carrying his black, domed lunch box.

Like her mother, Dorothy refused to drink milk. One frosty morning, Bert discovered frozen cream in the milk bottle. She scooped the crystals into a bowl, sprinkled them with sugar and *voilà*—ice cream. Dorothy thought it great and every morning that winter rushed to bring in the milk, hoping to find frozen cream.

Real ice cream was Bert and Dorothy's favorite treat. Arlo's Cousin Frank, who owned a creamery, always told Bert to bring her daughter by for a free cone. Of course, Dorothy wanted to go by the creamery every trip to town, but after two or three free cones, Bert's guilt complex took over. "I don't think we should take advantage of Frank's generosity." Dorothy ate few free cones after that. Instead, Bert encouraged her daughter to get a five-cent cone at Bailey's every day and while Dorothy loved them, they didn't seem as exciting as getting a *free* cone. Any trip to town, mother and daughter would be seen walking down the street, even in the dead of winter, each eating a cone or pint of ice cream.

CHAPTER 19

One day, Bert prepared to go to town despite the chilling drizzle, because Arlo was home to take care of Dorothy. A loud pounding on the door startled her. When she answered, an agitated tenant said, "I need to use the bathroom, but some damn fool's been in there two hours."

This was a common complaint, but two hours was excessive. Bert said, "I'll look into it." She determined Mrs. Eckerman was the malingerer. Her tenant was an average looking brunette, neither ugly nor beautiful, but she possessed one incredible feature: pale icy-blue eyes that gave the appearance of a drug-induced stare. In some light, they appeared almost wolf white. Bert found eye contact difficult. She felt as if the woman's eyes penetrated to her soul.

The woman was mentally unstable. No one would rent to the couple. Bert felt sorry for them and allowed them to move in when the husband assured her that his wife was not dangerous. They had given Bert no problem for four months.

Bert went to the bathroom and knocked on the door.

"Mrs. Eckerman, please come out, other people need to use the bathroom." No answer. "Come out and you can use the bathroom again later." Still no answer, Bert tried the door. Locked. No amount of pleading worked. *Why won't she answer? Dear God, did she die?*

The agitated complainer fidgeted. Arlo called the woman's husband, but Bert felt the cross-legged tenant couldn't hold out that long. Something must be done. The bathroom window over the tub opened onto the back porch roof. Arlo went for a ladder.

On the roof, he climbed the ladder and looked in the window. She wasn't there. Mystified, he wondered how the door could have accidentally locked. Arlo opened the window, put one leg inside and there she was—lying stark naked in the waterless bathtub, her blue eyes staring blankly into space. Stunned, Arlo lurched backward and almost fell off the roof. After regaining his composure, he pondered the problem, but didn't know what to do. He hated violating her privacy, but they needed a bathroom.

"Please, Mrs. Eckerman, if you'll open the door I won't have to come in," he said, looking at the bathroom door, the ceiling, the sink, anywhere but the tub. She didn't respond. An inflexible battle line was drawn, a challenge issued. He had no idea what she might do if he climbed in. His hands were clammy as he wiped beads of sweat from his brow. At last, he inhaled deeply, put one leg through the window and stared directly at her. Warm brown eyes met icy-blue eyes, locked in instant combat as he inched his way over the occupied tub. She never stirred, her eyes tracking his every movement. Breathing a sigh of thankfulness, Arlo unlocked the door as her husband arrived. He tenderly wrapped his wife in a sheet and took her back to their apartment—the squirming tenant bolted into the bathroom. Choked with emotion, Mr. Eckerman returned shortly and apologized, telling

Bert he was moving his wife to a sanatorium. She never saw them again.

A few weeks later, Bert rented the upstairs apartment to a couple from Big Sandy who wintered in Great Falls. He was a farmer and a plumber. Bert learned to barter watching her mother trade with the Indians, and she now did some fancy negotiating. She didn't charge them rent while he installed a desperately needed shower and toilet in the basement.

Bert's days were no longer fidgety from lack of work. In addition to daily chores, she cared for a youngster, cooked for a bachelor tenant, and managed an apartment house. She also tended her garden, but that was enjoyable work.

That October, Bert's garden looked sad and forlorn, so one glorious Indian summer day she advanced with a spade to prepare the plot for spring. The bright yellow and orange, long-stemmed zinnias and smiling-faced pansies had long ago spent their energy and surrendered to the grim reaper. A few dried red and yellow leaves still clung to tree branches, and there was a nip in the air. Remembering her first crop, Bert felt proud. Her mouth still savored the snap of the crunchy green onions she loved. She was glad she and Arlo had taken a risk and bought the house—they were on their way to the prosperous life he envisioned. A happy glow of contentment warmed her heart. Then a shadow crept across the garden as clouds blotted out the sun.

October 25, 1929, was a day like any other. People awoke, dressed, and went to work. Bert scurried about doing chores and hoped it wouldn't rain. She wanted to buy groceries. The business world opened its doors, and it happened. The U.S. stock market crashed. In mere hours, the market's paper value disappeared like bathwater down the drain sending Wall Street into a panic. Millions of people had speculated on the stock market and were wiped out when unable to pay for stock bought on margin. Wealthy investors jumped out of skyscraper windows rather than face financial ruin. Banks and businesses collapsed like falling dominoes. One in every four workers became jobless. Arlo and Bert felt blessed– trains were essential.

Dorothy's first birthday arrived as the world reeled in an anxiety-ridden atmosphere not conducive to partying. Bert baked two cakes, one for the family and a small one in a toy pan for Dorothy. White frosting with piped red edging and a single candle in a tiny filigree-glass candleholder decorated the miniature cake. Bert intended to set it in front of Dorothy and watch her dig in. "Oh no, don't let her do that," Arlo said, "it's too cute." The much-admired cake sat on the sideboard and became stale and dry. By then, Bert didn't want to throw it out. She put the cake in a red velvet heart-shaped box to keep until Dorothy's second birthday and enjoy it again. Eighty-eight years later, Dorothy still has the little cake preserved by dried frosting.

At Christmas, Bert once again tucked a small tree in the corner of their room. Dorothy was pampered beyond spoiling by the twenty-seven people who brought or mailed dime store gifts. And that didn't count presents from tenants and parents. Bert and Arlo's reward was the joy they felt watching their daughter's excitement over her new toys.

After Christmas, Bert, who was beanpole thin, made a doctor appointment and the doctor wanted her to gain weight. "I've tried. Nothing works."

"I'm prescribing a beer before dinner to give you an appetite."

"How can I drink beer? It's illegal."

"It's not if you make it yourself and don't sell it."

Bert wanted to gain weight. She bought bottles and a bottle capper and Bert's Brewery opened. She worried what the neighbors would think because the cellar emitted as much odor as the Great Falls Brewery when the wind blew from the west side, and visions of a police raid plagued her thoughts. While she was at it, she decided to make root beer. It was delicious. No one liked commercial root beer once they tasted Bert's homemade brew.

Bert's Brewery closed two years later. The boys in blue didn't raid her; the operation ceased because she didn't like beer—and she didn't gain weight. Clearly, she burned calories faster than she added them.

Arlo's cousin Marvin Courtnage visited often. The brash young man often bragged: "There isn't a woman alive I can't get. I can get poontang anytime I want." He used the derogatory term for "quickie sex" in front of Bert when they were alone in the kitchen one day.

She bristled. "Well, here's one woman you can't get."

Marvin grabbed her and Bert struggled to break free. Arlo's father, Frank, was also visiting. He heard the commotion, ran in, and slammed Marvin against the wall, chastising him severely. Only God and Marvin knew what his intentions were, but it seemed doubtful he would have tried anything with Frank in the next room. He probably wanted only to kiss her. The incident scared Bert and she was wary of him from then on.

At the same time, she felt great pity for Marvin. He was hopelessly in love with his cousin Grace, Arlo's sister, and depressed because nothing could come of it. Later, Grace told Bert she would have married him if they weren't cousins, so they obviously discussed their mutual affection. Marvin visited Bert and Arlo one day in 1930. He seemed more dejected than usual, but he didn't say anything about it. Bert thought it best to ignore him as she bustled about the kitchen. Using the hem of her red apron, she was removing biscuits from the oven when she heard horrifying shrieks coming from the basement. She ran downstairs. Marvin lay on a cot writhing. He reached up and begged, "Bert, help me, *p-lease!*"

"What's wrong?"

"I took poison." Chills raced through her veins as she ran upstairs to call Arlo and the police. Law enforcement arrived in minutes.

"What did you take?" an officer prodded

"Strychnine," Marvin said, his breathing labored.

The officer took Bert aside. "There is nothing anyone can do. It's hopeless." He asked Marvin where he got the poison and what he did with the bottle. His last strangled words were, "I threw the bottle in the furnace." His agonized screams ceased and he went into convulsions, his body rigid. His face distorted beyond recognition, and bloodshot eyes bulged in their sockets. When Arlo arrived, Marvin was still conscious but could no longer talk, his jaws locked. Conscious, but aware only of excruciating pain, he died minutes later. Marvin was only nineteen. Bert had never seen any living creature suffer such anguish, and she couldn't get the horrific scene out of her mind. She remained calm during the crisis, but afterward, she fell apart. Typically, she blamed herself for not trying to talk to him earlier.

Marvin had visited his cousin Harold and his wife Marge at the family homestead near Geraldine before driving to Arlo's. About the time of Marvin's death, Harold heard a knock on the door. He opened it and saw Marvin standing there. Before Harold could speak, Marvin vanished like a puff of smoke. In shock, Harold stood rooted to the floor. When he didn't come back, Marge called from the kitchen, "Who is it?"

Pale and shaking, Harold went back. He told Marge what had happened. "Was I seeing_things?" Then he answered his own question. "No. I *saw* Marvin." An hour later, the two were still stymied about the vision when Arlo called and told them about the tragedy. Harold and Marge could only believe Marvin came to say good-bye at the moment he died. No other explanation was possible.

For many years Harold and Marge didn't tell anyone about their mystical experience, because they thought no one would believe them. When they finally told Bert, she never doubted them for a moment. She'd too many premonitions of her own to be skeptical.

Bert had difficulty getting her life back to normal after Marvin's death. Everyday chores slowly restored her to routine. She owned a small collection of dime store trinkets that were of no great value, except to her. Everyone said, "You'll have to put the knick-knacks up high when Dorothy begins walking." Bert didn't believe in that method of teaching. She believed in reasoning.

The first time she caught Dorothy reaching for an ornament she scolded, "You can't play with that. It belongs to me. We'll go to Woolworth's tomorrow and you can pick out an ornament of your own." Shopping the next day, Dorothy selected a small ceramic dog, and when they went home, Bert placed it on an end table. "You can play with your ornament any time you want, but you can't play with my things."

Dorothy smiled. "Okay." A few days later, Bert began dusting and she picked up her daughter's dog to clean the table. Dorothy stomped her foot and lambasted her mother with, "You can't play with that, it belongs to me!"

Bert struggled not to laugh. "That's fine, but you have

to dust the table from now on."

Dorothy dusted the table twice and then conveniently forgot the chore. A few days later, Bert told her daughter the table needed dusting. Dorothy smiled innocently, "You can pick up my ornament as long as it's only to dust." Bert never put a single trinket out of Dorothy's reach—she didn't need to. Bert practiced child psychology before the term was invented.

CHAPTER 20

The Depression continued to intensify, and the Great Northern Railroad laid off more men. Eventually, word came down that one more man would be let go in the roundhouse; they couldn't lay off more and still operate. Arlo was terrified and worried about his friends as much as he did himself; they were all family men too. He considered the problem for hours. The next morning, he told the men, "If each one of us volunteers to work only three weeks a month, no one will lose their job." After some anguished thought, each man agreed that was the safest way to go, but none knew how to survive on three week's salary. Thankfully, unions didn't exist, and the supervisor approved the plan.

The loss of a week's pay was devastating. Bert tried to find ways to earn extra cash. That spring, she bought onion bulbs at Murray's Meat Market and asked the owner if he would buy the grown onions. He agreed and when they matured, she took three big bunches to the store where the tempting aroma filled the little shop. He bought them all after making her resize the bunches smaller. The next year, she added four long rows in

132

addition to those she grew for her family. The market bought them for several years.

Soon, money became a dire problem—Arlo and Bert's savings disappeared. The rent money paid the mortgage only if the apartments were full, and surviving on Arlo's reduced salary was impossible. Their garden and Bert's little onion business were only seasonal. Bert's talent as a money manager was amazing, but she couldn't budget money that did not exist.

Arlo and Bert, stretched to the breaking point, dreaded the arrival of each new day. They couldn't farm Arlo's property in Geraldine because he had no house or machinery. None of their family could help; their financial situation was the same. Arlo and Bert could see no way out of their dilemma and visions of the poorhouse plagued Bert's nightmares.

She not only had nightmares about the poorhouse, but her waking thoughts were saturated with anxiety too. Then the dreaded day arrived. The eviction notice arrived in the mail. Tears flowed—sleepless nights—all was lost.

On the morning of foreclosure, the sky filled with giant fluffy clouds that Bert loved, but now didn't see. Birds twittered in the trees while a dozen red-breasted robins worked at ridding their lawn of worms, oblivious to Bert and Arlo's pain. By habit, she fixed breakfast in stony silence. The aroma of butter and brown sugar oatmeal filled the room. She pushed her bowl away; Arlo didn't pick up a spoon. They sat staring at the clock watching the precious minutes tick.

Abruptly, Arlo jumped out of his seat. He decided to call a real estate and loan officer known for his compassion and helpfulness. They raced to his office. The man, impressed with Arlo and Bert's sincerity to make payments, agreed to help them. He stopped their expulsion with mere hours to spare. Two more eviction notices would later arrive and the same loan officer came to their rescue. Each time, Bert and Arlo counted their blessings; he kept a roof over their heads.

Being a landlady was a difficult job and required tact; some tenants were old enough to be Bert's parents. She didn't look or act her age, which didn't help. Still, she managed the apartments well, even when diplomacy failed. Dead-beat tenants were the plague of all landlords during the Depression. Hotel patrons sneaked out during the night without paying, and Bert had her share of these worrisome renters. The worst offenders were a couple living upstairs. They couldn't pay their rent and they wouldn't leave—they had nowhere to go. Remembering her and Arlo's near eviction, Bert felt sorry for them. She allowed them to stay three months hoping the husband might find work. He didn't. Finally, she told them they must leave. They refused. According to the law, she couldn't put them out on the street.

Bert was lost, not knowing what to do. Finally, she consulted a lawyer. Her story barely left her lips, when he told her bluntly, "There's nothing you can do, lady. That's the law."

Bert was stunned. "There must be something I can do—I can't support them forever."

"Well there's one thing," he admitted, "but it's awfully mean and lowdown."

"What is it? I don't have a choice; I need the money for my family."

"It's your house. You can turn off the heat in their room and take off the windows." It was January.

Bert turned off the tenant's heat and said, "The windows are next." Three days later, the couple moved still owing them back rent. The situation was common for the times.

The first time Bert saw the L-shaped, foyer staircase of their new home, she told Arlo, "What a perfect place for a Christmas tree." It was, but she hadn't realized how hazardous it was—at least for Dorothy. As a youngster, she fell down the staircase from the top step, rounded the landing, and rolled all the way to the bottom—twice. Bert feared the worst as she rushed Dorothy to the doctor both times. No bones were broken, she wasn't bleeding, and the doctor said she was fine.

Twenty years later, Dorothy developed severe back problems. Most people never heard of chiropractors, and those who did considered them "quacks." Manipulation or a brace as a youngster might have alleviated or at least helped her chronic rotary scoliosis.

Once, when Bert visited her adult daughter, her chiropractor told Bert that Dorothy could wind up in a wheelchair. Bert cried, "It's all my fault." Again, she blamed herself for something that wasn't her doing.

Bert was an attentive mother, but also a busy one. Dorothy disappeared one day and Bert couldn't find her. She looked all over the house, called down to the dark basement, checked with the tenants, and searched the yard and alley, but no Dorothy. The tenants joined the hunt and explored every nook and cranny in the neighborhood without success. Bert began to panic. About to dial the police, she decided to physically check the basement. She turned on the light and there sat Dorothy, playing on the floor in total blackness.

"Didn't you hear me call you?"

"I heard you."

Finding her little girl safe brought such relief, Bert couldn't punish Dorothy, but she did give her daughter a stern lecture clarifying how she must answer when someone called her name.

Because of the times, Bert was always seeking ways to earn money. A new fad swept the country, wood fiber flowers. Bert loved creating beautiful things, and she knew they would sell. The wood fiber material came in small, four-inch square sheets of soft velvety tissue-like papers, the thickness of a paper towel. The sheets came in a variety of colors: soft yellow, pale pink, and blushing peach, the most popular. Talented at fabricating anything, Bert soon created extraordinarily realistic flowers and within days began selling them.

George Phillips, Bert's boarder, suggested she make a box of corsages that he could take to a local bar he frequented. She did. He returned the box empty. Impressed, one woman asked if Bert could make her wedding flowers. Of course she could, and did. The flowers were cheaper than the real thing and since they could be used repeatedly, they were popular.

Bert worked long hours making corsages often turning on the radio. *Blue Moon* and other popular tunes helped pass the time. Working every spare minute, she couldn't keep up with the demand, so she hired a young woman living upstairs to cook and clean the apartment, which cut into her profits. Able to contribute to the family income in such troubling times made Bert happy. Her small business lasted about two years, but she continued making the flowers into the 1940s. Then, the supplies were no longer available and the fad passed into history.

Not seeing the circus as a child was a bitter disappointment to Bert. The harsh memory sent her dashing to the first show that came to town. Years of expectations had grown wildly out of proportion. Unimpressed, she felt disillusioned saying, "I can't watch three rings at once." She never went again. She loved attending various other attractions and was thrilled with the appearance of the Northern Montana State Fair in 1931. Leaving Dorothy in a tenant's care, Bert went to the fair. The exhibits and rodeo were free entertainment, and she loved the noise, rides, and excitement. Holidays were exciting too.

Bert's second favorite holiday was Easter. When Dorothy was three, she took her to Gibson Park for the city Easter egg hunt. When the city official cut the ribbon, the bigger kids knocked the little ones down in their rush to retrieve eggs. At the end of the hunt, the lawn was full of crying toddlers, while the older kids carted off egg-filled baskets. Bert told Arlo, "I'm not putting Dorothy through that disappointment again."

The next Easter, Bert bought baskets and straw and dyed two dozen eggs. Her flair had her mixing dyes and coloring some eggs half one color and half another. She drew wax patterns on some eggs so the dye wouldn't adhere, thus producing a design. Dorothy's Easter egg hunt blossomed as colorful as a bowlful of jelly beans on Easter morning. Bert saved the baskets and straw for next year.

Bert told everyone how well behaved her daughter was, but that didn't mean she didn't get into trouble. Missing once again, Bert began the search. A building across the alley from the family home housed a painting contractor, and there were always stacks of empty paint buckets in the alley for garbage pickup. Dorothy discovered the business when she was four. Curious, she pried off the can lids and saw a spoonful of paint in each one. She apparently thought dabs of paint in many buckets would make a lot of paint in one bucket—her mother did a lot of painting.

Bert found Dorothy sitting cross-legged on the ground pouring paint from one bucket into another. Her daughter looked up with a self-satisfied grin. If Bert weren't so angry, she might have laughed. Dorothy looked like a psychedelic rainbow from her shoes to the top of her head. Her lime-green face coordinated with blue hair that smelled like turpentine. The dress Bert made two days earlier was beyond even the rag box.

A hand-holding, lovey-dovey couple appeared at Bert's door one day to rent an apartment. They couldn't keep their hands off each other, and Bert suspected they were newlyweds. They were. They had each been married twice before—to each other. Apparently, they couldn't live either with or without one another.

Soon after the couple moved in, loud shrieks and cursing blasted from their room. Whenever the wife's piercing screams filled the air, the other tenants opened their doors for the free show. The husband would burst through their door like a greyhound leaving the starting gate and race down the stairs while she screeched obscenities and threw every dish in their apartment at him. Bert usually caught the act at the bottom of the steps; the show worthy of an admission fee. The couple would later kiss and make up, and go hand-in-hand to buy new dishes for the next time. It never took long.

CHAPTER 21

When Arlo and Bert bought their home, he told both their families, "Come stay with us when you're in town." Farmers couldn't leave their animals for days, but an overnight trip was easily arranged by going to town in the afternoon and getting back early the next day. Great Falls was the only sizeable town around, so all the family shopped there. Not surprisingly, they took Arlo up on his offer. None of them came often, but with such an extended family, plus cousins and other relatives visiting, Bert and Arlo's home rapidly became *The Courtnage Hotel*. Dorothy spent many nights sleeping on two hardback wooden chairs pulled together to make a bed with a folded-blanket mattress.

In summer, visiting children wanted to sleep in Bert and Arlo's tent, so she pitched it near the back steps. That meant additional work, but she didn't want to disappoint the kids. The visitors brought cream, eggs or some other farm produce and Bert appreciated it, but the free items never made up for the extra food cost. And the visitors not only required extra groceries and bigger meals, but also generated more dishes and bedding to wash.

Once a group of visitors was leaving as the next batch arrived—they passed each other on the sidewalk. After that incident, Bert kept track of their guests. During the next ninety days, the family ate only three dinners alone. Bert loved all her family and was always happy to see them; but because of the numbers, the work became overwhelming. No longer fidgety from lack of work, she now was a nervous wreck from too much work.

Arlo and Bert's home was a hotel for overnight guests, while relatives on both sides of the family stayed for longer periods. Della often visited for a week, seeking asthma treatments. Arlo's sister and brother were frequent visitors; Bert's niece and sister boarded with Bert for extended times during WWII. And in later years, both Max and Frank came for a week or two at a time. Bert invited her sister-in-law to stay while awaiting the birth of her first child and there were many others. The *Courtnage Hotel* was popular—and cheap.

Already exceptionally nervous due to her stressful childhood, Bert became tenser now and nearer to the breaking point. Arlo suggested she go to Seattle for a week or two to rest. She felt guilty about leaving him alone with Dorothy and didn't want to go. Ruth and Leonard, tenants and dear friends, offered to mind Dorothy and Ruth would fix dinner for Arlo. They didn't have children and Leonard worked at the corner Conoco gas station across the street. Finally, Bert agreed to go when Arlo said he would make a swing to occupy Dorothy's time, since there were no children on the block to play with. He hung the swing from the joists in the basement, which occupied Dorothy for hours.

Ruth prepared dinners for Arlo every afternoon. Then one day, Dorothy told Ruth, "You don't have to cook for Daddy—I'm going fix him dinner." Bustling about, she shooed Ruth out of the kitchen when she tried to help.

Dorothy made her daddy's favorite Depression cookies: Graham crackers spread with frosting. She pulled out everything she could find in the refrigerator, and bursting with pride she displayed dinner when Arlo came home. He dutifully ate his bread and butter, radishes, pickles, and Depression cookies. Later, with Dorothy outside playing, Ruth brought him a real meal.

Leonard gave Dorothy a billed cap emblazoned with the Conoco logo and Bert made her a matching uniform. Dorothy often went to the gas station to help Leonard. She did little work—she couldn't even reach the windshield.

Seattle did wonders for Bert's nervous condition, but returning home she faced the same financial problems. Arlo still worked only three weeks a month, so Bert was ecstatic when she found employment at the Deaconess Hospital. She worked in the dietitian section and sometimes in the ward with the new babies, where she was happiest. Hospitals didn't yet require a college degree for the same work any mother did every day. She began work in November 1932 and was thrilled with her first month's wage: 18.75 dollars, a lot of money when you had little.

Surgery fascinated Bert and she hoped to see an actual operation. Hospital regulations weren't stringent then, and a doctor gave her permission to watch a surgery. She and a male relative of the patient were allowed to observe providing "they wouldn't faint." The doctor warned them that no one could be spared to take care of them during surgery. The male relative became woozy before the first cut began. Bert helped him outside and returned to find the door locked. She was furious.

Years later, Bert would witness an operation of sorts. She and Arlo had agreed on having two children, and after the birth of their second child, Arlo had a vasectomy to prevent another "accident." Bert watched the procedure done in the doctor's office, but she never realized her dream of seeing a major operation.

The hospital where Bert worked used an elevator that hadn't worked properly for months. Employees needed to put his or her head in the shaft and call to have someone send the car up and down. One day, Hazel Cox—Bert would never forget that name—pushed the button while standing alongside Bert, whose head was in the shaft. The car began moving and caught Bert's head between the wall and the elevator door, lifting her to the ceiling. Her piercing scream sounded throughout the building's five floors. Blood spurted over the wall and ran in rivers down Bert's crumpled body that fell to the floor when someone opened the door. The entire side of her head was ripped open, her hair saturated with blood.

Bert couldn't have picked a better place to be injured; doctors and nurses surrounded her in seconds and she was rushed into surgery. Unbelievably, nothing vital was damaged beyond repair. She was hospitalized a week and the hospital administrator was *ever so* friendly. He came daily to visit—and to pressure her to sign a release form absolving the hospital of wrongdoing. She refused. Her practicality told her something could go wrong later. Needless to say, the hospital volunteered to pay all the bills, and she received meticulous care. She appeared to have no after effects from her injury, but within weeks needed eyeglasses.

Once home, she felt pressure from another source: lawyers who claimed she had an airtight case. The hospital not repairing the elevator was blatant negligence. Although she refused to absolve the hospital of fault, she wouldn't sue either. It was an accident.

Later, another opportunity for a lawsuit occurred, if Bert believed in such things. One day while she and

Dorothy bought groceries, a clerk carrying a large wooden crate of apples on his shoulder dropped it as he passed. His timing was abysmal. The crate struck Dorothy's back. She said she was okay, but it probably contributed to her chronic back problems that were to surface in a few years. Doubtlessly worried about a lawsuit, the store manager was there in minutes. Bert assured him Dorothy was okay. At least this time lawyers weren't harassing her.

Throughout Dorothy's formative years, Bert entertained her daughter with stories of her life, and she saved so much memorabilia that her chronological history could almost be written from that documentation alone. Incredibly, one vital piece of information was lost. Today, no one knows exactly when Arlo was reduced to part-time work or when he returned to full-time employment, but by the winter 1934, he once again worked an eight-hour shift. Little imagination was needed to know the great joy and relief they felt after years of hardship.

June Peterson, a lanky, young, fun-loving woman, lived next door to Bert and became her best friend. Bert loved June's hearty laughter. With only a husband and tiny house to care for, June had free time and visited Bert often, keeping her company while Bert worked. The women were a matching pair; neither of their husbands liked to dance, so Bert and June went together.

Whenever Max visited, he joined them. He didn't seem to have a problem allowing his children to become adults, and he treated them as such. It took many years, but Bert no longer 'hated her father.' She vividly remembered the beatings but had forgiven him, and they grew closer because they shared a love of dancing and old-time music. Max was proud of her calling.

June's mother, Belle, lived with her daughter. She

drove a black Cadillac and often left town for two or three days. Bert assumed she visited family or friends, never questioning her absence. While Bert worked in the kitchen one afternoon, Belle burst through the backdoor panting, her face flushed. "I want to rent your garage."

"Sure. Any time, I'm not using it."

"I want it *now*. I'm parked in back." Bert went for the key as Belle paced back and forth to the window. Bert was surprised by her anxiety but saw no reason not to rent her the garage. She could use the extra money.

What Bert didn't know was those mysterious trips were made to Canada via the Bootleg Trail, a seldom-used dirt road from Great Falls to Canada, roughly 100 miles north. There, Belle bought liquor and resold it in Great Falls at a handsome profit since prohibition was in full swing. That particular day, the police were watching and gave chase. Belle's souped-up Cadillac had outrun them.

The next day Belle told Bert the story. Bert turned pale, nervous the police would arrest her for hiding the Cadillac. She remained in a state of panic until Belle removed the hot car. Then she became worried. "How can I refuse to rent Belle the garage again?" She didn't have to face the problem; Belle was as scared as Bert and never made another trip.

Bert's boarder, George Phillips, eloped with her sister Charlotte, and they moved into Bert's upstairs apartment. The Depression still raged. Bert felt blessed to have so much in her life and she wanted to help the newlyweds get a start in their marriage. She gave them a ten percent discount on rent the entire time they lived there so they could save money.

One telephone, Number 6623, serviced the entire house from the foyer. Answering the phone for so many people proved a laborious task for Bert. Invariably, whenever she worked in the basement, the phone rang, so she climbed up or down the stairs a dozen times a day. Finally, she decided five-year-old Dorothy could handle the job; she'd tons of energy to burn. Bert instructed her to say "Hello" and politely ask the caller to hold on while she fetched the tenant. Dorothy could hardly wait for the phone to ring. When it did, she ran to answer.

George Phillips leaned over the balcony and called down, "If it's for me, tell them I'm not home."

Dorothy said, "Okay," and answered the phone. In her most serious grown-up voice she said, "Hello." Sure enough, someone asked to speak to George. Dorothy, ever so politely stated, "George said to tell you he's not home."

In despair, George yelled, "Never mind," and answered the phone, explaining to his friend that he believed it was his boss wanting him to work. When Bert heard the story, she winced, and Dorothy received more directions on proper phone answering technique.

Dorothy, the spoiled pet of all the tenants, spent a lot of time visiting them. Bert caught her coming out of Mrs. Decker's apartment eating a cookie one day when the tenant wasn't home. Bert started to scold her daughter. "But, Mama," Dorothy interrupted, "Mrs. Decker said I could get a cookie anytime I wanted." Knowing children's proclivity to lie, Bert doubted her daughter but held off any censure until she talked to her renter. When Mrs. Decker returned, she said, "Yes, I told her she could get a cookie any time she wanted."

Dorothy also "worked her grandmother" for treats. Bert and her daughter often took the train to Big Sandy for a day or two. Della had soda crackers in the cupboard, and Dorothy always pestered her grandma for one. Della spread the crackers with freshly churned butter, and

Dorothy sprinkled on salt for her treat. Anyone who hasn't tasted homemade butter has no idea what a pleasure it is.

On any trip to the farm, Dorothy spent hours in the attic with an enchanting kingdom of treasures. Several old trunks contained clothes, the attic floor littered with assorted broken, obsolete, or worn out items. However, what she loved most were the stacks of old newspaper comics from the late teens and early twenties. No one knew why Della saved only the comics, but all the grandchildren were happy she did. *The Katzenjammer Kids*, *Maggie and Jiggs*, *Mutt and Jeff*, *Blondie* and others sent Dorothy's imagination soaring like a kite in the wind.

Dorothy adored visiting her grandparents, and one day asked her mother, "When are we going to see Grandma again?"

"You can go anytime you want." Two days later, Arlo brought home a rail pass, and Bert took her daughter to the station. Dorothy wore a large tag around her neck with her name and destination. Bert told the conductor where Dorothy was to get off and he promised to put her off at the right stop. Conductors were obliging babysitters in those days.

The train began moving and Dorothy, nose against the glass, waved wildly to her mother. Grandpa met her at the station, and thereafter, she often took the train to Big Sandy, and to Chinook, Geraldine, and Shonkin to visit relatives. Later, her future sibling also rode the rails and both spent several weeks every summer at family farms. Sometimes they would be home only a week and then gone again. No parent would dream of allowing their child to ride the train alone today. But in those days, children went to town, the park, to a friend's house, and anywhere they wanted as soon as they were old enough to find their way home.

Whenever Dorothy visited the Clawiter farm, she shadowed her uncle Floyd everywhere, especially milking the cows. When the wind blew, the barn creaked, protesting the assault. Dorothy watched in wide-eyed wonder at the shafts of light that illuminated millions of glistening dust particles sifting down from the hayloft like snowflakes. Floyd always squirted milk at the waiting barn cats that were quite adept at getting their mouth in the right position. Dorothy wasn't that skillful and usually got soaked. However, it didn't annoy her enough to stop her cheery bellowing of *Spring Time in the Rockies* that she sang to entertain Floyd while he worked. The 'soaking' and the 'bellowing' were a nightly ritual.

CHAPTER 22

Once, when Bert and Dorothy visited the Clawiter farm, the family went to a dance at the Cold Creek School. Little Max and Floyd stayed home with Dorothy. While the dance was in progress, a man burst through the door shouting, "Fire! Fire! There's a big fire somewhere."

Everyone rushed outside and O.K. yelled, "Oh Lord, Max. It looks like your place." The men all agreed and Max's stomach churned. He asked Cecil Mack to drive him home—he had the only car.

Frantic, Della told Bert, "You go with Papa; I'll stay with the children." Bert sensed Della's anxiety, wondering if she would have a home to return to. The men all crowded into the car like pickles in a jar. When Bert arrived, the car was full—she piled in on top. Arriving at the farm, they found it wasn't the house but the chicken coop aflame. A full moon revealed choking black smoke billowing skyward, and an acrid stench assaulted everyone's nose. The coop was beyond saving, but the men rescued five chickens.

Characteristically, Max became outraged. He chastised Little Max. "You should've seen the fire and put it out," he ranted. Little Max and Floyd were asleep until someone pounded on the door yelling fire. The boys were spared a whipping that time, perhaps because there were so many people around.

How the chicken coop caught fire never was determined other than a possible chicken thief covering his tracks. Max told Bert he *knew* who did it. One man, his only enemy, had threatened Max that he would "get even" for an altercation Max no longer remembered. Max was convinced the man had his revenge.

Little Max didn't believe a chicken thief stole the birds, and the next day when his father went to town, he and Floyd dug down in the ashes and found the partial remains of both chickens and ducks. Little Max was too frightened to tell his father. The loss of so many birds was a terrible blow. A week later, neighbors surprised the Clawiters with a chicken shivaree and everyone brought two to five chickens. The family was grateful, but they received almost as many roosters as hens. That year, the cellar held an abundance of canned rooster.

Obviously, the subject of the burning coop never was discussed among the family after that day, and Bert and her father believed the arson hypothesis. Many years later, Bert and Dorothy were visiting Max Jr. on the farm. The trio was reminiscing and the chicken coop story surfaced. Bert's voice jumped an octave. "We never got the damn thief either."

Max wore a guilty grin. "It wasn't a chicken thief. I burned the coop."

Bert's eyes widened. "What?"

"It was my job to carry out the stove coals. That day, I laid them near the chicken coop. I didn't know Dad had put fresh straw around the outside because the ground was blanketed with two inches of new snow—I couldn't see the straw and the coals likely melted the snow, burned the straw and set the coop on fire."

Knowing his father's temper, Little Max made sure not to mention his suspicion, and for seventy-six years, the truth had lain buried as deeply as the chickens.

One day in 1934, Bert began pacing back and forth, a physical action that always accompanied those dreaded premonitions. Again, she didn't know what it was about, only that her family was doing something they were hiding from her. "Arlo, I have to go to Big Sandy."

Opening the door at the farm, her mother said, "What are you doing here?"

"I want to know what you're trying to keep from me."

Della's mouth gaped and she admitted Ella was about to marry Max Gerson. Della didn't tell Bert because she knew she would object to the seventeen-year age difference. Bert tried to talk her sister out of the marriage, but Della's influence was stronger. Della thought it fine; after all she still had three more daughters to marry off. The marriage took place, but after that episode, Bert's parents took her psychic ability more seriously—at least they didn't laugh anymore.

Dorothy entered first grade at the Great Falls Whittier School across the street in 1934. Entry age was six, but since classes started in September and Dorothy turned six one month later, Bert felt it was close enough. The principal agreed.

Dorothy needed a costume for the school Halloween party. Bert loved Hawaiian music and danced a bit of the hula. She made a hula skirt from brown crepe paper that she cut in time-consuming long, narrow strips. A flowered lei, ankle bracelet and small crepe-paper bra with a flower completed the costume. The outfit was so cute Bert made a larger version for her next masquerade.

She usually wore her hair in a bun, but when wearing the costume, her long hair cascaded down her back to give her *native* authenticity. Bert later made another hula skirt for Dorothy in 1940 for a Girl Scout party, because her daughter had outgrown the first one. She won first prize.

Dorothy had attended school only three months when Bert received a note from the teacher asking her to "come in for a talk." Remembering her own school days, she *knew* a note from the teacher was bad news. Her guilt complex shifted into high gear. Dorothy must be causing trouble. She fretted all day, her imagination running wild. The next day, the teacher said Bert should remove Dorothy from school.

Dorothy followed in her mother's footsteps and had difficulty concentrating. Being reared by a nervous mother, she learned to be nervous too. Miss Bratherferd, the teacher, told Bert, "Some children aren't ready to start school until later." She suggested Dorothy be enrolled in one of the new kindergarten schools that had sprung up around the city. Later, as an adult, Dorothy told her friends, "I hold the world record for being the youngest kid expelled from school—first grade."

Bert and Arlo made plans to visit his parents one weekend. When the time arrived, she didn't want to go.

"Why?"

"Something bad is going to happen if we leave."

"But we told them we were coming, and they're expecting us."

Arlo always claimed he believed her *feelings*, but he persuaded her to go against her wishes. Bert couldn't sit still at the farm and they didn't stay long. The moment they returned home, Bert dashed inside before Arlo was out of the car. Their apartment had been robbed. The loss wasn't a lot of money, but during those Depression years, the loss of a few dollars was a disaster. They never got their money back. And more bad news lay over the horizon.

Della frequently came to Great Falls for asthma treatment. An adrenaline shot was the only treatment at the time. Della's heart rate needed checking before the shot was administered. The doctor taught Max the procedure, and he had taught Bert so he didn't have to come in from the fields. After Bert left home, Little Max learned the method. The treatment worked fairly well for a few years, but when it ceased to give any relief, some type of "dope" was used. Max Jr. later thought it was morphine, but he wasn't sure.

Della's health became so precarious that Little Max stayed home with her for six years instead of working on the farm. The day after Christmas in 1934, Della suffered a severe attack. Little Max went into the bedroom and gave her the shot. Her eyes popped wide open in a shocked stare; she took two loud gasping breaths and died.

Everyone dreaded to see a Western Union boy appear at the door because no one used expensive telegrams for good tidings. They were always bad news. Trembling, Bert tore open the flimsy envelope. Telegrams charged per word so messages were cryptic: "Mother passed away 1:30 today will meet ten o'clock train tonight."

The news hurled Bert into shock. Her first thought was to wonder if her brother remembered to check Della's heart rate before administering the shot. That suspicion haunted Bert forever after, but Max Jr. had given Della the shots for so long it was unlikely he'd forgotten. Bert's mind reeled, searching for a reason, any reason, for losing her beloved mother. Della was only forty-nine.

That evening, deep snow blanketed the city as Bert made her way to the Great Northern Depot. Arlo would follow later with Dorothy. The fluffy snow compacted under Bert's galoshes as she trudged to the station platform. With each exhalation, smoke-like wisps escaped into the frosty air. The platform snow was beyond footprint decoration; it was packed and scarred like Bert's soul. As the train approached the station, its headlight beamed from a tunnel of blackness; its haunting whistle echoing across the still air, sounding an eerie death toll.

A raging blizzard had struck Big Sandy on Christmas Day; the snow was so deep the horses and sleigh were barely able to get through. At the station, Bert and Max said little. A bitter bite permeated the air as huge snowflakes accompanied them to the farm. A full moon shown between rolling dark clouds and, as far as the eye could see, glistening snow blanketed the world. The beauty of the night escaped Bert, who was too wracked with grief to notice.

At the farm, Bert wrapped her arms around her mother's cold stiff body and wept. *Oh, Mama, you had such a hard life. Why is God punishing you; why is he taking you so soon? It isn't fair.* After several minutes alone with her mother, Bert approached her task. No one had done anything with Della's body—they all waited for Little Mother to come home and take over. She knew her mother was dead, but her thoughts returned to the bewildered child of six, who swore on the Bible those many years ago. Silently, with a sharp knife, she opened a vein on her mother's wrist "to be sure." *Now I've fulfilled my vow.* At the same time she made her last vow: *I'll never again make a promise. They're too hard to keep.*

Bert washed her mother with homemade lye soap, and struggled with the unyielding body to get Della dressed in a fresh frock. She combed her mother's hair and applied a bit of color to her deathly-white cheeks. Bert had done her crying and no tears flowed as she opened the door and told the family their beloved mother was prepared for burial.

Della may have been ready, but during the long agonizing night, the family became snowbound. Opening the bedroom windows to keep the body from decomposing, everyone bunked down in the kitchen and dining room. Three long, grief-stricken days passed before they could take Della to Box Elder for burial alongside baby Evelyn. As her mother was lowered into the frozen ground, Bert appeared calm—her stomach, however, was in free fall.

After Della died, Max told Bert he was redoing his will and leaving her the farm. "You can pay the other kids their share."

"I don't want it. I don't like farming."

"Yes, but Arlo does." Bert didn't want to return to farming, and Arlo said it didn't make any difference to him, so, Bert suggested Max will the farm to Max Jr. and Floyd. He did.

Della's chronic asthma left the family with a staggering 4,000-dollar medical bill. Max didn't have health insurance. He paid two dollars each to the doctor and hospital every month. At that rate, it would take eighty-three years to pay the debt, but later, he increased the monthly payments. It still took almost thirteen years for Max and later Max Jr., then a married man, to pay the balance.

Dorothy was six when Della died, and although she'd visited her grandmother often, she was too young to have many memories. Other than begging for crackers, only one treasured recollection of her grandmother survived: the memory of a toe-tapping, fun-filled evening concert with Della and Max entertaining. To conserve kerosene, the lamp was turned low, but the spirited music lit up the room. The organ was tucked in the parlor corner and Max fiddled standing next to it, his shadow dancing on the wall.

The following Mother's Day, Bert bought one red and one white carnation. Dorothy wore the red one signifying her mother was alive, and Bert's white flower acknowledged her mother was deceased. Bert carried on the touching tradition for many years, but the ritual faded over time, which was a shame—it was a beautiful way to honor one's mother.

The next winter, the same plumber from Big Sandy rented from Bert again and her bartering continued. He installed running water in one apartment upstairs and in the two-room apartment on the first floor, which Arlo and Bert then moved into. She hated losing her back porch connected to their one-room dwelling, but the house had a side door to the backyard. For the first time, Arlo and Bert had a two-room apartment.

One room became multipurpose. The newly installed Murphy bed on the corner wall became the bedroom, and another corner was utilized as the kitchen. The round oak table with claw feet in the center of the room served meals and was used as a cooking counter. One set of double-sliding, pocket doors opened into the living room where Dorothy slept on a daybed, and another set opened to the foyer. Neither pair was closed during the day, so it made the two-room apartment seem larger than it was. The large foyer held only a stool and hall table for the telephone. Now—at long last—Bert could display her perfect Christmas tree.

155

CHAPTER 23

Bert never outgrew her childhood when it concerned Christmas. Her budget prioritized money all year to save for the holiday. Starting in late November, she made multiple batches of cookies and candy. It took that long to make sufficient provisions because *sampling* drastically reduced each new batch of sweets before it was ever stored. She made peanut butter fudge, chocolate fudge, penuche, and Bert's specialty, divinity. Divinity is fragile to make and Bert's was always superb. Sometimes her effort didn't turn out right. One goof tasted so scrumptious that Dorothy begged her mother to make it again. She did—three times—but she could never duplicate her original foul up.

Now, finally, after seven years of marriage, her goal of a six-foot tree was in sight. The pepper can she'd stuffed coins into all year for the event was full, and she was determined to make the holiday special, Depression or not. Bert could hardly wait to see her dream tree in the bend of the L-shaped staircase. She needed more ornaments and shopped store-to-store seeking the inexpensive, delicate glass decorations. Then she needed a tree. When they arrived, she searched every lot but none met her high standard. Feeling flustered, she rummaged around the last possibility, again failing to find a suitable tree. Loose branches on the ground drew her attention, and she approached the salesman.

"May I have some of those branches lying on the ground?"

"Sure, I'm just gonna toss 'em out anyway."

She selected several and stacked them. Then she bought a six-foot evergreen. Once back home, she drilled small holes in the tree trunk and attached the extra branches with wire. At last, she stood back and admired her work—the perfect Christmas tree.

Bert was particular about placing each colored bulb, often standing back to look and then move some to better locations. And heaven help anyone assisting if they tossed tinsel on the tree. She demonstrated—after scolding them—how to take only three or four strands and drape them on the tip end of each branch. She was a demanding taskmaster and few offered to help. That suited her fine.

And Bert was right. The placement of the tree was ideal, reaching almost to the second floor. It could be seen from the living room and the street, through the oval glass of the front door. And she fulfilled another childhood vow: the tree was trimmed by December fifth and remained in place long after New Year's Day. She maintained this tradition her entire life.

Bert had kept the small three-dimensional cardboard nativity scene she bought at the dime store in 1928 and added it to her 'perfect tree.' She didn't know in 1928 what that single purchase would hatch. Every year after, she added a few twenty-five-cent houses and by the time of her tree in the foyer, the nativity scene had become a village. Like a queen surveying her realm, she scrutinized the position of every item, often moving things around like a child with a dollhouse.

Bert and Dorothy sat in front of the tree nearly every evening enjoying homemade goodies. They sang Christmas carols and sometimes June and other friends, tenants, or relatives joined them. On special evenings, strolling street carolers sang outside their door, and Bert always passed around a plate of cookies. No one decorated the outside of their home in those years. The city always brought in a huge tree, placing it in the roundabout at the end of Central Avenue. The city also arched evergreen garlands with lights to lampposts on both sides across Central Avenue.

During the holidays, a parade of cars drove down Central Avenue, circled the roundabout holiday tree and drove back up the street as part of a traditional drive that continued to the pull-over parking lot at Black Eagle Falls. Gazing across the river at Smelter Hill, dozens of young evergreen trees bejeweled in glittering lights capped the evening ritual. Bert extended the popular tour by crossing the river and continuing on the road that curled around the hill and among the festooned trees for a closer view.

Taking her tree down in January, Bert recycled it even though the term was not yet in vogue. She cut off the branches and burned them one at a time in the furnace. Heavenly pine aroma wafted through the house, and visitors cocked an eyebrow and sniffed the air, never failing to compliment Bert on the lovely scent.

One year, Dorothy needed a white cape for a school Christmas song and Bert made one from an old sheet. The cape would be used only once, so she didn't want to spend money for material; she had a perfectly good sheet waiting for a second life. Dorothy hadn't developed Bert's practicality yet and she was mortified to wear it, but no one noticed. After the performance, the cape was retired to the rag box. The ubiquitous rag box never went out of style. In the hard times of Bert's world, nothing made of cloth was thrown away unless it was virtually in shreds. If an item was no longer fit for its original use, and had already led a second or third life, its final destination was the rag box. Bert used rags for everything from cleaning to sewing the two good ends of a hand towel together to make a dishrag. Worn out sheets were reused again and again; good halves or thirds could be stitched together becoming, once again, a useable sheet. When worn out again, they protected plants in unseasonable cold snaps, furniture during painting, and a number of other uses before hitting the rag box.

Later, in her nineties, Bert's finances were better, but she still stitched sheets together, saved rags, and made dishrags from parts of old towels. Lifelong habits were hard to break.

Boxes were another item Bert saved. "You never know when you might need a box." She saved all sizes, but her favorites were small, pretty boxes. She saved multiple dozens of them, stored, of course, in larger boxes. Everyone teased her about this obsession, but whom did they turn to when they needed a box?

Arlo's brother Harold and his wife stopped for a visit one day on their way to Choteau. Bert seemed nervous and upset, so after a while Harold and Marge decided to leave.

Bert blurted, "Oh, please don't go."

"Why?"

"Something bad is going to happen."

"What?" Harold said.

"I don't know—maybe an accident."

No amount of pleading could persuade them to

postpone the trip—they didn't believe her. A few hours later they came back, visibly shaken. They had been in a car accident.

Soon, another episode of those *feelings* troubled Bert deeply because of its persistence. Arlo, now a firm believer after the 'crooked car' incident, suggested she go see a fortuneteller. She went, but the psychic said, "I can't tell you anything—you're psychic yourself."

"No, I'm not."

"You can be if you try. Concentrate and you'll get better."

Bert's almost shouted. "I don't want to get better—I want the *feelings* to go away."

The fortuneteller did tell her she would have an extremely long life and three husbands. Two Indian women had already told Bert the exact same thing. She laughed—she was never going to divorce Arlo.

Melodic canaries enchanted Bert. She'd dreamed of owning one ever since listening to the birds trilling in the maple tree on Grandpa's farm. On the spur of the moment while shopping one day, she decided to enrich her life with a little song. She bought a gilded cage and a sweet, yellow warbler she named Spickie. But there was a problem. Spickie didn't sing. Not a note left his golden throat. Bert sang to him hoping he would join her. He never did. She tried whistling and playing music, still no song filled the air. Thinking he might be unhappy in his cage, she let him out every day to fly around the apartment, and when she held up the cage, Spickie flew right in the open door. Nothing worked—Spickie would not warble.

Bert taught Dorothy to cut and stack rounds of newspaper for the bottom of the canary's cage. When Dorothy scissored a dozen or more papers, Bert placed them in the bottom of the cage and removed a soiled piece every day. Dorothy cherished the canary.

One morning, Bert found Spickie dead on the floor of his cage. Dorothy was crestfallen. Tenderly, she wrapped him in a Kleenex shroud, lined a matchbox coffin with another tissue and buried him with prayer next to the house. He probably decomposed quickly—under the gutter downspout. Even though he didn't sing, Spickie was missed and soon Spickie II arrived. He was an identical clone of his predecessor—he didn't sing either.

Bert missed Spickie. She gave up on canaries and bought goldfish. One day she mentioned to Arlo, "I hate to see them swimming in such a tiny bowl."

"I can fix that." Arlo cut an old hot water tank in half lengthwise and placed it in the ground in the shade of the apple trees. To forestall cat feasts, he covered the tank with screen. At times, the tank held as many as thirty fish. In winter, Bert moved them to a big aquarium under the basement window during the winter.

The apple trees didn't shade the fish tank in the yard much longer. Abundant fruit grew, but kids sneaked in at night and climbed the immature branches, breaking them. Apple filching was the Olympic sport of the day, and the kids picked the fruit before it was ripe. Sometimes they ate only around the apple center, tossed the remnant on the ground and then picked another. The yard was always a mess. Arlo cut down the trees, permanently moving the fish to the basement. With the trees gone, Arlo built a small gazebo for shade. At first, the family ate in the summerhouse on nice days, but after the newness wore off, it didn't get much use. Soon, another backyard project emerged.

CHAPTER 24

Bert and Arlo wanted a sidewalk from the back door to the alley, but the long walkway was too expensive. Undaunted, Bert's creative mind sprang into action. "Okay, we'll make our own." On weekends they searched the Missouri River banks and hauled flagstone-style rocks home. Then Bert fit them together like a giant jigsaw. If a selected rock didn't fit, she hammered off a corner here and there until it did. A small pile of unused rocks sat stacked by the back door because they didn't work anywhere—at the moment. It took weeks of backbreaking labor, but eventually, a beautiful path led to the alley. Grass grew between the stones and Arlo mowed over the walk. Many years later, after selling the house, Bert drove by and was brokenhearted to see the new owners had ripped out her pretty sidewalk. Every muscle in her body ached once again, remembering the pain it had taken to create her masterpiece.

The Depression was still in full swing, and a steady stream of hoboes knocked on Bert's door that was next to the Congregational Church. Bums seeking money or food assumed the minister lived there and would be good for a handout. The men, dirty and unkempt, smelled of stale sweat from their lives of dire hardship. Some offered to work for food and sometimes Bert found a small job for them, but most of the time she asked them to wait on the porch while she made them a sandwich. As hard as times were, she never turned any away. Her own fear of the poorhouse was still vivid.

The Depression created countless door-to-door salesmen. They worked only for commission, so companies hired them by the dozens. They flooded the city, and it was a rare day when several salesmen didn't knock on Bert's door. She felt sorry for them too, but had learned to say, "No, thank you." She did welcome the Fuller Brush salesmen. She liked their products, and they handed out a small free brush for getting their foot in the door.

The previous Christmas, Bert had tried to tell Dorothy there was no Santa Claus, but couldn't bring herself to destroy the myth, deciding to wait one more year. Four months later, she gathered her courage, determined to tell her daughter that the Easter Bunny didn't exist, hoping to soften the blow about Santa Claus later. "Dorothy," she said, "Come sit down. I want to talk to you." She gently explained how the Easter Bunny was a fairy tale.

Dorothy looked perplexed. "Then where do the Easter eggs come from?"

"Daddy and I hide them for you."

After a few moments, Dorothy seemed to take it rather well and then made it easy for her mother. "Is Santa Claus a made-up story too?"

After Bert completed explaining the cruel facts of life about both holidays, Dorothy, somewhat downhearted, walked slowly to the window to look at the Easter eggs her parents had hidden. Suddenly she shrieked, "You lied to me! You lied to me," she cried and bolted out the door. Bewildered, Bert went to the window. Now there would be no convincing Dorothy the Easter rabbit was a fairy tale. There he sat, a tiny gray, escaped Easter Bunny sniffing a blue egg.

Bert had learned to sew as a youngster, and her new treadle Singer sewing machine hummed often. She designed and made both her clothes and Dorothy's without a pattern. If she felt she needed a pattern, she cut one from newspaper. Their Sunday-best clothes were always matching mother-and-daughter outfits.

Women of the day traditionally strolled out on Easter Sunday wearing a new outfit. On that holiday, a polished and combed Dorothy and Bert wore their new finery on their way to church. Bert surpassed her designing talent that year with stunning costumes. Everyone commented how spiffy they looked and asked where she bought their identical powder-blue dresses with the white-lined cape and matching pillbox hats. Bert glowed from hearing the compliments, and later, more happy news greeted her.

Arlo's sister, Grace, graduated from the Deaconess Hospital Nurses' Training School. Hazel Cox, who caused Bert's horrible elevator accident, was among the graduates. Arlo and Bert were proud of Grace; she was the only sibling on either side of the family to become a professional. One day in the future, they would be ecstatic because of nurse Grace.

Grace's future seemed bright, but because of the times, she had difficulty finding employment. She stayed with Arlo and Bert while seeking work. A letter Arlo wrote to their brother was full of clues about the terrible times. He wasn't a sportsman, but he wrote, "I'm going hunting Sunday in the Highwood Mountains. I hope I can get a deer because meat is awfully expensive." Grace added a note: "I am getting pretty desperate. I'm down to my last twenty-five cents."

The spring of 1935, Bert took the teacher's advice and enrolled Dorothy in kindergarten. Bert welcomed spending less time answering her chatterbox's hundreds of questions and was glad they could afford the three dollar monthly fee.

Bert's hiatus was brief. Three months later, her little chatterbox was again barely stopping for breath and Bert's days were hectic and time consuming because she walked everywhere. Frustrated with her busy workday, she told Arlo "I want to learn to drive."

"Okay, I'll teach you."

Starting the car, Bert shifted into first gear. Arlo said, "No, back up. Any fool can drive forward but they can't back up." She backed up, and backed up some more. It isn't known if she ever drove forward or not, but she became an expert at backing. Arlo and Bert's driveway lay between the house and church. The lane gave drivers only five inches clearance on each side, and it had a sharp bend in the middle. The driveway took skill to maneuver and Bert became the official car backer for more than one tenant.

Anytime Dorothy rode in a car, she vomited. Bert tried withholding food and drink beforehand, but nothing worked. June suggested putting Dorothy in the front seat, so the next trip she sat in front with her daddy. Hallelujah! No nausea—but her innards still did a wild tango.

The second problem was more serious, somnambulism. Once, Bert found Dorothy sound asleep drawing pictures on the blackboard, and another time standing in front of Spickie's cage waving her arms

Houdini fashion as if hypnotizing the helpless bird. Another time she located Dorothy asleep, curled up behind the bathroom door. Bert wasn't concerned until June told her about a neighbor with the same problem. She'd left her home and walked down the street in the middle of the night sound asleep—buck naked. After hearing that, Bert slept fitfully. Finally, she noticed whenever her daughter had a bedtime snack, she walked in her sleep. That ended Dorothy's evening goodies, and Bert got some sleep. Logic won after all.

One month shy of seven, Dorothy again entered first grade in 1935. Bert worried for a month before she visited Miss Bratherferd, who assured Bert that her daughter now seemed able to concentrate better and enjoyed school more—until a few weeks later. Dorothy came home for lunch in tears. Bert said, "What's the matter?"

Dorothy sobbed. "I wanted to play with a ball, but the teacher said, 'they're only for the boys,' and she took the ball away from me." Still sniffing, she asked, "Why do the boys get a great big playground and balls to play with, but we have to bring our own jacks and play on the street sidewalk? It isn't fair." She was right; the boys had the only playground. Dorothy wailed long and loud about the bias. She didn't know it, but she was a feminist many years before the word became a popular movement. It troubled Bert too, because logic failed to solve the problem. She couldn't ease Dorothy's angst while she still suffered the same discrimination trying to become a caller. Neither knew it would be more than seventy years before for the most diminutive changes would take place.

As a youngster, Dorothy was a mischievous imp, but that didn't discourage Arlo and Bert from wanting another child. Bert had two miscarriages at home, both boys; the loss haunted her the rest of her days. After her second miscarriage, she and Arlo had agreed to postpone having another child until times improved. The Depression still lingered in 1935, but Arlo was again working full-time and he said, "If we're ever going have another child we better do it now." Bert agreed.

One cool November day, Arlo labored in the yard pulling dandelions that bounced back quicker than Mexican jumping beans to annoy him. He looked forward to a hard freeze to end his weed battle for the year. Times still weren't good and President Roosevelt's New Deal Program didn't appear to be making progress. It was a beautiful day and he had faith things would get better. His reverie was shattered when Bert called, "Arlo, your father's on the phone." When Arlo answered, he paled. His mother had died from dropsy, an old terminology for congestive heart failure. She and Arlo had been very close. Once again, Bert buried a beloved family member while getting ready to bring another soul into the world— she was pregnant. Now, neither she nor Arlo had a mother; Dorothy was left without a grandmother. Her soon-to-be sibling would never know one.

Arlo still worked the swing shift. To fill the lonely evening hours, Bert and Dorothy attended movies several times a week—cheap entertainment. Dorothy got in free and the ten-cent adult admission allowed them to go often. They went to anything but the horror flicks and the crude science fiction films of the day. Their favorites were the musicals with Fred Astaire and Ginger Rogers and Nelson Eddy and Jeanette MacDonald. They sat through those twice.

Bert could afford the movies often for another reason. George Phillips and his buddy, Herb, who also rented an apartment from Bert, were both ticket takers at the Town Theater. If the boss wasn't around, George or Herb let them in free. When they left the theater for home, they passed the Rainbow Theater. The box office closed ten minutes after the last film began. Anyone could walk in because the theater managers assumed no one wanted to see a film in progress. They were wrong—Bert and Dorothy always went in. This was after they'd already seen a newsreel, previews, cartoon and a double feature.

The movies were cheap, but snacks were expensive and Bert didn't buy any. Like everyone else, they wanted "munchies," so one evening Bert sneaked in a sack of green grapes she'd picked off the stem for easier eating. Passing the sack back and forth, they fumbled and it dropped to the floor with the grapes rolling down to the front row. They didn't return to that theater for two weeks—Bert was afraid to go back.

Bert, an avid film fan, had assembled a movie star scrapbook, a popular adult hobby in the thirties. Dorothy was mesmerized by the Colgate smiles of the beautiful people. One day, Bert bought a ten-cent movie magazine, and Dorothy wanted to cut out six little pictures of her idol Buck Jones for the scrapbook. Bert was ironing, so she brought out the book, glue and scissors for her daughter to use. Dorothy became absorbed with her project and Bert took advantage of fewer interruptions to complete her task.

When she finished ironing, she asked to see the scrapbook. Dorothy showed it to her. Weird polygon, octagon, trapezoid and other shapes that didn't have names shone from Bert's carefully crafted scrapbook. Dorothy had simply cut around her cowboy hero on his bucking horse. The pictures looked funny; however, the scrapbook still sold for a good price sixty-five years later when Dorothy sold it for her mother who needed to dispose of some of her collectibles when moving to smaller quarters.

CHAPTER 25

Shirley Temple was the most famous person in the country in the mid-1930s. She earned more money than the president—and she was more popular. Every little girl in town wore Shirley Temple curls. Bert thought they looked adorable and took Dorothy for a permanent. Her hair was so thick the operator needed to use two wave machines, one on each side. Dorothy's head became so heavy she started to cry and Bert cupped her hands under her daughter's chin and held her head up for a long time. The torture results: elongated-sausage curls covering Dorothy's entire head when Bert rolled her daughter's locks in metal curlers. The hair was only the beginning of the Shirley craze.

A Shirley Temple doll hit the market and every little girl in America wanted one, including Dorothy. The family's financial situation had improved, but Bert wanted to teach her daughter the value of money and how to save to buy things she wanted. Her parents told Dorothy she must earn the money for her doll, and they offered her two cents if she dried the dinner dishes and five cents if she did the dishes herself. Washing and drying all the dishes seemed like a daunting task, and at two cents for drying, her savings progressed slowly.

Discouraged at the snail pace growth of her doll fund, Dorothy complained. Arlo came up with another scheme. The family lawn was the most beautiful one in town; dandelions were rare because Arlo continually dug them out. He told Dorothy he would pay her five cents a pound for weeded dandelions. He showed her how to dig deep to get the root and how to shake off the dirt before putting it in her pail. Five cents a pound sounded better than two cents for drying dishes. She grabbed a bucket and ran outside. Because of Arlo's continual assault on the pesky plant, the only dandelions she found were small, young sprouts weighing little. She wore off five cents of shoe leather the first day rushing to the basement to weigh the weeds every time she pulled two or three. At day's end, she was disgruntled with her pay.

The church next door didn't have dedicated weed pullers, and gigantic dandelions grew against the back wall. The next day when Arlo wasn't looking, she sneaked over and pulled several. When she produced her pail for weighing, five dandelions filled the small bucket. Arlo pulled them out. "The weeds have to come from our yard." That ended Dorothy's weeding—dandelions didn't weigh enough to suit her. It was back to drying dishes.

By mid-December Dorothy had saved half the money for the precious doll. Arlo and Bert told her they would "match her savings" and buy the doll for Christmas. Days before the holiday, Arlo needed a hemorrhoid operation, a painful procedure at the time. He opted to use McCleary Hospital in Excelsior Springs, Missouri, where they specialized in pain-free rectal surgery. Determined to preserve the family holiday, Bert said, "We'll celebrate when you get home."

When the holiday arrived at last, Dorothy became

despondent. Unable to bear it, Bert told her she could open one gift and Dorothy was ecstatic seeing the doll. Her joy was the only present her mother needed. Dorothy treasured her doll and never allowed anyone else to play with it. Bert had taught her well, and her doll looked like new for fifty-six years. When she moved to Georgia, the change in climate cracked the doll's composition face in two places. Other than that, it remained in mint condition along with the original dresses. Afraid it might develop still more cracks, Dorothy sold the doll in 1993 for 200 dollars—finally, a handsome profit for her dandelion weeding.

After Dorothy opened her one gift, the other packages remained under the tree until mid-January, and Bert fielded dozens of queries about the strange scene. When Arlo returned, the long-delayed Christmas took place. Dorothy thought two Christmas' were wonderful, and Arlo and Bert soon celebrated another event.

Arlo and Bert attended his Uncle Will and Anna's golden wedding anniversary in 1936. Bert, pregnant and embarrassed because she was so big for her five-month pregnancy, insisted Dorothy stand in front of her to hide her condition when Arlo took pictures. Women of the era hid their condition rather than flaunted it.

While Will and Anna were in the autumn of their marriage, Bert's sister Mamie was ready to spring sprightly into hers. She married Arthur Gerson, the brother of Max Gerson who married Ella. Two brothers married two sisters. Later, when Charlotte and George moved out of Bert's apartment, Mamie and Art moved in, and Bert gave them the same ten percent discount. Again, she wanted to help them save money to buy a home. Arthur worked in the coal mines and later the smelter, but in his youth he was a hobo. Dorothy adored him and she pestered him to tell her stories about his days of riding the rails in filthy, cold or boiling-hot boxcars depending on the time of year. Arthur's embellished tales were likely more fascinating than the real event.

After several years, Mamie and Art saved a nice nest egg and they bought a new car. In no uncertain terms, Bert let her sister know she believed it wrong to put a car before a home—she could not stop being Little Mother. Later, they did buy a summer retreat on the border of Glacier Park. Again Bert felt their priorities were in the wrong place, but at least they had made an investment.

Pale green walls, intended to soothe anxieties, weren't working for Arlo and he paced back and forth in the Deaconess Hospital waiting room. Bert's labor with her second child was far easier than the first. The doctor delivered eight-pound, four-ounce Earl Raymond on July 13, 1936. Bert wanted to name him Arlo, but again her husband balked, so neither of their children was named after anyone.

Earl was only seventeen-and-a-half inches long, a perfect size eleven: an eleven-inch head, abdomen and chest, a round little ball with his mother's hazel eyes. Ironically, the infamous Hazel Cox, who caused Bert's elevator accident, was now the supervisor of the third floor where Bert and Earl received visitors. Arlo was thrilled to have a son and the feeling was more than mutual—Earl very soon obsessively idolized *his daddy*.

A cranky baby, Earl started cutting teeth early, twelve in fifteen months, and he was completely opposite of blabbermouth Dorothy. He hardly talked at all. When he did, he couldn't say Dorothy and called his sister Do-Do—for the next seventy-five years.

Bert was washing clothes in the basement and she called to Dorothy to bring Earl downstairs. Dorothy said, "Okay," and seconds later the air was fractured with a penetrating scream. Chills ran up Bert's spine. She dashed to the stairs to see Dorothy plunging down the steps on her back, her elbow-locked arms holding Earl high in the air above her, protecting him.

Earl never liked to be cuddled—unless it was by *his daddy*. By age two, he toddled along wherever Arlo went, holding onto his finger or the seam of his pants. He insisted on taking a bath, emptying the garbage, and going to the toilet with Arlo. Once, when Arlo urinated, Earl, absorbed in the process, said, "Will my little wee-wee get as big as yours when I grow up?"

Caring for her home and family, gardening, running an apartment house, providing for a boarder, finding ways to earn extra money, and operating a part-time hotel was more than a full-time job, yet Bert always made time to play with her children.

Dorothy's favorite playtime came when Bert read her the Sunday funny papers, a single comic strip filling an entire page. Sitting on the foyer floor with the pages spread out before them, Bert read them all. Dorothy's favorite was the *Katzenjammer Kids* because Bert made them come alive using a strong German accent and Dorothy giggled at every guttural "*ach.*" Once was never enough, and Dorothy insisted her mother read that particular comic at least twice. Her mother never refused.

Dorothy loved coloring books and Bert made sure she always had one or two. Sometimes they colored together, but usually Dorothy colored while Bert ironed.

Like all little girls, Dorothy loved to play "dress-up" in her mother's clothes. When Bert finished pinning Dorothy into one of her gowns one afternoon, the radio began playing *The Continental,* a popular song in the mid-thirties.

"Oh, listen, Mama, it's the song they played in the

movie." Dorothy began to whirl around the floor. "Look, Mama, I'm Ginger Rogers," she said flipping her long skirt around in imitation of the Hollywood star's latest movie.

Bert laughed, walked over, bowed deeply, and said, "May I have this dance, Miss Rogers?" Fred and Ginger spun merrily around the floor.

Earl's favorite game was "store." Bert cut out letter postmarks to use for make-believe money. Whenever she brought out the ironing board, Earl took out the cupcake tins to collect his inventory: food, toys, thimble, or whatever he could find. When he gathered sufficient items for sale, he knocked on her ironing board. "Come in," Bert sang out and he proceeded to show her his stock. She inspected it. "Oh, that's nice, how much is it?" When she made her selection, she counted out her postmark money. Earl learned to count to ten and to make change playing the game—ironing was extra time consuming.

Bert bought miniature farm buildings, fences, human and animal figures, and she made little sheds for animals. Then, she and Earl played "farm," moving the animals and fences around while she spun barnyard tales. She loved her children deeply—but could not tell them so.

Bert never heard she was loved when growing up, so she never said those words either. Her children didn't doubt her devotion, because of her actions and tender care, but she never actually used the word "love."

When Bert was in her seventies, Dorothy began saying "I love you" when she hung up the phone. Soon her mother said it too and once verbalization started, it became consistent, deeply felt and often voiced first by her.

CHAPTER 26

Cleaning house one afternoon, Bert listened to KFBB radio and was surprised to hear a square dance caller. The next week she went to the station to meet him. A few observers watched the affair through a large window, and Bert joined them. She hadn't called since volunteering in Manchester. After the program, the caller came out and Bert introduced herself, saying brashly, "I can call square dances just like that." He blinked, his face registering surprise, but he was polite and they talked about square dancing. The conversation resulted in her calling square dances on KFBB radio. She was ecstatic—even if she wasn't paid.

Two years later the broadcast was dropped. The dancers so enjoyed their dancing evenings that they began meeting in the basements of various homes to dance. The group soon outgrew cellars and they rented the hall of the Independent Order of Odd Fellows Lodge naming themselves the Merry Makers. Phonograph records provided the music and Bert called. As news of their good-time evenings spread, the dancers increased in number and they outgrew the hall.

Bert searched and found a new hall for the group at the Elks Lodge. When she heard the lodge's "condition for the hall's use," she was stunned. The Merry Maker's dance *must* be open to the public and The Cascaders and Pokarney's Old-Time Orchestra would provide the music. She could hardly believe her ears. After eleven years of being refused work in Great Falls, she would be calling for a public dance. Jubilant, she raced home. Arriving nearly breathless, she told Arlo the wonderful news. Knowing how desperately she wanted this recognition, he was overjoyed. Counting the years she called for country dances in Big Sandy, she'd performed for eighteen years as a volunteer.

Bert's skin tingled in anticipation on the day of her official debut. Her long years of frustration were over—but now the minutes before the bewitching hour dragged on and on; she looked at the clock every few minutes. After washing the dishes, she began to prepare. Skin gleaming from her bath, Bert donned her freshly ironed flared red skirt and tucked in a ruffled white blouse. She dabbed Evening in Paris behind her ears, and twirled in front of the full-length closet-door mirror to inspect her image. Ready to join the ranks of the professional square dance callers, Bert smiled.

As she sat to put on her black ballerina shoes, the memories of her long struggle washed across her mind disrupting her joyous mood. Irritation surged through her body and she stood quickly. *Well, the male callers might not be ready for me, but here I come.*

When Bert arrived at the lodge for her first appearance, her stomach and backbone did a *do-si-do.* Inhaling deeply, she stepped in front of the musicians seated on a low platform and looked at the crowd already formed in traditional squares. "Howdy," she said wearing a broad smile. "Are you ready to square dance?" When the musicians struck the first note, all the tension drained from her body and her deep booming voice resonated across the hall.

"Allemande left with your left hand,

Right to your partner with a right and left hand.

Meet your honey and promenade.

Chicken on the fence post,

Fox on the rail,

Meet your partner and everyone trail."

Ending the call, she rolled her hips in a saucy hula flip. "That's all there is, there ain't no more," and the hall exploded with cheers and applause. At the fulfillment of her dream, tears of joy rolled down her cheeks. At last, she was a professional square dance caller—she was paid.

Being hired as floor manager, caller, and official greeter at the Lodge Old-Time Dance in 1937 was a goal she'd fought to achieve for almost two decades; Bert would be the only female caller in the state for the next twenty years. She was also the first woman floor manager. When she applied for the combination job years earlier, she was told, "Women can't handle the drunks. We only hire men." Now the dance hall overseer wanted her as floor manager because he thought a woman *could* handle the drunks better. And Bert managed the drunkards fine—her way.

One night, the ubiquitous drunk was pestering all the ladies to dance. The women complained to Bert, "He's drunk and obnoxious."

"His hands stray, too," said another.

"I'll take care of it," Bert promised. The music started and the staggering wolf wove toward his prey. Bert intercepted him at the pass. "Say, you promised me this dance."

"I di—did?"

"Yes, you did." He belched and lurched toward the

dance floor. He was so inebriated he didn't realize she was leading him—leading him straight to the door. As they neared the entrance, she told two men standing there, "He's drunk, throw him out." They did, and order was restored with only minor damage to Bert's dancing shoes.

A woman caller was such a surprising novelty in the thirties that everyone wanted to hear her—everyone except the male callers who verbally sabotaged her whenever possible.

Bert's sister Erna attended a country dance in Chinook and someone suggested they hire the new woman caller in Great Falls. The current male caller heard them.

"Oh, you don't want to hire her. She can't call."

"I think we should at least give her a chance," one lady said. Several others echoed the sentiment, but the men threatened to boycott the dance if a squeaky female called. Bert didn't get the job. When Erna told her sister, she cried.

After the lodge broke the ban on female callers and as more and more of the square dance public heard Bert, she began to get gigs for other dances. The dancers couldn't get enough of her deep, husky tones. Her booming voice carried throughout the hall without a mike. The people could understand every word; that wasn't always true of some male callers.

Bert couldn't call whatever came to mind at the moment. She needed to plan a pattern to bring each dancer back to his or her partner. New callers needed to learn more than 200 commands, but she'd known them for years. She did both patter and singing calls.

Times were still difficult and prices high, so when Bert received an occasional gig for a dance, she was happy to add to the family income. However, choreographing, rehearsing and calling brought additional work to her already full schedule, as well as additional ironing. And none of the money she earned for calling, selling onions or wood fiber flowers could be depended on. Still when she looked at the plight of others, she felt lucky.

During one of those ironing sessions, nine-year-old Dorothy sat at the table flipping through the latest issue of Life magazine. She stared at one page, finally held it up, and said, "Mom, isn't this beautiful. If I *ever* get to Louisiana, I want to see this house." The antebellum ruin had no roof and according to the caption had giant white pillars on all four sides. Spanish moss hung from the live oaks around Belle Helene, all reflected in a nearby pond.

"Yes, it's pretty, but if you ever go to Louisiana, you'll never remember where it is. You need to write it down." She gave her daughter a small loose-leaf notebook, and Dorothy dutifully labeled the first page, "Louisiana." Thereafter, anytime she saw something interesting in the paper, a magazine, or heard something later on television, it all went into the notebook that would grow into four big binders. Bert couldn't have known her idea would be future guidance for the many trips she would make with Dorothy and her husband. Ironically, twenty years later, Dorothy and her husband did see the spectacular structure pictured in Life magazine still standing serenely among the moss-covered oaks in all its faded grandeur. Enjoying the beautiful sight, Dorothy smiled, thinking of the day when Bert interrupted her ironing to fetch the little book.

Ironing was such a time-consuming chore that Bert taught Dorothy to wash and iron her own clothes when she was nine to ease her workload. If Dorothy's dress was exceptionally detailed, Bert ironed it and let her daughter do dish towels, tablecloths or pillowcases instead.

Dorothy sat coloring at the kitchen table one day while Bert chopped onions for the dinner meat loaf. "Dorothy,"

Bert said, "would you like to help me so you can learn to cook?"

Bert gaped at Dorothy's casual and innocent reply, "I don't think so."

Bert hadn't expected that response. She tried to get Dorothy's interest on several occasions, but something else always seemed preferable to her daughter. Bert, often forced to cook for her entire family at nine years of age, refused to do the same thing to her daughter. Fortunately, Dorothy's future husband didn't mind being a guinea pig, but he probably wished on more than one occasion that Bert had insisted a wee bit more.

In the summer of 1937, Bert invited Arlo's four nieces and nephews to spend a week at their home. That meant eight people sleeping in two rooms. Warm bodies were bunked down everywhere except hanging from pegs. She devoted the entire week to entertaining her guests, playing games, going to the movies or to the park. One day, they made a huge picnic lunch. Their car wasn't available so they walked the three miles to Giant Springs. Earl, who was one, remained behind with Mamie. The group spent the day eating, playing games, exploring and taking pictures. Then they walked three miles home. Bert's nephew Kenneth later wrote in her ninetieth birthday memory book. "She is my favorite aunt, and I will never forget the wonderful time she created especially for us."

Max Jr. bought his first car in 1937, a Chevrolet—the world beckoned. The 'world' had to wait awhile, but in September 1939, Max Jr. and his father set off on their first vacation. Arlo and Bert went along leaving the children with Mamie, who still lived upstairs. Bert packed enough camping gear and food for four. Driving into the wild unknown, Bert felt overjoyed.

On their way to Butte, the so-called *Richest Hill on Earth,* they stopped to watch a fascinating, massive gold dredging operation. Camp that evening was at a grassy clearing in the bend of the Missouri River. The next day, they drove to Polson to visit family who took them to a big dam with power generators. Again, they'd never seen anything so extraordinary, but it didn't take much to impress people who had seen little of Montana, let alone the world. The most impressive sight was yet to come.

Glacier National Park—a wilderness wonder consisted of more than a million acres. Blasting the Rocky Mountains for eleven years had produced the spectacular *Going to the Sun Highway* in 1932. The fifty-two mile road climbed 3,000 feet amid glaciers, lakes and waterfalls plummeting from snowcapped peaks.

The park was free but furnished few amenities, unless you stayed at the expensive Glacier Park Lodge. Only the hoot of owls and wolf serenades disturbed the campers' slumber. A torrential rain almost washed their tent away one night, and it leaked, soaking everything. In the morning, bedding flapped in the stiff breeze, turning their camp into a Chinese laundry when Bert hung everything in the trees to dry.

She wore a pair of slacks for the occasion, but still hated them. Cooking and making beds was mostly her job, but she was having so much fun she didn't care.

Driving through the park, alpine meadows splashed with colorful wildflowers startled her senses. Bert's eyes darted from side to side—she didn't know where to look next. She had the only camera and took pictures of everything that didn't move. The towering waterfalls mesmerized her. She swore to return—it would be a long wait.

The five-day trip was a fabulous adventure for people with no travel experience, and the vacation cost little since gas was only seventeen cents a gallon. Their wonderful adventure would be the only vacation Arlo and Bert would make during their entire marriage, hardly balancing out their many trials and tribulations.

CHAPTER 27

Bert had two horrifying experiences with Earl as a youngster. One day, at ten-months-old, he lay on the bed while Bert talked to Grace who was visiting. Suddenly, Bert noticed Earl was blue and appeared lifeless. Grace, a nurse, knew he wasn't getting oxygen. Bert's heart pounded like a jackhammer as she watched Grace turn a limp Earl upside down and slap him repeatedly on the back. It didn't help. She then put her fingers down his throat and found the item obstructing his breath. She couldn't extricate it. "If I pull it out, it might damage his pallet so bad he won't be able to speak; but if I don't, he might die. What should I do?"

It was not a choice. "Pull it out," Bert screamed, blood draining from her face. Grace did and Earl's complexion turned rosy in moments. Later, when he learned to talk, an attractive and unusual accent on certain letters bestowed him with a distinct style. The object that turned the letter "R" into a lisp—a toy jack.

Playing Jacks was Dorothy's favorite pastime, and she used them every day. Bert had cautioned her daughter several times not to put the jacks down where Earl could reach them. After using them earlier that day, Dorothy carefully put them on the windowsill where they were high and safely out of his reach—until the Murphy bed was lowered.

The second traumatic event happened when Earl was a toddler, about three. He was still unsteady on his feet, often plopping down in one-point landings. Arlo worked on the roof one Sunday making repairs while Earl followed *his daddy's* every move from the fenced yard. Bert came out of the house to check on Earl. She couldn't find him. She looked up, adrenaline-fueled panic froze her in mid-step. Grabbing her throat, she struggled to halt the blood-curdling scream that surged upward as she saw Earl tottering along the edge of the roof on the two-story house. Unbelievably, Earl had somehow climbed the ladder because he so needed to be with *his daddy*.

Bert didn't dare shout for fear of startling Earl, making him lose his balance. "Arlo," she called softly, "Whatever you do, don't yell. Earl is on the roof behind you." Bert started walking under the eaves, her eyes turned skyward, all the while holding her arms out to break her son's fall if the worst should happen. Arlo turned around. Beads of sweat broke out on his forehead and his hands were shaking as he held out his arms. Earl wobbled—lunging forward, Arlo snatched his son, crushing him to his chest. Bert always had an amazing ability to remain calm during a crisis, but when the calamity was over, she fell apart. That day she splintered into slivers.

If Bert had seen Dorothy's horse riding accident, she would have been panicky too. While visiting family on the farm, Dorothy, her uncle, and cousin were driving cattle down the road on horseback. Her horse bolted and appeared to be a runaway. The mount galloped on and on. She struggled to rein him in until she could hold on no longer. She threw herself off sideways. Her uncle said she fell. Dorothy knew better. When she regained consciousness two hours later, her aunt wept at her bedside. Dorothy felt sore but no bones appeared broken. Her aunt felt Bert would blame her when they took Dorothy home, but Bert was only happy Dorothy seemed okay.

Later, Dorothy had another equine accident when the animal she galloped bareback stumbled in a gopher hole. She flew over the horse's head and the steed then soared over her head, hooves flying. Fortunately, she was unhurt other than bruises and probable back damage. Bert was getting used to her accident-prone daughter's hazardous adventures.

When Earl outgrew his crib, it presented a predicament. The apartment was already over-crowded and there wasn't room for another bed. Bert pondered the problem and then cleverly modified Dorothy's daybed by sliding a board in at night turning one bed into two. It functioned so well Dorothy later didn't catch Earl's chickenpox.

It was Dorothy's job to mind Earl when her mother was busy. She was reading when Bert instructed her to watch Earl while she went to the basement. When she returned, Dorothy was still reading.

Bert snapped, "You were supposed to be watching Earl."

"I was. He was quiet as a mouse."

He was quiet all right—playing Van Gogh on Bert's freshly painted walls. He decorated his canvas with crayon hieroglyphics for five feet, as high as he could reach. Bert fretted because she didn't have enough paint left to re-do the wall and she didn't want to buy another gallon for that small space, and the area was too big and too low to hang a picture. As always, she found a practical solution. She bought a long blackboard to cover the area, giving Earl a place to practice his brush strokes. Then he lost all interest in his artistic endeavor.

Every August, Bert enjoyed the Montana State Fair, which ran for a week. She went at least twice, taking the kids when old enough. As well as the carnival, there were free exhibits, animal barns, horseracing, a rodeo, and a ticketed evening show with fireworks. Bert enjoyed the races, and she and Dorothy guessed which horse would win, but she never placed a bet. They both loved the Penny Arcade and were fascinated with the mutoscope that held hundreds of photographs stacked in a metal drum with a viewing slot. It was mounted on a pedestal and by turning the handle very fast, the figures jumped around and looked like early nickelodeon movies. Penny Arcade entertainment could last hours for mere pennies.

Sometimes they took in the freak shows when a barker tempted them, but not often. They felt sorry for the "special people." During those years, pitiful souls with untreatable medical abnormalities—such as the Siamese Twins—usually wound up in freak shows where they were shamelessly exhibited. But if not for the existence of these carnival shows, most of the "freaks" couldn't earn a living, so the situation was a double-edged sword.

One time, Bert became fascinated by a particular game of chance. She could win the stuffed panda that smiled at her from a shelf. She needed to sink three nails in a rail with only one swing of the hammer. She'd swung many a hammer in her day and was confident she could do it. The "carny operator" started the nails and handed her the hammer. She succeeded with two nails every time but one always bent. After several attempts, Bert whispered to Dorothy, "There's something crooked about this game." She told the proprietor, "I want to start my own nails." He wouldn't let her. Today we recognize it as a scam, but back then, much of the public didn't realize flimflam artists abounded everywhere at fairs. Disgusted with herself for losing what she considered a lot of money, she felt guilty and agitated for being taken in. She was never conned again.

Unbelievably, Arlo and Bert never had a fight during their entire marriage. Not one. This wasn't due to her, because she was a little domineering, stubborn, and had a temper. Her anger didn't surface often, but when it did and she became irritated at him, Arlo snatched his hat and went outside to work in the yard. Later, he would return, open the door, fling his hat into the room, poke his head in, and say, "Is it safe to come in yet?" When Bert saw the hat sailing in, she couldn't help but laugh and that ended the matter. Her thinking was always so practical and logical that later, when disagreements arose, Arlo said, "You're usually right, just do what you think best." Perhaps that is why the yard had so few dandelions.

Bert could not understand how Arlo kept his temper under such tight control. When her father-in-law visited, she asked him. Frank told her that when Arlo was a teenager, he got into a horrendous argument with his brother Harold. Arlo became infuriated and in blinding rage, he grabbed a pitchfork and was about to stab his brother when their father walked in. Frank pounced on Arlo. Then he sat him down for a long serious talk—with Frank doing the talking.

When Frank told Arlo how he'd almost killed Harold, the blood drained from Arlo's face. He broke into a sweat. He couldn't believe it. Arlo had been so out-of-control he had no memory of the event. Traumatized, he swore he would never, ever lose his temper again. And he never did.

After Della died, Max visited Bert and Arlo often, bringing his fiddle along. He spent his days helping Arlo rid the lawn of those wretched dandelions. In the evenings, he often provided a fiddle recital. In the midst of a lively tune, he'd abruptly stop playing and gargle out a loud "*ach*" followed by a whooping German spiel of some sort. Dorothy always giggled and pestered him to do it again.

During one of Max's future visits, Dorothy played a new record she'd bought, *You, You, You Are the One,* by the Ames Brothers. "I've always liked that song," Max said.

Startled, Dorothy smiled. "But, Grandpa, it's a new song." Apparently not—it was an old, old tune and Max sang her the entire song in German.

Max always joined Bert and June for dances. Remembering her own great joy when learning to dance at six, Bert had taken Dorothy to the dances at the same age. In no time, she knew all the round dances and could square dance too. Max always danced with her; and, at her insistence, all the round waltzes. She adored them because they whirled round and round like a spinning top. The happy-go-lucky side of Max's dual personality was always great fun. Dorothy cherished her grandfather—she never knew the raging, out-of-control Max. With his children now grown, he seemed to have little need for wrath around his family.

Box socials were a custom of the times, and Bert used them for her dance clubs and they were tastily successful. Each lady brought food in a fancy decorated package for auction. The highest bidder was privileged to eat with the designer and have the next dance. Supposedly, no one knew who made the lunches, and the men bid on the mystery boxes. Often the bidding soared, because a lady told her beau which box was hers.

The lunches were usually acquired for a nominal price, but, occasionally, beautiful ones sent the bidding skyward. Artist that she was, Bert took extra time creating her donation and once she twisted crepe paper—a favorite decorating tool—into long ropes and glued them around the box. Flowers covered the top, and the bidding went on and on until it reached fourteen dollars, the highest price her crowd ever paid for a box lunch. Bert kept one of her favorite boxes all her days.

One warm July day, Bert worked in the garden. Puffy clouds dotted the sky as the afternoon breeze caressed her cheek. A friendly chickadee serenaded her as she worked, and she felt a glow of happiness. Despite their stiff struggles during the Depression, she felt lucky because her life was complete: a loving, hard-working husband, the two children they had wanted, and the income from renters paid their mortgage. She was in high spirits. Her life was percolating merrily along on the front burner, and getting better every day as they worked toward culmination of *His Plan*. But sometimes plans go awry.

CHAPTER 28

Arlo had worked at the Great Northern Railroad for nineteen years, and according to *The Plan* he would continue until retirement. Buying one apartment house at a time, he hoped to be landlord of two or three by then.

Arlo called Bert from work one hot day in 1940. She was surprised because he rarely called from the job. "Bert, I don't feel good. Please have some hot food and plenty of hot water so I can take a bath when I get home."

"Are you in pain?"

"No. No pain, I just feel strange. I can't describe it."

When Arlo came home, he looked pale. "Where do you hurt?"

"I don't hurt. I just feel funny."

"I'll call the doctor."

"No, I don't want to go to the doctor. I'll get some rest. I'll be better in the morning." Arlo ate little dinner, took his hot bath and went to bed. Unable to sleep he arose early, as did Bert. His eyes looked strange and his fingernails were turning blue. She called the doctor.

When Bert described Arlo's symptoms, the doctor said he would come right away. He arrived in minutes and after examining Arlo, he took Bert into the hall. "Get him to the hospital immediately; he has problems with his heart." Bert told Arlo he needed to go to the hospital.

"No! I don't want to go to the hospital."

"But the doctor says you have to."

"No," he begged, "p-lease, Bert, don't let them take me. They'll kill me!" Bert was mystified. *Why is he so terrified of hospitals? Did he hear scary childhood tales? Is it a premonition?* She could not persuade him, and her emotions were shredded. In complete despair, she felt like she had no choice but to go against his wishes. She called for an ambulance. Earl was visiting Grandpa Courtnage and Bert called the farm. "Bring Earl home. Arlo is in the hospital."

The doctors worked frantically. They couldn't find anything wrong. By the time Frank and Earl arrived, Arlo could not talk. Frank took his son's hand. "Earl is here. Squeeze my hand if you can hear me," Arlo was so weak his fingers barely moved. He died July 26, 1940, mere hours after admittance. He had turned thirty-seven three months earlier.

When Bert went home with the dreadful news, relatives and friends gathered around to support her, but they couldn't help her tell her children their daddy would never be home again. She took several deep breaths trying to calm her shattered nerves; dry-eyed she explained the loss to her children as best she knew how. Earl had turned four, thirteen days earlier. Dorothy was twelve. Bert, a widow at thirty-four, mentally screamed: This is not part of *The Plan.*

That night, after everyone left and the children were asleep, Bert slumped in a faded overstuffed chair she inherited from a departing tenant. She disliked the chair because it seemed to envelop her entire body as she sank low in its depths. Now, strangely, in her black hole of desolation, she felt wrapped in familiar comforting arms, but it did little to relieve her foreboding. A heavy lump of fear lay like stone in the pit of her stomach. Innumerable thoughts ricocheted across her mind, jumbled thoughts having no connection to anything, but intertwined with terror and confusion.

Arlo was gone. She had two children to rear. She was in debt. The apartment income barely paid the mortgage, and her occasional calling gigs brought in little money. She had no idea how long she sat there. Time vanished. Near dawn she straightened and slapped her own face, leaving a bright red mark on her cheek. *I can't cry and feel sorry for myself—I have to be strong for my family.* She didn't cry again.

When she met with the autopsy doctor, he said, "We could have saved your husband, if we had known what the problem was."

Bert shrank back as if punched in the stomach. A shriek rose from the core of her being; "You mean to tell me Arlo didn't have to die."

"Yes, we didn't know the problem was a blood clot."

Bert began to shake. The doctor helped her to a chair. *Oh, my God, if I had only told them about the lump in Arlo's leg*—torrents of guilt washed across her.

When Arlo and Bert married, she'd asked him about a small lump on his calf. "Oh, it's been there for years. It doesn't hurt." In those days, people only went to the doctor when they were in pain, something was broken, or they were bleeding profusely. The average person didn't know their blood type, never heard of cholesterol, and knew little about their bodies. Shortly before his death, Arlo had noticed the lump moved higher up his leg but didn't think anything about it. Then it disappeared. He told Bert, "That lump went away." It did—straight to his heart.

The doctor told Bert, "The clot probably was caused by getting up too soon with a high fever." At fifteen, Arlo came down with the Spanish Influenza, the pandemic of 1918 that killed millions of people worldwide. When the rest of the family caught the flu, Arlo got out of bed to care for the others—he still had a high fever. If the clot had remained in place, it wouldn't have been problematic. In the stressful situation of Arlo's sudden illness, neither he nor Bert thought to tell the doctor about the lump in his leg that went away.

Bert never forgave the doctor for telling her about the needless death. It was a dreadful thing to tell someone who had just lost the love of her life. The doctor's words and those of Arlo, begging her not to take him to the hospital haunted the rest of her days. She never could erase Arlo's plea from her mind, and she cried and cried in her nineties repeating the story for this book. The death of a loved one is always traumatic, but Arlo died of pure ignorance.

Over the next five days, several times a day, Earl asked to go to the mortuary to see *his daddy*. With business matters and funeral arrangements needing attention, Bert couldn't take him as often as he wanted to go, so her brother-in-law, George, took him. The mortuary owner brought out a stool and Earl climbed on it, putting his hands around Arlo's frozen face. "Don't worry, Daddy; I'll take care of Mommy."

When they returned home, George said, "Oh God, Bert, it was awful. Earl talked and talked to Arlo. I couldn't stand it and left the room." George, and later Arthur Gerson, Earl's uncle, became surrogate fathers and he remained close to them the rest of their lives. But they were not *his daddy*.

Strangely, Dorothy retained only two memories of her father's death: She remembers only the shock of touching his cold, hard face at her mother's suggestion, so she "would know he was gone." and utter contempt whenever the family mourners' photograph before the funeral surfaces, because she remembers posing to be certain her handkerchief trailed from her hand for everyone to see. How could she have been so callous? Later, she learned the emotion was not unusual for a twelve-year-old, but today her only memories of the funeral are of self-loathing.

Courtnage and Clawiter relatives, Great Northern personnel, friends and tenants filled the Methodist Church. Twenty-seven bouquets and eleven floral sprays surrounded the casket. The organist played *The Old Rugged Cross* and *In the Garden,* hymns that brought tears to Dorothy's eyes forever after. The same two hymns had resonated throughout another church for Arlo's mother and later three other family members thus becoming a family tradition. Both hymns would one day be played at Bert's funeral.

Arlo eternally rests on a grassy knoll in Highland Memorial Cemetery. It was a beautiful sunny day, a sharp contrast to the heaviness in the hearts of the mourners.

For weeks, Bert's surface-deep tranquility was deceiving. In a daze, she automatically fed her children often unaware what they were eating. For months, her days were a foggy limbo. Friends and family believed she was bearing up well because she didn't cry—they didn't know she was falling apart. Finally, she went to the doctor, because she could not function.

During the examination, Bert admitted she'd not cried since the day of Arlo's death. The doctor shook his head. Then he chastised her severely. Startled, her eyes widened and she stared—then she began to cry. Then she sobbed, and couldn't stop weeping. Again, the typical prescription of the day: rest.

Both children were at family farms, so Bert was free of responsibilities, and she went to Seattle, even though Arlo's free railway passes were a thing of the past. Seattle was her nerve-soothing treatment center. Her solution worked well in the past and while it didn't relax her completely, it did help her to get on with the grieving process.

Dorothy wrote her mother, "Stay as long as you want to, Mom, as I am having a wonderful time and don't mind staying longer." In Bert's world, any separation required letters back and forth. She gave both children stamped, self-addressed envelopes to ensure they wrote. When Dorothy and Earl came home, Bert's nerves were slowly improving—her finances were not.

CHAPTER 29

Arlo had a 5,000-dollar life insurance policy. "If anything ever happens to me, you can use the money if you must, but please try to save it for the children's education if possible." Determined to honor his wishes; difficulties developed quickly. Soon she had no choice and she spent 3,000 dollars. She managed to save the rest for Dorothy and Earl; how, can only be imagined.

Bert still planted her garden and called at dances, but financially she was in dire straits. Unable to hire out as a live-in domestic because of the children, she once again applied for jobs at the Woolworth and Kress dime stores. Her grammar had improved since her first attempt, but without job experience or a high school diploma, she still couldn't get hired as a dime store clerk. No one else would hire her either.

The one bright spot was square dancing, which seemed to be gaining in popularity again and she was asked to call more often. The male callers still resented her, but the public adored her. Even with more dancing gigs, her financial struggle intensified. Bert often recalled how Arlo had wanted to buy the apartment house, but she was afraid of being in debt. Now she felt thankful for *The Plan* even though it wasn't fulfilled. Because of Arlo's dream, she wasn't homeless—yet.

When life was at its darkest, she heard about jobs being offered at a seed house near Giant Springs. She applied and was accepted. Apparently, a high school diploma wasn't needed to qualify a person to pick out a bad pea or bean as the vegetables came down a long conveyor belt in front of several women. She was delighted to get the job, but it didn't ease her angst. The employment was only seasonal and she would soon be out of work again.

Charlotte and George, who still lived upstairs, were avid fishermen and often took Bert and the kids on fishing trips to give them an outing. Bert loved these jaunts. Other than Glacier Park, she'd never traveled anywhere except to visit family, and she was thrilled with the beautiful Montana scenery. With each exploration, she yearned to see more.

All farmers kept cats to solve the barn mouse problem. Arlo's brother Harold had a typical feline population that recently increased in number. He knew Earl loved cats and thinking it would help ease the sadness of his first Christmas without *his daddy*, he asked Bert if he could give Earl a kitten. She agreed. On Christmas Eve, Harold brought Bert an adorable black and white bundle of fur. She put the boxed feline under the tree moments before Earl came out Christmas morning. When he saw the kitten, his eyes rolled in their sockets; he was so excited he couldn't eat breakfast. He named the kitten Felix, after the cat in movie cartoons.

Bert developed a strong bond with her daughter, but for reasons she never understood, she couldn't establish the same relationship with Earl. Theirs was one of almost constant dissension. In desperation, she sought help from a medical doctor. His conclusion: "Earl had *obsessively* bonded to his father, and Arlo's premature death *marked* him." Hard as she tried, she couldn't overcome the problem. Earl wouldn't bring his troubles to her or confide in her. Her feelings were easily hurt, now they were crushed. Bert felt she must be doing something wrong, and as usual, she blamed herself.

Bert had pestered Arlo to have his portrait taken, and he did—two weeks before he died. She wanted the photograph in her bedroom, but Earl insisted on having the picture. He missed *his daddy* so desperately she gave in. Often, she found him crying and talking to the picture. Even in high school he wept and took his problems to the picture instead of her. Sixty-six years later, that picture hangs by Earl's desk—there is none of Bert.

Finding a method to punish Earl for typical childhood misdeeds was difficult—nothing worked. Not logic, spanking or guilt trips. Taking away his movie privileges succeeded only a short time. In later years, Dorothy asked Earl why he didn't confide in their mother. "I didn't want to worry her." While it was true Bert was a worrier, confiding in her would have forged a closer relationship. Instead, she heard about incidents from his friends, who were then shocked she didn't already know. He had a bad motorcycle accident, never mentioning it and he didn't tell her when he was nearly killed water skiing. She found out only because he could barely walk the next day; and his body was so black and blue he couldn't hide it. This time, she insisted, and he finally told her the story.

Water skiing on the Missouri River, he spotted several girls watching him from the shoreline. He made a few passes by them, deliberately going closer and closer to the bank. The closer he went, the more the girls yelled, and he was showing off to impress them. During the next swoop, the girls blew kisses—he blew kisses back. Then he saw the dock looming in his path and realized the damn thing wasn't going to get out of *his* way—it caught him just above the waist. Earl admitted what the doctor had said, "One inch higher and you wouldn't have survived."

Bert's tremendous guilt over not establishing a close relationship with Earl made her doubt her mothering ability. She often told Dorothy, "I don't think I was a good mother." Like all parents, she made mistakes rearing her children. Her error was due to the stilted guidance she received at home. Remembering her childhood whippings, she was determined not to abuse her children when they needed to be punished. When correcting Dorothy, she talked to her instead of swatting her, but she didn't realize using the wrong words were more damaging than a spanking. Dorothy never had a single spanking because logic and reasoning worked well. But Bert's idea of logic was actually guilt trips. They worked wonders producing the results she wanted. Bert, who learned her guilt-trip skills from her mother as a child, didn't recognize them as that; she felt she was reasoning. When Dorothy needed punishment, Bert used her version of logic: "You are going to grow up to be absolutely worthless." Sometimes she substituted worthless with "good-for-nothing," but those words were equally as bad. Dorothy, a scamp, heard those statements often. Like most kids she shrugged off the admonishments, or so she believed. The verbal abuse only retreated, hid and festered deep in her subconscious. The repetitive negative comments left her with powerful feelings of inferiority and a total lack of self-esteem.

Twenty-five years later—during great stress—the quagmire of infection would erupt in Dorothy's quaking body that she clawed at uncontrollably. A doctor administered a shot for the hives-like itching that raged across her body. She already suffered recurring anxiety nightmares, tingling fingertips, sudden sweats and piercing headaches, some lasting days. Dorothy realized she needed help.

Dosed with Valium by an inept psychiatrist who told her only what a "terrible mother she had," Dorothy became angry. She didn't have a 'terrible mother,' only an uneducated one who didn't understand *verbal* abuse. The psychiatrist insisted that Dorothy confront her mother to bring closure for herself. She refused. Nothing could change the past. Her mother already suffered deep guilt about her failure as a mother to Earl and learning she verbally abused her daughter would destroy her.

Dorothy joined a group in Gestalt Therapy where she learned her "stylized thinking" was the cause of her instant, blinding headaches. Eventually, she became a more self-assured woman with her humor still intact. Told she would "always battle her demons" she considered the therapy helpful, but it was not a complete cure—she was shrink resistant.

Earl didn't appear to have low self-esteem. He had the same life-of-the-party personality as his mother, sister and grandfather, but all his emotions lay buried behind a high wall he built the day his father died. Other than joy or sudden anger, he never expressed any kind of emotion toward his family.

Bert reared her children as best she knew how, and considering her history she made great progress, primarily of which was breaking the pattern of physical abuse in her family, possibly a long ingrained pattern on her father's side. Bert played with the children, was generous with treats and money when she had them, dressed them well, and was always there to help them with their problems. When she used her version of logic to train them, her verbal skill was lacking, but she was a great mother in every other way.

Bert's home became a gathering place for her children's friends. Each week, she welcomed Dorothy's grade-school club and furnished snacks. One of Dorothy's first grade friends would later write in Bert's ninetieth birthday memory book, "I always wished I had a mother like Dorothy's. She talked to us like adults. If we were about to go forth on some adventure, her mother included us when she advised Dorothy to be independent and think for herself when away from home."

As 1940 came to an end, Bert looked forward to the impressive new decade. Ladies nylon stockings took the market by storm, and the forty-hour workweek was about to become law. Welcoming the new developments, Bert hoped for a little more prosperity in her life.

CHAPTER 30

Bert still called square dances at the Elks Lodge every Saturday night. One brisk November evening, she showed off a new outfit. The full-circle red skirt depicted hand-painted dominoes and was paired with a white blouse. Circulating and talking to the crowd, she noticed a distinguished-looking man in a dark blue suit standing in the doorway. He never danced, only watched. After a while Bert went over.

"Hello, I'm Bert Courtnage, the floor manager. Do you like to dance?"

"How do you do? My name is Arthur Moore, and yes, I do like to dance."

"Would you like me to introduce you to some of the ladies?"

"No, not yet."

Bert excused herself and danced a number or two and when she looked, he still stood in the doorway. She walked back. "The next dance is number thirteen, Ladies' Choice. May I have this dance?"

He accepted.

Traditionally, number thirteen was always ladies'

choice, and Bert claimed it was her lucky number. Some men considered it to be an *unlucky* number because no gentlemen dared offend a lady by turning her down—fat, ugly, wearing too much perfume, having B.O. or being a terrible dancer, it didn't matter. Turning down an invitation to dance was considered poor manners. Women also were expected to dance with any man who asked, unless he was drunk. Bert and Art danced twice and she thought him a good dancer.

"Would you like to dance with anyone else?" she asked.

"Maybe later."

He danced a few more times with Bert, but never with anyone else.

The next Saturday, Art arrived at the hall before Bert. "May, I pick you up next week? There's no use taking two cars."

"I like having my own car so I can go home whenever I like."

"I'll be happy to take you home anytime you want." Nothing more was said—but he didn't wait for next weekend.

Three days later, Bert was working on one of the home ownership's never-ending repair jobs, a leaky pipe. She did whatever job she could herself, because hiring help was too expensive for her finances. That day, wearing an old checkered housedress saved for such occasions, she stood on a stepladder up to her elbows in a damp musty hole in the ceiling. She nearly fell off the ladder when June burst through the door. "Stop whatever you're doing—you don't have time for that."

"Yes, I do. It's important."

"Not right now—you've got a date."

"What on earth are you talking about?"

"I saw Art Moore at the dance last night, and he asked

me what religion you were. 'Why do you want to know?' I asked him. He said, 'I want to invite her to a formal Masonic Lodge dance, but it wouldn't look right if she were Catholic.'"

"What did you tell him?"

"I told him, 'I think she's Methodist. I'm not positive, but I know she's not Catholic.'"

Like the town crier with exciting news, June left as abruptly as she entered. Unconcerned, Bert returned to her smelly leak. Thirty minutes later the telephone rang; Art invited Bert to the dance the coming weekend. She accepted; her first date since Arlo's death. Since she neither owned nor had time to make a formal, she rushed to town to buy one leaving the hole in the ceiling. She bought an inexpensive, powder-blue gown with puffed sleeves. At thirty-six, it was her first evening gown and one of her few store-bought dresses.

Bert enjoyed the dance. She liked her lean nearly six-foot-tall date. Art had ash-gray eyes and wore rimless glasses. His facial expression was rather stern and he didn't smile much, a misleading appearance because he was a friendly and likeable man. A shock of wiry, salt and pepper hair was so thick he used a foldable currycomb to groom it; a deep wave created a natural high pompadour.

Feeling like Cinderella after the ball, Bert smoothed out her gown on the bed. A faint scent of *Evening in Paris* lingered, reminding her of the swirling waltzes and gliding foxtrots; it seemed strange not to square dance, but she enjoyed the formal affair. Still, she couldn't help thinking the dress was a waste of money. *I'll never have a chance to wear it again.*

Art apparently enjoyed their evening too, because he called again the next day for a second date that night. During dinner he said, "Would you mind if I called you

Bertie? Bert sounds so masculine." When she first adopted the nickname Bert two decades earlier, she believed she would never change it. Now, the new sobriquet charmed her. Thus, Albertine Roseline, Albertha, Bertha, Bert became Bertie. To her siblings she forever remained Bert.

During their date, Bertie learned Arthur was born near Valentine, Nebraska, in a sod house with a dirt floor kept hard by daily sweepings. His family later moved to Rimini, Montana. He learned algebra in sixth grade and excelled at math. He could add a double-digit column of figures—in his head. In 1907, he went to work for the First National Bank in Great Falls as a stenographer and transit clerk, working his way up the ladder to assistant cashier, his dream job. It was the only job he would ever have. He likely had been at his desk the day Mrs. Graham helped Bert open her first bank account, and she could have seen him on the bank's open floor plan. Perhaps she did.

Art asked Bertie out again the next night and after six consecutive dates in as many days, she thought surely he wouldn't call so soon again. After all, even the Lord rested on the seventh day. The call came early Thanksgiving morning as she prepared for work at the seed factory. The seasonal job lasted only a few weeks, so the crew worked seven days a week.

After the first "Hello" and "How are you" greeting, Art casually said, "Let's drive to Choteau and get married."

Bertie felt she must have misunderstood him. "What did you say?"

"I said, let's drive to Choteau and get married."

I didn't misunderstand! She was stunned. "I can't. I–I have to go to work."

"You won't need to work if you marry me."

205

"But I-I haven't eaten yet," she stammered.

"We can get something in Choteau."

She made another limp excuse or two, but the more she excused herself, the more he persisted. Finally, her confused mind could think of no other pretext and she blurted, "I like you, but I don't really love you."

"No, but you will, I can promise you that."

They talked about their brief acquaintance, raising her children and their nineteen-year age difference. Art said, "I would be honored to support your children. I won't interfere with raising them, and you can handle all the discipline."

A fusillade of thoughts crossed her mind: *We're both adults. We've both been married before. We know what to expect.* And, she thought of her fatherless children. She accepted.

Minutes later, Bertie told Dorothy that she and Art were getting married, asking her daughter how she felt about it. Dorothy, who had just turned twelve, liked Art and didn't object. Bertie thought five-year-old Earl too young to understand, so she didn't tell him. Later, she learned his feelings were hurt. He had promised his daddy, he would "take care of Mommy," and she hadn't asked him if it was all right to get married again.

Within two hours, Bertie was on her way to becoming Mrs. Arthur R. Moore. Because of the whirlwind courtship, she didn't have a wedding dress so she wore one of her dressier outfits. They didn't have witnesses, so the minister's wife and son filled the role. They exchanged marriage vows on November 26, 1941, ironically in the same town she'd wed Arlo. Because of the hasty wedding and rushed nuptials, there wasn't a wedding photograph.

Until Bertie signed the marriage license, she didn't realize that both hers and Art's initials were the same. She and Arlo had also had the same initials, and both times the initials spelled a word. She shivered. *Was it an omen?*

Art was a sociable man who belonged to many clubs. Everyone in town seemed to know and like, Art Moore— Bertie was having doubts. After she rebounded from the hasty wedding, Bertie's emotions plunged. She hated herself for being weak and allowing him to talk her into marriage. Certain she'd made a dreadful mistake, Bertie cried every night for two months—the man lying next to her in bed was a stranger. She kept her tears a secret, but Art had been right—she did fall in love with him.

Bertie kept her house but moved into Art's home at 1625 Central Avenue. Bertie liked the home with one exception—it had no room for a garden. The family began adjusting to a new life.

When they were children, Bertie read Dorothy and Earl numerous fairytales. If the story featured an evil stepparent, she always explained the tales were made up and that not all stepparents were mean. After the wedding, she had a long talk with them, and her children accepted Art immediately. They called him daddy without asking. Overjoyed, he offered to adopt them. Bertie asked if they would like that, explaining their last name would then be Moore. Earl and Dorothy both wanted to keep the Courtnage name and Art understood. He was an amazing man and exceedingly good to Bertie. Like Arlo, he let her do anything she wanted within reason. He was also kind to her children, denying them nothing, supporting them happily and most of all, loving them. He and his first wife were childless, and like Bertie, he found it impossible to express his love to the children verbally.

Art had only told Bertie that his first wife had been killed. Bertie didn't want to pry thinking questions might upset him. After a few months, several neighbors who knew Art and his first wife, told Bertie "they had never seen Art so relaxed and happy," something they didn't witness when he was married to his first wife, Ethel McCollim. Art and Ethel had married in 1913, but it wasn't a particularly happy union. Ethel wasn't an awful person—they just lived in different worlds. Art was a down-to-earth guy who liked to hunt and fish; Ethel was a socialite who belonged to numerous sewing and bridge clubs. Every table, chest and closet in the house overflowed with gorgeous fancy work.

Art had never cleaned out Ethel's closet. When Bertie asked if she could, he said, "Sure, do whatever you think best with the clothes." Other than a few housedresses, Bertie counted thirty-nine suits and dresses for entertaining and social events, many with matching hats and gloves. Ethel also owned a thousand dollar tri-colored Hudson Bay seal coat, a very luxurious item for the times. Bertie donated the clothes to the Salvation Army, but kept the coat, only because Art seemed so proud of it. However, she wasn't the fur-wearing type, and wore it only twice. She sold it forty years later for twenty-five dollars to a lady who made fur teddy bears.

Ethel had died tragically two years before Art and Bertie met. Her nephew, Bob, lived with Ethel and Art. Bob and Ethel erupted into an awful argument one day. She'd promised him the car and after he invited friends for an outing, she reneged. He became incensed and got his gun. They scuffled and the gun fired, killing her. At the trial, Bob said he only meant to scare her—it was an accident. Only God and Bob knew what was truly in his heart that terrible day, but the jury didn't believe him. They found him guilty.

Art wanted to teach Bertie to hunt and fish so she could accompany him. He said she needed a pair of slacks for their activities. She disliked pants of any kind, but because he suggested it, Bertie made a pair of flaming-red ones and wore them a few times. Still, she hated wearing trousers and finally threw them into the rag box. No one ever saw her in slacks again.

Bertie tried, but she couldn't work up any enthusiasm for the sports Art enjoyed; however, she loved going along. She'd lived so many years on flat, treeless plains that she found Montana's beautiful scenery intoxicating. It inspired her to set a new goal: travel in all forty-eight states. While Art fished, she and the kids hiked to waterfalls and enjoyed the scenery. She always accompanied him, drawing the line only at ice fishing.

Art didn't care for movies. However, he went if a classical singer or musician was in a film, and he took the family to see "Chopin." During the movie, Dorothy whispered, "I must find out the name of that beautiful music." Art knew it was Chopin's *Polonaise* and Dorothy, who now received an allowance, bought the record. At a later movie, she fell in love with an aria from *La Traviata.* Again, Art recognized the melody and Dorothy bought the record. He had been puzzled as to why she often came in from playing to tune the radio to The Lone Ranger. Then when the story began, she left. One day he asked her why. She wasn't interested in the story; it was the music she liked. He was pleased and encouraged her interest in classical music.

Bertie preferred the old-time tunes and the classics of pop music like Lawrence Welk. Art and Dorothy were the only ones in the family who had a penchant for classical music, and Dorothy became a collector extraordinaire. She bought everything from cowboy yodeling to grand opera *yodeling.* Her collecting days ceased only with the arrival of heavy metal and rap. To her ear that wasn't music, it was noise.

Bertie had yearned for a piano ever since leaving

home, but she and Arlo couldn't afford one. She saw an old roller piano for sale in the classified section one day and bought the 1908 Armstrong upright for twenty-five dollars. It included nearly 100 rolls. Family and friends often gathered around the piano singing the words printed on the paper rolls.

Bertie hoped Dorothy would take piano lessons, but she wasn't interested. Later, she took violin lessons, likely due to the influence of Grandpa Max. She participated in the Great Falls High School orchestra for four years—then never played it again.

Art owned a beautiful Gibson mandolin and played it almost daily. He and Dorothy often played together using sheet music. Bertie couldn't join them, she couldn't read notes, but she often chorded on the instrument by herself.

The problem with Earl's discipline was ongoing. Nothing worked. He had developed an annoying habit of coming home minutes before dinner and Bertie would caution him not to leave, dinner was ready. Five minutes later he was nowhere to be found. Sometimes he ambled in halfway through the meal or after everyone finished eating.

Bertie wracked her brain to find a new punishment. Earl loathed washing dishes, and she told him, "The next time you're late, you have to wash and dry the dishes." Since tardiness was almost a daily event, she felt sure he would be late the next day in spite of the new rule. She used every dish in the kitchen whether she needed it or not. Dirty dishes, some only swished with meat drippings, filled the sink. As dependable as snow in January, dinnertime arrived and ended without Earl. The chore took him more than an hour. The plan worked—he wasn't late again. Only afterward did Bertie confess to the relief she felt when Earl *was* tardy. Otherwise, the monstrous intentional mess would have been hers to clean.

CHAPTER 31

Art only rented his home and Bertie missed her garden, so the next year, the family moved back to her apartment house, turning it into a private home—almost. They didn't need the upstairs apartment, so Mamie and Arthur continued living there, still receiving a discount on their rent. And there was still the problem of only one bathroom. *The Courtnage Hotel* reopened with Art's blessing. Not many men want to share their home with another couple, related or not. But Art would do anything to make Bertie happy. In the twelve years Dorothy would live at home, she never once saw Art angry.

The basement boarder's room became Art's sports haven. A gun rack filled one wall and he used the long workbench in the cellar for ammunition reloading.

Earl and Dorothy each had their own upstairs bedrooms—when they didn't need to surrender it to "hotel guests." Earl's small room was next to the bathroom; Dorothy occupied the largest bedroom, and she adored the bonus step-down glassed-in porch. Her delight didn't diminish even when Bertie said she would have to clean the room herself. She didn't realize until later it wasn't fair; Earl didn't have to clean his room.

Art came home from work one day and told Bertie the bank offered him the presidency, again. "Should I take it—it pays more?"

"That's up to you; it doesn't make any difference to me."

Art smiled. "If you don't care, I prefer keeping the cashier's job. It's the one I set my sights on the first day I went to work there. I wouldn't be comfortable out front wearing a suit and meeting people. Working in the back with the girls, I can roll up my shirtsleeves."

After numerous attempts over the years to promote him to an officer's position, the bank solved what it considered a problem—they reclassified Art's job. He became an officer whether he liked it or not. Now it suited him fine; he still worked in back with his sleeves rolled up.

Art used his math skills at home too. He always helped Dorothy with the arithmetic she hated, and he tried to help with the detestable shorthand, but he had learned Pittman style, more complex than the Gregg she studied. He couldn't help her. Art studied shorthand forty years earlier and remembered it still. Dorothy forgot her chicken-scratching hieroglyphics the next year. And there were other things she wished she could forget.

Bertie stunned Dorothy one day saying, "I never would have married Art if it weren't for my children. I believe you're old enough now to understand."

Dorothy understood, felt deep guilt and was unable to forget it. Although Bertie saw it more as an explanation, it was a heavy burden of guilt to put on an immature child of fourteen. Bertie did learn to love Art, but her initial acceptance was for the sake of her children.

December 7, 1941, was a beautiful sunny day, so warm that a coatless Dorothy played hopscotch on the front sidewalk. Her amusement was interrupted: "Extra! Extra! Pearl Harbor Bombed." Newsboys all over town hawked the extra edition with gigantic black headlines. Dorothy wondered where Pearl Harbor could be and rushed inside to tell her mother the exciting news—the "extra edition." She'd never seen one before. Like the rest of the country, the family listened to the radio and heard President Roosevelt describe the "dastardly attack" and declare a State of War against Japan and Germany.

Rationing soon became a way of life. Buying coffee, butter, sugar, meat, fish, cheese, gas, shoes, and more required either coupons or tokens. The family drank tea instead of coffee and used saccharin so Bertie could hoard her precious sugar ration for Christmas goodies.

Recently invented margarine looked like Crisco. The substitute butter included a packet of yellow coloring to be mixed into the product. Everyone took turns stirring the tint into the niveous mass that didn't actually taste bad.

Bertie and every housewife in America kept a can near the stove to save meat fat for Uncle Sam's needed explosives. Depositories were scattered about town for the donations. School children pulled their wagons door-to-door collecting scrap metal. Bertie's family walked everywhere and saved their valuable gas coupons for fishing trips and family visits. Shoe rationing, however, was a problem because Dorothy wore out a pair in three months. Fortunately, other family members were easier on shoes and she used their coupons. Not everyone had the heaviest requirement for the same items and a system for bartering ration tokens and stamps developed among friends—every city had a swap club.

The wondrous new nylon stockings were one of the

first things to become nonexistent—parachutes required nylon. But ladies met a niche of need with a new solution. They covered their bare limbs with leg makeup that looked like stockings from a distance. To complete the realistic look, women helped one another draw seams down the back of the leg with an eyebrow pencil. The big bonus: no more runs—now their stockings only rubbed off on the sheets.

Like millions of Americans, Art and Bertie bought a Government Savings Bond each month, and later when Dorothy went to work, Bertie devised one of her *practical plans*. If Dorothy bought a bond a month for thirty years, she could then cash one every month for thirty years and have a small pension that would last her a lifetime because life expectancy was then sixty-eight. Dorothy duly bought a bond every month for thirty years. However, she didn't receive the pension because later she cashed them, using the money for better investments. Without Bertie's pension plan, it's doubtful she would have had money to invest.

Bertie called square dances at the Great Falls Air Force Base NCO and the Officers' Clubs to entertain the soldiers, and she often invited one or two airmen for Sunday dinner. She admired them, but she couldn't help feeling relieved her son was too young for the draft.

Max Jr., who now worked at an aircraft factory in California, became engaged to Jean. Bertie offered her home for the ceremony. She prepared dinner, a cake, and took the wedding photographs. After the war, the couple would return to join Max Sr. and Floyd on the farm.

When Max Jr. and Jean returned, the catchall farm attic still held the bits and pieces from Della and Max's earlier years, a treasure trove of antiques, collectibles and pure junk. "Come take whatever you want," Jean told everyone. "I'm going to burn whatever is left." Bertie took her framed baby picture and others took ornate framed pictures, little else. Antiques were not yet in vogue and no one believed Jean would actually burn everything, but she did. Flames and smoke curled a lifetime of memories skyward.

When Dorothy graduated from eighth grade, Bertie was happy her daughter could attend high school, but she didn't encourage her to set goals, which was strange since she was a consummate goal setter. Instead, she said, "I'm not telling you that you must get all "A's" in school—a "C" is fine, just so you pass."

That comment didn't inspire Dorothy, and like many teens in school, she was lazy. She might have applied herself if she'd more motivation—or maybe not. She would never know.

Dorothy never had a date in high school due to her severely protruding teeth. All the popular girls—those deemed cute or girls with questionable morals—belonged to elite cliques. Dorothy dressed *de rigueur:* full circular skirt, form-fitting sweater with shoulder pads and white anklets worn with black and white saddle shoes or penny loafers. Nothing helped. If you didn't belong to the inner circle, you were a *nobody.* Dorothy did belong to a clique—a clique of other *nobodies.*

Dorothy knew her mother's financial situation had improved, and she wanted to have her teeth straightened. She'd suffered horrendous teasing in school and was willing to undergo barbed-wire fence jokes to correct the abnormality. When she asked her mother to get braces, Bertie said, "I am so grateful to Art for unquestioningly supporting my children that I can't bring myself to ask him to spend so much money." Art could afford it and Dorothy felt he would be glad to do so. Bertie's guilt was too strong to ask, and Dorothy's low self-esteem didn't allow her to broach the subject either.

Typical of Bertie, she offered a *logical* solution. "Maybe it would help if you pushed on your teeth." Using the edge of a table, Dorothy pushed and pushed, every day—without success. As a last resort, she stood in front of a mirror day after day practicing her smile and laugh while jutting her lower jaw forward, and amazingly the protruding teeth were not quite so noticeable.

With Art's blessing, Bertie invited her sister Charlotte to come live in their home while George served overseas. Charlotte turned down the offer, so Bertie asked Lois Courtnage, her niece, to move in. Lois worked at Great Falls Air Base and accepted the invitation. Then Charlotte changed her mind. Bertie didn't want to tell her sister she couldn't come, so Dorothy suddenly found herself with not one, but two roommates.

Charlotte and Lois each paid Bertie twenty dollars for room and board—an extremely reasonable rate—and Bertie then cooked for six people. Dorothy's room was crowded beyond belief with a double and single bed, a dresser, library table, and a couple of chairs. Charlotte wasn't easy to get along with and she and Lois took an instant dislike to each other. They couldn't agree when to clean the room. Each cleaned her few square feet on different days—then, the dust migrated. Later, Bertie removed the table, and added another single bed because Charlotte said she couldn't sleep in the double one with Dorothy. How they managed with one closet is a mystery. Lois moved out first, easing the situation, but Bertie sighed in relief when Charlotte left too. Bertie had heard complaints from all of them for three years. However, this annoying experience never stopped her from helping others in distress.

When Arlo's younger brother Chris married, his bride

Kay ordered the cake from the bakery. The day before the wedding, she realized the cake wasn't big enough for all the guests. She panicked. "Oh, don't worry," Chris said, "Bertie will make a cake for us." At the last minute, she produced two sheet cakes—she never failed her family.

Art came home from work one afternoon and told Bertie he had a chance to buy some land at an unbelievably low price. "I can't make up my mind whether to buy it or not. It's a terrific deal."

"Where is it?"

"The sand hills on Tenth Avenue South. It's being offered for a dollar an acre." They discussed it, but neither could think of any reason anyone would want to buy block after block of sand. They turned the offer down. Today the street is lined with stores and one of the most heavily traveled streets in the state. Art and Bertie were clever and smart people in their fields—real estate wasn't one of them.

Art always wanted Bertie to accompany him on any trip, but one day he came home and said he needed to go to Wisconsin for a couple of days to straighten out some bank's mess. Bertie was delighted. "Wonderful, I'd love to see Wisconsin."

"Oh, there isn't any use in your going this time; I'll be busy the whole time and you'd be stuck in the hotel room."

"That's okay; I'll enjoy the scenery on the way."

"There isn't any point of your going; I'll be gone only a few days."

Bertie's feelings were hurt—she wanted to go. She didn't say anything more, but she felt perplexed why he didn't want her along. She didn't know it then, but those mysterious trips would happen again and again.

CHAPTER 32

When Art failed to interest Bertie in his favorite sports, he focused on Dorothy. She didn't have any patience for fishing, tangling more flies in the bushes than she put in the water. And she was not about to kill a critter of any kind. Art still fished and hunted alone. Later, he finally had a companion in Earl who loved both sports. Art taught him everything he knew, and Earl became quite an expert at skeet and won many prizes.

Because Art didn't have children of his own and was fifty-six when he married Bertie, he didn't know *how* to be a father. Once when Earl was learning to fish, Art grew snappish when Earl asked, "Why do we have to throw parts of the fish away?" Art was embarrassed; he didn't know how to answer Earl's innocent question. It was the one and only time anyone found fault with his treatment of his ready-made family. Earl hunted and fished for many years with Art. In later life, like Dorothy, he too came to hate killing animals and he quit both sports.

Art finally found one sport Bertie liked: archery. The family joined the Great Falls Archery Club. Art put up

218

hay bales in the backyard for practice. He became quite proficient and always broke 500 in competitions. Bertie did well too, but Dorothy mostly scraped her arm raw from the bowstring—while wearing an arm guard. Earl was too young to join in, but he soon enjoyed his own special event.

Because Earl missed the daylong outing when Bertie took Dorothy and the Courtnage cousins to Giant Springs, she wanted to give him a similar day. She made a picnic lunch and invited his friends to his birthday party at the springs. The kids thought it a marvelous place for a party, but Earl's day wasn't quite the equal of Dorothy's outing—they didn't walk six miles.

Like most young boys, Earl was on the puny side. He wanted to build some muscle and he asked Bertie to buy him a punching bag. They were expensive and Bertie knew his passing fancy would fade, so she created a bag with pillows stuffed in a canvas sack and hung it in the summerhouse. Earl spent many hours punching away at his homemade bag. It must have worked because he did develop muscle—ten years later.

When Dorothy had asked her mother if she could go on a double date at thirteen, Bertie said, "I don't want you to go. But you can do as you want." Dorothy didn't go. Later, because of her protruding teeth no one asked her out and she had her first date at seventeen, if it could be called a date. Two cousins were in town with dates and brought a friend along. They asked Dorothy to go out with him. Bertie happily passed on her special date-dressing technique. She showed her daughter how to wrap a few coins in a hanky for mad money. "Now you can tuck it in your bra." Dorothy did, and they both heard clunk. Her badly curved spine made her pigeon breasted—the packet dropped straight through to the floor. Bertie laughed. "I guess you better carry a purse."

The so-called date was a flop; but soon, serious dating began.

Dorothy won a pair of tickets for Frank's Roller Rink in 1945 and took a friend with her. They enjoyed themselves and thereafter Dorothy went two or three times a week. She learned skate dancing and appeared in a skating show. Bertie made several costumes for her daughter that drew raves from friends.

Because of her horrible teeth, it wasn't surprising Dorothy never had a date in school, but at seventeen she'd practiced her *specialized* smile to perfection. She began dating airmen from the local base that she met at the rink. Bertie still seemed unconcerned about her daughter's total lack of sex education. Then Dorothy began dating a divorced, twenty-three-year-old man who managed the roller rink—and lived in the apartment upstairs.

Bertie thought it was time for the "birds and bees talk." She would have answered any questions her daughter asked, but unlike most children, Dorothy never asked. She heard nothing from her *nobody* peers, and she was enormously ignorant for seventeen. Bertie's one sentence sex education had been worthless. Dorothy's was twice as good—she received *two* blunt sentences. Bertie described the act, why it was necessary and then handed Dorothy a book. "You can find anything you want to know in this book." Bertie believed she wasn't educated enough to tell her daughter the facts of life. The answers *were* in the book—Dorothy never read the book.

In her sophomore year, Art asked Dorothy if she wanted to become the bank's messenger during the summer. She jumped at the chance to earn some money and still have time to skate with her boyfriend after work. Her job involved making daily runs to the courthouse and local banks to exchange checks. Bertie was concerned because the job had Dorothy going into bars to return bum checks. Art assured Bertie that her daughter wouldn't go anyplace unsafe. If checks were bounced from the Red Feather or other bars with a bad reputation, one of the men took them. After his reassurance, Bertie agreed to let Dorothy accept the job. Dorothy was seen about town carrying a purse-like leather pouch leaving the Mint Saloon and other local bars in the middle of the day. She received some strange looks from people on the street, and Bertie waited for someone to tell her Dorothy was drinking. Surprisingly no one did. Soon, new employment opened for both Dorothy and Bertie.

When Art and Bertie married, he was the pari-mutuels cashier at the Northern Montana State Fair. He would hold the job for more than forty years. In 1944, he needed to hire another worker, and he asked Bertie to be his assistant.

Bertie was surprised. "Golly, I don't have any experience handling money."

"Trustworthy people are far more important than experience."

"If you think I can handle it, I'll be glad to help." She helped Art with paperwork, and counted and wrapped coins. The other workers despised wrapping dimes because they were small and difficult to handle. Nimble-fingered Bertie wrapped the dimes easily so coin counter's hands from every direction slid dimes over to her after each race. Both Dorothy and Earl would work as "runners" fetching change for the ticket agents. Who says nepotism is bad?

Besides being a fishing fanatic, Art became so proficient at archery he decided to try combining the two sports. He drove out near the west side bridge on River Road and was successful after only a few tries. He enjoyed his new hobby and went back to the river often.

One day in 1945, a *Great Falls Tribune* reporter drove by and seeing a man standing with a bow and arrow pointed at the water aroused his curiosity. He stopped. He and Art chatted resulting in an article with several pictures in the paper. It was a unique way to fish. The next day, the newspaper reported bigger news.

Art took the family out for an early dinner and leaving the restaurant they were stunned to see the streets swarming with people running around helter-skelter, screaming and waving. Car horns blared and people plastered complete strangers with hugs and kisses. It was May 8, Victory in Europe (V-E) Day. Dorothy wanted to join in the universal party, but Bertie and Art were so relieved at the awesome news they only wanted to go home and drink it all in.

Charlotte, George, and Bertie's family usually drove to Highwood to visit George's brother in the summer; there was a lovely swimming hole nearby. Ten people gathered for a picnic one Sunday, and everyone brought their bathing suits.

A hot day by Montana standards, Bertie appreciated the fluffy round-topped cumulus clouds that provided shade. The men rocked in the watermelon in the creek as the women set the table, and then everyone headed to the creek.

Bertie had a bathing suit, but couldn't swim and always felt frightened in or on the water. As everyone splashed in, Bertie said, "I can't swim, so watch out for me. I'll hold my arm up if I get in trouble." Everyone hooted at her joke. By mistake, Bertie found herself in a deeper part of the creek and was floundering. She called for help and sank. Surfacing she called again. Everyone laughed—Bertie was such a kidder. She now coughed and sputtered at full throttle, but she wasn't screaming—she was perfectly calm as she went down the third time waving her hand above the water with one finger stuck straight in the air. That finger wave was a lifesaver.

Bertie's brother Floyd met Lorraine at Bertie's square dance club and when they became engaged, Bertie once again offered her home for the ceremony, prepared a lovely meal, and baked the wedding cake. She loved being able to do this for them. Lorraine played the piano and soon joined Art and Dorothy for jam sessions.

Bertie adored Lorraine and the feeling was mutual. They were like sisters, calling each other almost daily. When children came along, Bertie thought of the little ones as her grandkids, often giving them little gifts. Once she took their son Cliff to Yellowstone National Park for a "just for the two of us" trip. She geared all the activities around him. Bertie was his favorite aunt, but then she was the favorite aunt of most of Dorothy's cousins. Later as a widow, Bertie would spend every Christmas holiday with Floyd's family playing Santa in her Ho-Ho-Ho red suit.

While cleaning out some of Bertie's memorabilia boxes in later years, Dorothy found a 1983 letter that Lorraine wrote Bertie for the express purpose of telling "Dearest Bertie" why she loved her so much. In part it read: "There were so many countless times you kept me from going to pieces, and you always offered me a shoulder to cry on. Without you I don't think I could have survived—you have made my life worth living rather than only existing. You have understood me and shown me love when I felt quite unlovable."

When Dorothy finished reading the emotional letter, she smiled. If she hadn't understood as a child, the letter was further proof how her mother expressed her love with deeds and understanding, not words.

CHAPTER 33

On a sweltering August day in 1946, Bertie, Art, and Dorothy were working under the grandstand at the fair pari-mutuels. Earl and Mamie, sitting in the last two seats of the grandstand next to a horse barn, were watching the races and rodeo. As the first race ended, three Army Air Force A-26 Invader Bombers demonstrated precision flying in front of a grandstand crowd of 20,000. The planes whooshed into view at almost 400 miles per hour as thousands of awestruck spectators craned their necks skyward to stare at the mesmerizing maneuvers. During the first minute of the show, the planes zoomed directly toward the grandstand in a low dip, trailing red, white, and blue smoke. Suddenly, the unimaginable happened. The second plane clipped the tail of the lead aircraft destroying its wing and then veering north crashing a few miles away near Bootlegger Trail. The lead plane, with its tail sheared off and lying in the racetrack twenty feet from the grandstand, wiped out a fence and hurtled more than 900 feet plunging into the nearest horse barn. The barn exploded into a towering inferno shooting flames skyward.

Earl and Mamie felt the heat blast on their faces and raced to safety. Others scattered, but hundreds more stood rooted to the grandstand in shock. Some cried and others stared blankly as stomach-churning screams from the trapped horses horrified the spectators. A lone frightened horse, rescued from the burning barn, whinnied pitifully and trembled in fear. Grim-faced jockeys sat dejected on a fence rail watching volunteers, army personnel, and firemen who eventually quenched the fire. Inside the barn, only blackened timbers lay among the charred bodies of once sleek racehorses. Four army personnel were killed, two people in the horse barn and nineteen magnificent racehorses perished.

Despite the gruesome disaster, fate was kind. If the lead plane had veered left instead of right, it would have killed thousands of people in the grandstand including Bertie's entire family, two sisters and their husbands, as well as Mamie. Two minutes later, eight more horses, jockeys, owners, and trainers who were returning from the first race would have been in the barn. The horror lingered on Bertie's mind for days, so she was happy when another job got her mind off the tragedy.

The Scottish Rite Lodge held monthly dinners for its members, hiring a cook and crew for these occasions. Bertie had volunteered for kitchen duty and table setting shortly after her marriage. She refused payment saying, "I want to help the lodge, and I enjoy it." The work was a school of opportunity where she learned to make the world's best gravy. All day the chef kept a pot of water simmering on the stove. After washing the produce, the crew put seeds, peels and onion skins into the simmering pot. Meat scraps, chicken skin and bones were added. Like witch's brew, the cauldron bubbled, filling the air with mouthwatering aromas. Minutes before serving the dinner, the chef strained the water and made his mouthwatering gravy. Then Bertie became the gravy chef for most family potluck gatherings.

When Bertie retired from kitchen duty thirty-four years later, the lodge presented her with a beautiful silver and gemstone bracelet. Bertie was the only one of the staff to receive an appreciation gift, but she was also the only volunteer.

Becoming a professional square dance caller had been a long, constant struggle for Bertie. The male dominated profession would not step aside and allow a young, insignificant female to join their ranks. None of the men said anything to her face, but comments about her talent were made behind her back and found their way to her ears. The male callers never recommended her as a last minute substitute nor offered her encouragement or assistance, but she had struggled on.

Great Falls hired a new City Director of Parks and Recreation who wanted to learn to call square dances. Bertie gave him free private lessons. He was in a position to help her career, but never did. The worst insult came when he later published a book with square dance calls most of which came straight from her, yet he never mentioned her name nor credited her with the calls she'd composed. Feeling the discrimination, her feelings were hurt again and again.

About the time Bertie had begun drawing attention as a caller in the late 1930s, square dancing lost popularity. In the mid-forties a revival boomed. Once again, a female caller with a deep robust voice competed in the exclusive male occupation, whether they liked it or not.

Bertie had called only occasionally the last few years, but with the revival, came a constant demand for her robust voice. She now called twenty-eight days a month for more than two-and-a-half-years. The pace was exhausting—she loved every fatiguing minute.

During the 1940s and 1950s, Bertie taught and called square dancing in Fort Benton, Belt, Cascade, Geraldine, and other small towns around Great Falls. She called for the Sons of Norway, Great Falls Shrine Club, Eagles and Elks Lodges, the Senior Citizens Center, the NCO and Officers' Clubs at Malmstrom AFB, private affairs, and at her own dance clubs.

Now there wasn't enough of Bertie to go around. More people danced than ever before and a shortage of square dance callers emerged. She approached the city director and suggested they begin a caller's clinic to teach the craft. He agreed and they produced many future callers.

Great Falls didn't have a square dance club. Bertie decided they needed one, and she organized the "Four Square Club." The colorful swinging skirts first swirled to *Bird in the Cage* in January 1946. Unable to afford live music, the sixty members danced to records. The group first met in the Old Veterans Hall and then moved to the Latter Day Saints Hall. Bertie and the city director collaborated later to form the Promenade Club.

Art was proud of Bertie and she appreciated his help toting the heavy PA system and cases of records for her gigs. She taught him to call, and sometimes he took over at her dance clubs to give her a chance to square dance.

At one particular occasion, a couple from a Wyoming dance club visited and couldn't believe the caller would be a woman. They were overheard saying she can't be any good. Apparently, they changed their minds. During a break they asked her if she would come to Wyoming to call at their club. Calling square dances plus free travel was a dream offer she happily accepted.

When not calling, Bertie danced, and she could *do-si-do* with the best of them. She designed and made all her full-circle, square dance dresses. One creation, a white dress with fifty yards of silver rickrack, caused a sensation wherever she wore it. A tiny handbag matched the dress and the outfit was worthy of museum exhibition. Lawrence Welk's orchestra made a personal appearance in Great Falls and drew an enormous crowd. Bertie attended wearing her stunning white dress. The costume may have been what inspired Welk to single her out for a dance. Bertie retired, but the dress didn't. Her sister Ella's granddaughter now wears it performing in her combo in California while playing her great grandfather Max's fiddle. The dress continues to draw raves.

Bertie's name appeared in the National Directory of Square and Folk Dance Callers until she retired. The square dance craze lasted about forty-years before again losing some of its popularity, but square dance clubs still exist.

One night, Bertie told the ladies in her Four Square Club she wanted to make a friendship skirt. The women looked puzzled. Bertie smiled. "If anyone can donate a swatch of cotton fabric, I want to make a crazy-patch skirt." At the next dance the ladies flooded her with samples. She made her skirt, and wore it to the club asking the women if they could find their 'donation.' Everyone swarmed about her, turning her around, laughing, and pointing. Bertie always used some gimmick to keep the dancers' interest in more ways than kicking up their heels. Fifty-years later, Dorothy found Bertie with *that* skirt spread out on her bed, tearfully reminiscing about the wonderful people who had contributed. She no longer wore it, but she kept the skirt the rest of her life, along with her wedding dress, and the red outfit she wore the day she met Arlo.

Bertie loved the crazy-patch design and made throw rugs, a housecoat, and a bed coverlet. Later, when

Dorothy moved into her first home, her mother made her three throw rugs. When a saleslady came to measure for a new living room rug, she asked Dorothy where she'd bought the beautiful throw rugs. Bertie loved anything odd and made innovative dresses for herself. In the thirties, no one wore their hair swept back on one side, but Bertie did. If she wore a neck chain, she might loop it around a pin on her shoulder to change the look. Her character had a spark of flamboyance that never flickered out with age.

Neither did her love of taking pictures. Bertie was an avid photographer. At family gatherings she insisted everyone get together for a group picture, difficult because people were involved in separate conversations. Once a relative became irritated and said, "Surely you have enough pictures by now." The subtle hint fell on deaf ears.

By 1947, Max's children were all married. That Easter, the entire family assembled at Bertie's sister's home in Big Sandy. Ella's small house couldn't hold everyone so tables and chairs were in the garage. No one cared; it was an insignificant price to pay for a gathering of the clan. No one knew this was the last time the entire family would ever be together.

Prior to graduating from high school, Dorothy told her mother, "I think I'll apply for work at Malmstrom AFB. They pay better."

Bertie frowned. "That's six miles from here. Surely, you don't want to drive that far twice a day." She *reasoned* Dorothy out of the idea, but her daughter later regretted it. Had she followed through with her idea, she could have retired at age forty-nine. Ironically, she ended up working for Civil Service anyway. By then she drove thirteen miles to work twice a day and couldn't retire until fifty-eight. Practical advice wasn't always perfect.

Art and Bertie gave Dorothy a garnet ring for graduation, but Bertie wanted to do more. Senior trips didn't yet exist, so she offered to treat Dorothy and six of her closest friends to dinner at the Stockmen Supper Club that Art had recently joined. It had a restaurant, bar and dance floor. Bertie had called to the music of the Kornpoppers, and KFBB radio broadcast the grand opening. The club seemed the perfect treat for this special occasion.

Bertie crisscrossed town picking up the girls and transporting them to the west side club. After dinner, Dorothy called Bertie and she chauffeured all the girls back home. Fifty-eight years later at a girlfriend reunion, one of them reminded Dorothy of that special evening. "I couldn't believe your mother went to all that effort for us." Dorothy saw nothing unusual about it.

College wasn't considered essential in those days and Bertie didn't urge her children to go. She told them, "If you want to go, I still have the 2,000 Arlo left each of you for your education," and then she left it for them to decide. Like her father and his father before him, she didn't stress the importance of a good education. Instead, she strove to teach her children to be logical, responsible, and practical above all else, the same values her mother taught her. Over the years her attitude changed, and later Bertie said, "Not getting more schooling was the biggest mistake of my life." Definitely her mother's daughter, Dorothy didn't have a specific career in mind; therefore, it didn't seem *practical* to go to college and spend all that money.

On graduation night, an immature child wearing a long blue robe and tasseled, flat square cap, was— according to tradition—magically transformed into an adult. But Dorothy didn't feel grown up. The last day of school she arrived home at noon. Art said, "You better hurry and eat because you start work at one o'clock." She'd worked at the bank part-time since her sophomore year, but this was the first she heard of a full-time job. She ate fast. She went to work as a transit clerk, earning sixty dollars a month.

As her mother had with her first paycheck, Dorothy felt rich envisioning how to spend all her newfound wealth. The Paris window displayed a cute black cocktail dress, and the red high heels were adorable, and... Her feeling of wealth didn't last long. "Now that you're working," Bertie said, "you can pay board." Art was against the idea, but Bertie wanted Dorothy to learn responsibility. "You don't have to pay for your room because it would be empty anyway, but you can pay one-fourth of the food bill." It was a good lesson—and cheap board.

And Bertie's logic wasn't through. She had learned well from Mrs. Graham's lessons, and she sat her daughter down for a financial discussion far more detailed than the earlier birds and bees talk. This was Bertie's forte. "You need a budget. With a good financial plan you'll have money available when vacation and tax time come around." Together they compiled a list of estimated yearly expenses, and then divided that sum by twelve. Dorothy deposited that amount in a savings account every month. It required limited bookkeeping, but all or most of the money was available when needed. The original four or five individual needs multiplied during her life, and Dorothy used the system until her eighties. The budget worked—at least for her. Later, Dorothy learned her mother taught the same budget to her sister's granddaughter, who also still uses it today as well. Dorothy considers her stylized budget one of the most important lessons her mother taught her. She learned having spending money did bring happiness and she soon spent some of it.

In 1948, movie star Nelson Eddy was to perform at the Liberty Theater. The city rarely had big-name entertainers and Dorothy bubbled with excitement. The timbre of Eddy's voice had made him her favorite singer. Bertie's interest wasn't as keen—Jeanette MacDonald wasn't with him. Dorothy wasn't about to miss the event but she didn't want to go alone. "I'll treat you, Mom." She stood in line early and bought tickets in the fourth row. During the performance Bertie whispered, "He's singing to you. He always looks right at you." Sure enough, he did, but Bertie didn't realize performers on the stage are blinded by footlights so they pick certain spots in the audience to keep them looking in different directions. Dorothy was a spot. And later 'the spot' got Eddy's autograph.

CHAPTER 34

Dorothy felt uneasy working at the bank, assuming everyone would think any future promotion would come because her stepfather was an officer. She worked there only eighteen months before quitting with Art's blessing. He understood. She needn't have worried about a promotion—tire-tread wrinkles and gray hair would have found her before any of the female tellers died, leaving an opening. Tellers were the end of the promotion line for females.

Dorothy found another job at Strain Brothers' Department Store, as a stock procurer, but the store was sold three months later and she lost her job. She found another, but didn't punch a time clock—nor receive a wage.

Bertie's house needed painting, and she and Art were stunned at the thousand dollar price tag. A two-story house with full attic was a big job, but they felt the fee too high. They were debating what to do when Dorothy heard the discussion. "I'll paint the house," she said.

Bertie and Art were delighted. "We'll help as much as we can. You needn't hurry and we'll support you while you work." So Dorothy painted a few days and then took a day off to go to the Mitchell swimming pool or some other fun activity. Bertie paid for all the movies and skating Dorothy wanted, giving her a little pocket money as well. Art built a small scaffold the family could move, but much of the work required a long ladder. Art often painted after work and Bertie pitched in whenever possible. Dorothy's current boyfriend painted an hour or two in the afternoons, but Dorothy did most of the work. The venture was successful and saved Art and Bertie money—and it started a trend.

Bertie and Art appreciated Dorothy's boyfriend's help. Bertie invited him to dinner every night, and she and Art gave him a rifle for Christmas. Soon he became a problem. At first Bertie liked him. He was charismatic, courteous and always cooperative. After the house was painted, he still came over early every day and Bertie invited him to dinner. After many conversations, she realized he couldn't possibly have done all the things he claimed he had. Bertie knew he must be lying about several things, among them how he had been able to drive to their house every night in a military truck while in the Air Force. As a civilian, he lived on unemployment benefits, and she doubted his reason—a metal plate in his head causing headaches—for not being able to work.

Bertie suffered the anguish of all parents because she knew the more she told Dorothy he wasn't any good, the more she would lean toward marrying him. Desperate, Bertie felt she must do something. She created The Bertie Detective Agency. She questioned local people, wrote inquiries and placed several expensive long-distance phone calls.

Dorothy had dated the young man about a year, and she knew her mother didn't approve of him—Bertie spouted some mighty strong hints. Dorothy finally told her mother, "I won't marry him until either you change your mind or I change mine." Bertie pursued the truth relentlessly. When at last she produced her written evidence, Dorothy changed her mind.

Bertie was right. The young man was a first-rate liar and couldn't, or wouldn't, work. Bertie knew he would ruin Dorothy's life and she felt tremendous relief when he left town after their breakup. Later, the Air Force called Bertie; they wanted to prosecute him for misuse of military equipment. He'd already left town, and Bertie never learned the outcome. Dorothy also learned a bitter lesson. Her boyfriend left owing her seventy-five dollars, a handsome sum for that period. He had borrowed the money over time and never repaid the loan before "desperately needing" to borrow again. Immature and in love, Dorothy was an easy mark for a charming con artist.

After the house gleamed in new paint, Dorothy needed a paying job. Her cousin Lois worked for Civil Service in Brazil. Dorothy loved Latin music, food and dance and told her mother she wanted to get a job in South America. Bertie's shocked reply: "Oh, no you don't—you'd come home with one of them." She knew Dorothy's proclivity for dark-haired men with piercing black eyes. Dorothy was an adult, but until she left home and matured, Bertie's influence always won out. Dorothy didn't consider the matter further, but she regretted never getting to tango with those dark-eyed men.

In the summer of 1949, Max Jr. and Jean decided to sell their harvesting service to ranchers in Kansas and perhaps other states. Max Jr. didn't know their destination or how long they'd be gone. The project was an exciting experiment, but unluckily timed. Max Sr. died suddenly of a heart attack in July—still not knowing if he was 73 or 74. To add to the problem, Floyd and Lorraine were traveling in Yellowstone National Park.

Bertie told the family they simply could not bury their father without both his sons there. No one knew how to reach Max Jr., who was somewhere in Kansas, maybe. Bertie contacted the Kansas State Police for help in finding the caravan, not holding out much hope. Amazingly, they located them quickly. Max and Jean drove back at once, leaving their equipment behind. Yellowstone officials never found Floyd and Lorraine, but her mother knew they planned to visit Lorraine's brother after the park, and she notified him. Floyd and Lorraine walked in the door, received the terrible news, and turned around and walked out.

Burial took place in Big Sandy because Max no longer attended the Box Elder church; the family agreed to move Della and Evelyn's bodies to Big Sandy. Little Max and Max Jr. now became just Max. After the funeral, the family gathered at the home place for the reading of the will, and to allow each sibling to select an heirloom from the family treasures. As the oldest, Bertie chose a beautiful Michigan glass berry bowl set, her parents wedding gift. The set was now a lovely antique— purchased from the dime store in 1905.

No one argued about the keepsakes, but there were hostile feelings because Max and Floyd, who inherited the property, could only afford to give each sister 200 dollars temporarily for their share. The farm was valued at 14,000 dollars. Charlotte was the most bitter because she and Bertie labored so intensely as children to help create the farm. Two years later, Floyd sold his half of the homestead to his brother.

Max Jr. did eventually give his sisters 2,000 dollars each, so they ultimately received their fair share, but not for many, many years. His sisters knew he could have afforded to pay them sooner because he'd become a millionaire speculating in the stock market.

When Della and Evelyn's remains were moved, Bertie drove to Big Sandy because she wanted to see her mother's body. She knew Della was dead before burial— she'd made sure. It was merely curiosity to view a person buried that long ago. No one wanted her to look, but Bertie insisted. They opened the casket, Bertie looked and caressed her mother's face but did not faint as the men predicted. No one else looked. After all those reminders of man's mortality, she needed some cheerful news.

That news came in the form of the city's first square dance festival that occurred a few months later. A hundred squares filled the Great Falls High School gym with spectators overflowing the balcony. Dancers from Montana, neighboring states, and Canada attended, and Bertie made an elaborate red skirt encrusted with sequins for the occasion. Many visiting males were surprised to meet a female caller. And as usual, the dancers loved her deep voice.

Art was a wonderful husband and like Arlo, he and Bertie never had a single fight during their marriage. This amazing achievement was possible because she married such remarkable men. Art and Bertie had only one disagreeable discussion. He felt Dorothy's dates were spending too much time at the house and "Mr. Painter" was, but Bertie said she would rather have them at home than out somewhere. Art never mentioned the subject again. Another thing he kept his mouth shut about were those sudden mysterious trips he took.

Art was on another there's-no-use-your-going-along-trips. The first time it happened, Bertie suspected another woman, but that didn't seem probable because he never went back to the same place. As before, she felt irritated because she wanted to go along, but she was still unwilling to demand an answer as to why. Then, an enjoyable event soothed her aggravation.

When Dorothy entered grade school, Bertie had tried to give her a birthday party, twice. No one would come. Dorothy wasn't as popular as "trick or treat." When her twenty-first birthday approached, Bertie felt it the perfect time. She prepared the food and conspired with Dorothy's current boyfriend to keep her away from the house until the celebration. A dozen guests enjoyed the evening party and Bertie was as excited as Dorothy was surprised.

Bertie's fishing trips with Art soon made traveling a high priority, and her feet were forever itching to go to other states. She started late in life but serious travel was about to begin. A magazine advertisement fascinated Art and he studied it a long time. The object of interest: a Cree Coach, the forerunner of the modern motor home. It rested inside the six-foot bed of a pickup truck. When the requested literature arrived, Art and Bertie studied it and agreed it would be a wonderful and inexpensive way to travel. In those days you didn't need to overnight in a secure campground; you could park in the woods or store parking lots.

Bertie bought the first Cree Coach sold west of the Mississippi with her square dance money; Art paid for the new Studebaker pickup. The coach didn't extend over the truck cab as later models and was only about six inches beyond the rear bumper. The rig was a diminutive dollhouse. Amazingly it slept three, one in a rollout-canvas hammock over the table that lowered into a bed. A butane tank sat on the truck running board, and a bucket placed on the ground under the drain hose caught the gray water. Primitive compared to recreational vehicles today, it was the ultimate camping experience at the time.

Bertie searched the city for miniature supplies for the coach, like the toy broom and dustpan she bought to sweep the floor. The coach had everything required except a bathroom; she even baked in the miniature oven. Floor space was big enough for only one person, so when she cooked, Art and Earl either went outside or sat at the table. Their Lilliputian rig housed them quite comfortably.

The family took short trips around Montana to learn the "do's and don'ts" of miniature camping. Eagerly, they waited for Art's retirement and their first big adventure. That day arrived June 1951. Art retired from the First National Bank after forty-four years. The years had passed quickly because he loved his work, but now he looked forward to retirement and travel.

Art, Bertie, and Earl left within days. Dorothy, already working, fumed; she wanted to go, her travel notebooks already contained hundreds of ideas.

Bertie asked Floyd and Lorraine to care for their home while they were gone. Dorothy still lived at home but didn't need a babysitter at twenty-two, and Bertie's sister Mamie and her husband lived upstairs. The house didn't need a watchdog, Bertie wanted to give Lorraine a break from the daily grind in her miserable living conditions. Floyd was in the process of building their home, and the family temporarily lived with their six-month old baby in a cramped, one-room apartment at the Elmore Hotel. Bertie sympathized with apartment-bound Lorraine. Later, Lorraine told Dorothy, "She saved my sanity."

Art and Bertie took enormous pleasure in their Cree Coach, but from the first day they discovered one major disadvantage. The rig was such a novelty that everyone wanted to see it. At first, they delighted in showing it off, but after numerous meals were interrupted it became a nuisance. Finally, in desperation, they took their camp chairs after dinner and sat away from the coach, enjoying the evening and watching curious people tap on the door and peek in the windows—they were no longer tour guides.

When they returned from the first trip, Bertie began planning the next. She never had traveled anywhere by car except one trip to Glacier Park. Once ignited, her curiosity about the rest of the country burst forth like a rocket on the Fourth of July. She became as obsessed with traveling as she was dancing; she wanted to see every state—even those without waterfalls, her new passion. And she would do much of it by herself.

Two weeks after their first adventure, the bank called Art. The president asked him to return to work. Art wasn't interested. Then he heard his job description: picking up repossessed cars and driving them back to Great Falls. He was ecstatic—*another* dream job. He discussed it with Bertie, and in minutes he called back to accept.

For the next six years he traveled across the country retrieving vehicles over-eager buyers couldn't pay for. Occasionally, there were two automobiles close together and Bertie went along to drive the second car. Then they detoured off the main highways to see the countryside. Bertie was disappointed that there were never enough cars close together for her to go along.

Their Cree Coach was not only fabulous for traveling, but also wonderful when Art went ice fishing. He was the envy of every fisherman on the ice. The coach also came in handy when Bertie called square dances at nearby towns. Then she and Art stayed overnight and drove back fully rested in the morning. If Bertie went alone, she parked "her motel" on the property of one of the dancers.

CHAPTER 35

Dorothy loved dogs. "Mom, would it be okay with you if I bought a dog?"

"Fine with me. What kind do you want?"

"A dachshund."

After their conversation, Bertie came home one day from shopping, all excited. "I've just seen the cutest dog I've ever seen in my life. I asked the owner if you could come over to look at him. She gave me her address."

"What kind is it?"

"It's a Pomeranian."

"Does it have short hair? I don't want a longhaired dog."

"No, it has long hair, but you simply must go see it—you'll adore the breed." Dorothy went and when she saw the dog, it was love at first sight. She agreed. A Pomeranian was the cutest breed she'd ever saw. She wanted one.

After looking at "Dog World" magazine, Dorothy bought a seven-month-old, five-pound, orange male for sale. The puppy's pedigree sported a U.S. and International Championship making his price 100 dollars.

That came to a hefty twenty dollars per pound, an expensive tab for a pet in 1951. She bought the dog sight unseen because the kennel owner said, "You can return him if you don't like him."

When Dorothy told Bertie about the guarantee, she laughed. "He knows very well once you see how adorable he is, you'll never return him."

Bertie was excited as Dorothy waiting for the dog's arrival. Bertie warned everyone about the danger of introducing a young puppy to Felix because the cat had been the only pet in the house all his life. She worried that a single swipe of the feline's claw could put out one of the dog's big black eyes. The Great Northern Railway office called on a cold icy evening. Tell's Sparkling Mike, a precious orange ball of fluff, had arrived. Art drove Dorothy to the railway station to retrieve the wooden crate.

Once back home, everyone—including a curious Felix—circled the crate eager to meet the new family member. Dorothy opened the door. Everyone held their breath and watched Felix. The puppy, crated three days on the train, staggered immediately over to Felix, gave him a sloppy kiss, and promptly walked off as the hissing cat's hair stood on end. Felix was a treasure; he never, ever took a swipe at Mikie. The dog loved that mysterious black and white creature—whatever it was. The feeling was not mutual. But after a worrisome beginning, they got along fine.

A sweet aroma filled the kitchen as Bertie removed a sheet of her famous cinnamon rolls from the oven. Art sat at the sun-drenched kitchen table bent over a miniature vise tying fishing flies, and growing more aggravated by the minute. His every movement demonstrated frustration and finally, Bertie said, "What are you doing?" He showed her the fly he was attempting to tie. She studied it a moment, then sat down, and tied it for him. Art couldn't believe it. She did it with such ease that he taught her to tie other flies as well. At last, Bertie found something about fishing she liked—something creative. She tied all Art's flies from then on.

Art taught a night fly-tying class once a week at the Whittier School across the street. On one of his car retrieval trips, he called Bertie. "I'm not going to get back in time for the class. You'll have to take over for me."

"I can't do that; I've never taught before."

"What do you mean you've never taught before? You're a good square dance teacher, and there's no reason you can't teach fly tying too." She finally agreed, but on the way to the class her stomach did flip-flops. She worried for nothing. Bertie succeeded so well that Art said, "You might as well take over the class and I won't have to worry about getting home from a trip on time." She taught for two years.

One warm autumn day, Bertie sat on a crystal-clear creek bank near Augusta, happy to be out in the wilds of nature. She tied flies while Art fished. A western grebe with his white necktie sat on a nearby limb casting a beady-red eye at Art to see if he might toss back a too small fish. The sun warmed Bertie's back, and she smiled at the insistent rat-a-tat-tat of a determined woodpecker staking claim to a resistant cottonwood. She tied a dozen or more flies watching Art reel in fish after fish. Two nearby fishermen weren't catching anything. Finally, the nearest man approached Art. "I'm not hooking a thing. What kind of fly are you using?" Art showed him.

"I've never seen one like that, where did you buy it?"

Art pointed to Bertie. "My wife ties them."

The man walked over to Bertie. "Would you consider selling me some of your flies?"

"Sure, I'd be happy to."

When he paid her he asked, "Where did you ever learn to design such beautiful flies?"

Bertie shrugged. "I just make 'em up as I go along."

Then the second fisherman joined them. He bought what was left of her stock and ordered more, picking them up a few days later. A month later he came back for another special order. He must have lost as many flies in the bushes as Dorothy when Art attempted to teach her.

Now Bertie was in the fly-tying business. She sold some to a local sport shop, but she couldn't make them fast enough to supply their needs; it was back to word-of-mouth customers. She no longer needed to earn extra money, but she loved the creativeness of her new hobby.

"Mothering" was still important to Bertie. She always told Dorothy to call if she'd be home late. "It doesn't matter what time because I don't sleep until you're home anyway." Dorothy, a woman of twenty-two, still had a worrying mother. Fifty years later, Mother would still worry.

One night in 1951, Dorothy tested her mother by creeping to her door and calling softly to see if she was asleep. She wasn't.

"Oh, Mom, I found him," Dorothy said, her voice high-pitched.

Bertie must have thought, "Here we go again," because Dorothy had already been engaged three times—twice to "Mr. Roller Rink." This time was different.

George Dewey Wilson Jr. was a twenty-three-year-old buck sergeant stationed at Great Falls Air Force Base. Knowing Dorothy's proclivities, Bertie wasn't surprised he stood tall and slender with dark hair and deep brown eyes—he was also movie-star handsome. Dorothy, who still had ugly protruding teeth, showed her co-workers his

244

picture and their shock that this striking man was dating Dorothy registered plainly on their faces.

Dorothy met George at the roller rink. He offered her a ride home because it was raining. He asked if she planned to go skating the next night. She said no, and the next day when she came home from work, she was stunned to find George already there, as he was every afternoon thereafter. They were dating "steady" without him ever asking for a single date. He told Dorothy from the beginning he would never marry, because he didn't want to burden anyone with his medical problem. He repeated his vow often. Japan had surrendered only days before his ship arrived in the Philippines, but hundreds of Japanese soldiers fought on. George fully expected to meet his end by a sniper's bullet. A bullet didn't do him in—an insect did.

George, an aircraft mechanic, worked out in the open and the mosquitoes were thick as the humidity. One particular species, a day-biting insect that preferred human blood, found George's B negative tasty. He got dengue fever and his 105 degree fever couldn't be broken. The overwhelmed hospital moved him to another tent with other cases awaiting death.

The men received only the basic necessities because the hospital was beleaguered with patients they hoped to save. But George was an enigma—he refused to die. Finding him still alive a few days later, the hospital moved his skeletal body back into the infirmary. His five-foot, eleven-inch body weighed less than 100 pounds. He once weighed 165 but never again tipped the scale more than 125 pounds the rest of his life.

George still suffered monthly, recurring attacks of fever. He explained what Dorothy needed to do when an attack occurred. In reality, she could do nothing but dry the rivers of sweat that flowed like Niagara Falls, and try to keep him covered while he thrashed about in overheated frenzy that alternated with teeth chattering cold. The attacks lasted about thirty minutes. To keep him from kicking off the blankets, she developed her own system. She threw herself on top of the covers. It was a bumpy ride.

Dorothy felt confident George would change his mind about marriage, but a year later he hadn't. One day, Dorothy was in the process of telling her mother that they wouldn't be getting married when the phone rang. Bertie left to answer it. George said, "What were you going to say."

"I was going to tell her we weren't getting married."

Expressionless, he said, "I wouldn't say that." He didn't say another word, and never did *ask* her to marry him. So Dorothy's proposal was as strange as both of her mothers were.

CHAPTER 36

Dorothy's mind was full of future wedding plans as she walked home from work one afternoon. A woman walked up behind her and tapped her on the shoulder. "Dearie, you need to see a chiropractor," and walked on without stopping. Stunned at the bizarre behavior, Dorothy just stood there. At home, she laughed as she told her mother about the weird lady

Bertie didn't say anything for a moment—one could almost hear the logic wheels grinding. "Maybe you should. You know how much pain you're in when you come home from work." Dorothy made an appointment. The visit produced an amazing three dollars' worth of information.

The doctor asked her to stand straight in front of him. "You often stand on one foot, don't you?" Dorothy was shocked. She hadn't mentioned that. "You're resting your back," he said.

For years, Bertie had chastised her daughter about standing on one foot in every picture ever taken. "Why can't you stand up straight?" Now, as Dorothy stood in front of the doctor, her arms should have touched her hips and her right arm did. The left hung five inches away. She had chronic rotary scoliosis. Three falls down the stairs, two horse accidents, an apple crate striking her back, and dozens of falls roller skating had caused major damage. She began a lifelong relationship with chiropractors because there was no cure, only temporary relief.

The chiropractor's visit also solved a year's long mystery for Bertie. She'd always pinned the hem of a new garment while Dorothy modeled it. On the clothesline, one side hung five inches shorter than the other. When she put the skirt back on Dorothy, it hung straight. Now she knew why—just in time for the wedding gown fitting.

Dorothy's coming wedding was a special time for Bertie. She was determined to make it the wedding she never had—either time. This time, Bertie approved of Dorothy's choice and said she and Art would pay for everything.

They went shopping. Bertie, exercising her great need to be practical, hinted that one of the more inexpensive gowns was a nice selection. "You can wear the dress without the accessories for a later occasion." Such an occasion never occurred, at least not while Dorothy still had that twenty-four-inch waistline. They selected everything together and Bertie sagely advised picking out china patterns. "Be sure you get one with a lifetime pattern." Bertie planned two receptions while carefully watching costs. She still felt she took advantage of Art's generosity when spending money on her children. He never, ever complained.

Since her father couldn't walk her down the aisle, Dorothy wanted Arlo's father Frank to have the honor. Bertie talked to Art and he not only understood but thought it the right thing to do. Since childhood, Dorothy yearned to do the old-fashion hesitation glide to the altar, appearing to float. However, Frank couldn't master the steps at the rehearsal, and they would later simply walk down the aisle.

The invitations were mailed, cake and flowers ordered, and minister and singers engaged when George came to the house the day before the wedding with alarming news. The previous day, the Air Force searched the entire base for him to fill a twenty-four-hour emergency TDY at another base. When George couldn't be found, they sent someone else. Such situations were rare, but Bertie paled at the news, insisting George stay at their house that night—just in case. She had visions of calling all those out-of-town guests, as well as an avalanche of bills for items they wouldn't use. She needn't have worried, at least not about the groom.

On the big day, the family awoke to a deluge of rain—and a torrent of tears from the bride. Dorothy did not inherit calmness from her mother. Bertie darted from job to job like a hummingbird seeking nectar. At last, prayers, tears or chance worked their magic. At noon, a dazzling sun broke through, wrapping the world in dewy freshness.

Reverend Adams officiated at the two o'clock ceremony at the Methodist Church on June 1, 1952. The bride's family more than made up for the groom's small representation, George's mother. At the last minute, in full wedding regalia, Dorothy called Lorraine and asked her to bring a small picture of Arlo from her room. Dorothy tucked it in the little white Bible she would carry down the aisle, a gift from Grandfather Courtnage—Arlo accompanied his daughter after all.

As Frank and Dorothy, in her white lace over taffeta gown, walked toward the altar, she carried a bouquet of pink roses and lily of the valley resting on the Bible. The ceremony took place without a hitch. Tears seem mandatory at all weddings, and this one was no exception—the bride cried all the way down the aisle.

After the church reception, Bertie had a second one at her home for relatives, the bridal party and close friends. During the planning, Dorothy had doubted the need for a second gathering. Bertie said "You cannot expect all those people to drive back home without giving them something to eat." She worked for days preparing the food. The guests went through the buffet line and out to the backyard filled with borrowed tables and chairs.

Bertie had worked in high-pitched anxiety preparing for the big day; afterward, her emotions plummeted. But she never regretted anything—it was a labor of love. The newlyweds honeymooned for a week in Banff, Alberta. Because they would be entering another country, Dorothy's little Pomeranian, Mikie, stayed with Bertie. She was already missing Dorothy and welcomed the company. The only one upset with the arrangement was Mikie.

When Dorothy and George returned, they stayed at Bertie's house while she and Art were Cree Coach touring. When they returned, Bertie felt rested but still downhearted at losing her daughter. She didn't know it, but she wasn't about to lose her for a long time—a very long time.

Before Dorothy and George moved out of Bertie's home, the Air Force issued George orders for Saudi Arabia. While Bertie longed to see only the U.S.A., Dorothy dreamed of seeing the world. She was overjoyed. A nanosecond later, her bubble of joy burst when she learned wives weren't allowed. She was furious. George had applied for overseas duty three times and was refused because of a shortage of aircraft mechanics. Then, twenty-eight days *after* he wed, he received orders. So Dorothy never left home and the wedding gifts were stored. Bertie felt sad for Dorothy, but secretly happy to have her daughter one more year. Dorothy was glad she hadn't quit work yet.

Dorothy worked at the Great Falls National Bank, and one day a middle-aged woman walked to her window wearing teeth braces. Dorothy blinked, unable to believe her eyes. Orthodontists wouldn't accept patients older than sixteen when she was a child, so she felt doomed to have Bugs Bunny teeth the rest of her life. She made an appointment. The year George sweated buckets in Arabia, Dorothy greeted customers with a happy barbed-wire smile.

When George returned, Dorothy would be far better prepared to set up housekeeping than her mother was. Bertie had made sure of that. She taught Dorothy embroidery as a youngster, saying, "You'll need dish towels, pillowcases and tablecloths when you marry, and you can have pretty things if you start now." After Dorothy stitched a few things, Bertie made her a birthday gift hope chest that she'd covered with wallpaper.

Bertie wanted to spare Dorothy the newlywed financial hardship she went through. She always saved little cans of money stashed all over her house for specific purposes, and now she suggested Dorothy start filling a can with spare coins for that first huge grocery bill. Her daughter even added one for bathroom necessities. Then to be sure she had a honeymoon, she added a can for that—a good thing since she married a man whose only possessions were uniforms and one civilian outfit with deep empty pockets.

Because Dorothy didn't marry until she was nearly twenty-four, she possessed everything she needed to start housekeeping, including a dust rag. Bertie and Art's wedding gift was a set of stainless steel cooking pans and the relatives did their shopping at Duval's where the couple had registered for china. And the 'lifetime pattern'

Dorothy selected—discontinued the next year.

George never went into debt starting married life. Even their wedding license was a gift from "Mr. Roller Rink," who now worked in the license bureau. The only thing Dorothy needed to begin housekeeping was a broom and mop. George's cost was his outlay for a new suit—it's a wonder Dorothy didn't have a can for that too.

For some time, Bertie had wanted to sell her home for something smaller. With Dorothy leaving soon, it seemed the perfect time. Bertie found a house both she and Art liked. The one-story home with an attic and front porch showcased two beautiful blue spruce trees framing the front. The backyard was big enough for Bertie's prized garden, and Art appreciated the long storage area and workbench in the basement for his sporting gear. The house was a winner.

Bertie sold her home on a sad August day in 1952. Mamie and Art, who had lived there for thirteen years, now paid undiscounted rent somewhere else. Bertie had spent twenty-three of her twenty-six years in Great Falls in that home. Leaving the house for the last time, tears filled her eyes as she relived those indelible memories etched forever in her mind—Arlo's wonderful *Plan* for the future and the three times they came within hours of losing their home. Bertie had both wonderful and terrible times in that house; now she was leaving it forever. It was a bittersweet moment.

CHAPTER 37

Bertie and Art's new house had only two bedrooms so Dorothy said she would rent an apartment. Bertie wouldn't hear of it. Earl volunteered to sleep in the partially finished attic, making room for Dorothy.

When George returned from Arabia, he was stationed for only three months in Washington to await discharge, so Dorothy still didn't leave home. Like Dorothy, George had been angry with the timing of his shipment to Arabia. "When I get back, I'm getting out of the service." After his discharge, he changed his mind and wanted to re-enlist in California.

Bertie wasn't surprised. She had predicted him changing his mind while he was still overseas.

Dorothy was shocked. "I don't want to be a serviceman's wife."

"It has some good benefits," he said, so they sat down and discussed the pros and cons.

Still not convinced, Dorothy finally said, "Well, I wouldn't mind if I thought we'd go overseas sometime."

George laughed. "You'll probably go two or three times."

That was the *convincer.* He re-enlisted. In his next fourteen years of military service, he never went overseas again.

"If you're making the Air Force your career," Dorothy said, "I'll join the WAFs and then I can be stationed at the same base as you."

George said, "Fine with me."

Bertie objected because Women in the Air Force had a bad reputation at the time. Dorothy was a twenty-four-year-old married woman, but Bertie's influence was still strong. It took complete removal from Bertie's proximity for Dorothy to become independent. Had she enlisted she could have retired at forty-five instead of fifty-eight and with the same perks as George.

Before leaving for California, Dorothy had an inspirational money-saving idea. "If we'll be moving from base to base, why don't we buy a trailer? Once paid for, it will be cheaper than rent." George thought it okay, but as always, Dorothy sought advice from Bertie. She agreed it was practical, and Dorothy and George bought a used thirty-three foot Columbia trailer. Moving the wedding presents inside was hopeless. They were stored at Bertie's for many years.

In December 1953, Dorothy, George, and little Mikie left for California towing their trailer with a 1950 Oldsmobile they purchased for the job. Despondent at losing her daughter, Bertie struggled not to cry. She was also anxious about the icy roads and feared they couldn't get over Gore Hill, so she and Art followed them all the way out of town to be sure they made it. At the top of the hill, they all said good-bye again with Bertie no longer able to hold back the tears—she was losing her twenty-five-year-old "little girl." It was difficult for Bertie to get on with her life, but soon a happy event provided some distraction.

The newspaper wrote that the famous Pappy Shaw's School of Dance was coming to Great Falls for one week. Overjoyed, Bertie signed up. Shaw was surprised to find a woman caller in his class. When she performed, he praised her calling and asked her to perform a "Mike Hop." They stood side by side while he called the square. With her never knowing when, he handed the mike to her to continue the call. It kept them both on their toes when spontaneity prompted more callers to jump in. The event created a joyful week, but Bertie still missed Dorothy.

When Bertie learned her two sisters and their husbands planned to visit Dorothy when driving back from California, in 1954, she gave them a message. "Tell Dorothy if she'll ride back with you and visit a week or two, I'll pay her way home." The offer was too good to miss. Dorothy joined them when George's mother, Bessie, agreed to take care of Mikie.

The following year, Bertie still missed Dorothy and told Art, "I want to see where they're living." She drove to California. Dorothy and George's entire home measured eight by thirty feet. The living room utilized a divided-couch. Each section opened to two narrow, single beds. Dorothy and George moved them together and rolled towels to fill the deep cross-shaped indentations. Bertie insisted she slept fine, but Dorothy knew her mother wouldn't let a minor thing like discomfort interfere with a visit.

Bertie made sure to return home by June for Earl's high school graduation. She and Art gave him a watch for the event. College didn't interest Earl; he only wanted to be free of all school. Bertie felt happy he was graduating, but didn't fancy facing the empty-nest syndrome. Earl saw no reason to spend money for his own place—he already had a home. He didn't move out for many years. Bertie didn't let his reluctance to leave the roost tie her down. She flew the coop often.

That first visit to see Dorothy and George's new home gave birth to Bertie's newest ritual, visiting whenever they moved. Since they lived in California, Florida, Georgia, and Louisiana, Bertie saw a lot of the country driving from Montana to Dorothy's latest home. She drove across the entire country by herself, stopping to see things along the way. Whenever Bertie visited, the three of them gallivanted. For a woman who never traveled until Art retired, she was fast becoming a dedicated tourist. Now she struck states off her "to see list" at record pace.

Art didn't usually accompany Bertie on trips to Dorothy's. He wanted to be available when the bank needed him to retrieve a car. He was picking up a car in Los Angeles and stopped to visit Dorothy and George overnight. George came home that afternoon with news. "I've received orders for Robins AFB, Georgia." In those days the military didn't pay to move trailers, and servicemen made their own arrangements. The government's per diem came to six cents a mile whether you pulled a trailer or not—it didn't cover expenses. While their Oldsmobile had done a good job hauling their trailer to California, George was skeptical about using it again to cross the entire country. On his lunch hour, he'd found a suitable pickup truck for sale. Because her husband was in the military, Dorothy couldn't get banking employment in San Bernardino, and making payments for a trailer, car, and orthodontist had left them living on potato soup and pancakes. The twenty-seven cent newspaper was beyond their means.

George said, "We can move the trailer ourselves with the pickup, but we need a loan."

"How much do you need?" Art asked.

"With trade in we still need 200 dollars."

"Taking out a loan for that much is crazy." Art whipped out his checkbook. "You can pay it back whenever you're able." When Art told Bertie, she was thrilled with the news. In her mind she checked off those states she would see driving to Georgia. The first time, Art went along because they planned to tour Florida.

Art and Bertie visited them in Georgia on their way to Florida in 1956. Bertie wished Dorothy and George could accompany them, but the coach only slept three. After the move, George had traded their pickup for a car and Dorothy said, "We'll take our car and I can sleep in the back." As soon as George received leave papers, the caravan headed south. On balmy nights Art preferred to sleep outside on a foldable cot, Bertie then occupied the rollout hammock, and Dorothy and George used the bed. The group played musical beds and cars often.

The two vehicles traveled south on the west coast to Key West and back north on the east coast. The trip was great fun and Dorothy's first real vacation with her family—but this time Earl wasn't there.

Sunlight streamed through the kitchen window one morning as Bertie opened the newspaper. "Look at this," she said to Art, who was still eating. "It says we'll be able to drive from New York City to San Francisco without ever stopping for a traffic light because of a new project President Eisenhower signed." Innumerable possibilities flashed through her mind, one being displaced by another as quickly as she thought of it. She was fifty-years old—will we live long enough to see this wonder. Was it another premonition?

When Art saw the new Volkswagen Bug, he visualized zooming over those Interstates too. He loved the small car that used little gas. To surprise Bertie, he bought one. He was the one surprised. She hated it on sight. And she didn't mind letting him know how she felt. But it wasn't her dislike of the car that bothered Art. He wasn't feeling well.

CHAPTER 38

Art was a healthy individual who rarely ever caught a cold, and he'd quit smoking six years earlier. In January 1957, he began suffering pain that worsened daily. The doctors did multiple tests but couldn't find anything wrong. They finally did exploratory surgery and then simply stitched him up again. Two different cancers had eaten away at his body and were too far advanced for the limited treatment of the day.

The doctor took Bertie into the hall. For days, her *feelings* had warned her of impending doom, and she braced herself for terrible news. The surgeon told her it was hopeless; he suggested they not tell Art, a common practice in those days. Eyes shimmering with unshed tears, Bertie told Art she wanted to go eat dinner and would be back soon. Once in the car, the emotions she had kept in check burst forth. Sitting in the car, she cried and cried. *Not again! It's not fair—first Arlo and now Art. What have I ever done to deserve this?*

Under a crystal-clear sky, the air crackled in the bitter cold temperature. Crusty snow covered the ground and sheets of ice glistened curb-to-curb. Bertie sobbed, not feeling the chill in the Volkswagen, until her body began to shake. Frost fairy etchings covered the windshield, and she got out to scrape the glass. Brushing off the frost she remembered her angry disapproval of Art's new VW Bug and guilt replaced the ice in her veins.

Bertie drove Art's beloved car back and forth to the hospital two or three times a day for weeks, and she changed her mind about the car—it was the only vehicle in the neighborhood that would start that bitter cold February. At the hospital she told Art how wrong she'd been, that she was glad he'd bought the car. When Bertie knew she was wrong, she was a person who could say so—sometimes it took a little convincing her that she was wrong.

Bertie called Dorothy. She was on the next flight. George drove up later. After surgery Art's cancer advanced at lightning speed, and he never left the hospital. He suffered horrendous pain because the hospital refused to give him pain medication often enough. The staff said he would get used to it and the medication wouldn't work anymore. No one knows what medication the hospital used, but morphine existed and there was no reason for him to suffer such horrible pain.

Bertie challenged the strategy, but the hospital wouldn't budge from its policy. The doctor's only solution for the horrendous pain was to remove Art's feeding tube so he would die sooner. After his strong, persuasive conversation, Bertie agreed because she couldn't bear to see Art's atrocious agony. He suffered on. Then, Bertie couldn't stand to see his emaciated, pain-wracked body dying of starvation, and she tried to have the tube reinserted. The doctor said they couldn't, his veins were collapsing. So was Bertie.

Art was in such unbearable pain that Dorothy stood outside his door every day praying for him to die. A longtime friend visited, walked in the room and walked right out. "I must have the wrong room. I was looking for Art Moore." Poor Art was unrecognizable when the Lord took him home. He was seventy-seven when he died after sixteen years of happy marriage, still with a thick, full head of hair. At fifty-one, Bertie became a widow for the second time.

Bank officials, Art's club and business associates, square dancers and the Courtnage and Clawiter relatives attended the funeral. There were few vacant seats in the church, but hardly anyone went to the cemetery because of the bitter cold day. Art was buried in a family plot he'd bought in the Masonic Section of the Manchester Cemetery a few miles from Great Falls.

A week after Art died, Charlie Klau, an officer at the First National Bank came to visit Bertie, and she received the shock of her life. Art had lived a secret life. He was a Special Undercover Agent for the FBI.

When Bertie heard that, she shook her head. "Charlie, that can't be true. He never told me—and we shared everything."

"Bertie, he couldn't tell you; the FBI wouldn't let him. I knew because someone at the bank needed to give him permission to be off work whenever they summoned him."

Bertie was used to Art bringing bankbooks home to straighten out various financial messes, and that action made his trips to other city banks believable. The FBI called him in whenever an embezzlement or fraud case was suspected anywhere in the northwest. Art, ingenious with figures, was the perfect choice for the job. At last, those mysterious trips when he didn't want her along made sense. And now her guilt blossomed anew, when she remembered the times she'd been irritable with him.

How she wished she could apologize. It was too late.

But Art was still with her.

For months, Art's withered body floated in Bertie's nightmares. His moans of pain awoke her screaming, drenched in sweat, her heart pounding. Hours later, when at last she drifted off, the moans returned again, night after night. Bertie felt she was losing her mind, and her anguish soon combined with financial reality.

Art had left 20,000 dollars of life insurance that sounded sufficient when he signed the policy, but it did not keep up with forty-four years of inflation. As prudent as Bertie was, she knew it wouldn't last long. Even worse, Art worked much of his career before Social Security began in 1935, and in those days widows received only a portion of their husbands' benefits. Her check was very small.

When Art's insurance money ran out, she was once again in financial crisis. She'd always wanted to learn to play the accordion and bought a nice one years earlier. She took lessons and did well, but during this period of financial hardship, she sold the instrument. She told everyone she'd made the mistake of buying one too heavy. Later, Dorothy learned she sold it because she needed money. That broke Dorothy's heart. Bertie had never mentioned her dire situation to either Dorothy or Earl—they could have helped her.

Dorothy suggested Bertie sell the few stock investments her brother Max had persuaded her to buy. Then she could qualify for food stamps and welfare. "No!" Bertie snapped. "I've never been on charity and I'm not starting now. Besides, I want to leave something for my kids."

Dorothy frowned. "We can take care of ourselves." Bertie wouldn't budge.

That summer, some surprise income drifted her way.

The Montana State Fair hired a new pari-mutuel cashier from California and asked Bertie to stay on as his assistant. She was overjoyed. It meant extra income. Because the cashier wasn't local, she had more responsibility. She interviewed and hired all the prospective employees. One year, the cashier became ill and was hospitalized *en route* to Montana. Frantic, the fair board called an emergency meeting. The assembled officials talked and talked, but they didn't know what to do. Bertie interjected, "Don't worry about it, I can do it." And she did.

Afterward, the fair board congratulated her on a job well done. She glowed all day. *Now the job is mine and the pay is much better.* After living in her dream world for months, she learned the fair board again hired another man. *How dare they tell me what a great job I did and then hire a man.* Bertie had long suffered the discrimination between the sexes where it concerned employment. There was nothing she could do other than quit—not an option if she wanted to travel. The pari-mutuels and her calling gigs were her only jobs and that money went mostly to her travel fund. Her original goal had been to see all forty-eight states, but with Alaska gaining statehood in 1958 and Hawaii in 1959, her objective had increased by two.

Realistically, Bertie couldn't afford to travel on her income. Her extreme frugality and the austere measures she instituted saved a few dollars for that purpose every month. She picked up aluminum cans to recycle, shopped at the Salvation Army Store, and qualified for free butter and cheese. At the end of every month, she divided any leftover money into several individual funds with the travel one receiving the biggest share. As every spare dime collected and multiplied, she worked on her goal of traveling in every state. She traveled on half-a-shoestring budget but allowed for at least one splurge. Art's beloved little VW Bug carried her across the country using little gas, she didn't eat in fancy restaurants, and she often stayed with family or friends so motel bills were low. These bare-bones trips were her only extravagances during years of financial struggles.

She returned from one trip to sad news. Now Arlo's children had no grandparents. Arlo's father Frank had died, surviving his son by eighteen years.

Bertie drove across the country by herself for years, but as she grew older she felt unsafe being on the road alone. The dilemma troubled her because she yearned to travel, and typical for her, she solved the problem using logic. She promptly submerged herself into a passionate and long-term affair with Sylvester, who liked to travel as much as she did. They were an amicable couple who never argued. He agreed with anything she wanted to do, and they traveled all over the country in her Volkswagen Bug.

Sylvester was her safety net—a stuffed dummy she created with a pillowcase head. She dressed him in Art's clothes and for fun stitched on two shiny black buttons with silver-center eyes. Sylvester, hat pulled over his eyes, slept in the car as she drove, pumped gas, or checked into a motel. At night, she pushed *him* down on the floor, putting his hat on the back of the seat so people would think a man was in the motel. Their hot affair lasted many years and added countless miles to her Volkswagen.

Bertie liked the Volkswagen Bug, but when the Karmann Ghia came out, she fell in love. Her car fund had received a few dollars every month for years and was sufficient with a trade in. Signing the papers for her new Ghia, she experienced a guilt twinge but felt Art would understand. Within days, she and Sylvester were on their way to Arizona to visit her sisters Ella and Mamie. Any trip Bertie made, she and Triple A planned the route to see special attractions along the way.

In the winter of 1958, Bertie and Sylvester headed for Georgia to visit her daughter. Whenever Bertie arrived in any large city, she tossed her map in the back and drove wherever her curiosity took her, paying no attention to landmarks. When she was ready to drive on, she looked at her map or asked directions. She wasn't lost—she just didn't know where she was at the moment.

Dorothy and George lived at the Robins AFB trailer park. Their lot included a storage room in an old barracks building they converted to a guest room. They made a plywood folding-screen to block the window at night and wood apple crates, painted burnt orange, made a nightstand and storage shelves. Dorothy borrowed a bed and tossed a throw rug on the floor. The rustic *décor* was quite comfortable, at least more than the split couch in the trailer Bertie had slept on before. Sylvester didn't agree— he hung on a peg.

When Bertie arrived, they all drove to Montgomery, Alabama, to visit Earl at Maxwell-Gunter AFB where he studied medical training for the Montana National Guard. The four enjoyed a family reunion and two fun-filled days before returning to Georgia. Dorothy, like Bertie, had set a goal to travel in all fifty states. Neither had yet been to South Carolina, so one weekend they drove to Edisto Gardens in Orangeburg, South Carolina to strike that state off their lists. Then they drove home.

Bertie planned to stop in Missouri on her way home to have hemorrhoid surgery where Arlo had gone. Dorothy had fissure problems and decided to accompany Bertie and have surgery too. She took leave from work, and they did some sightseeing on the way.

After surgery, their only recovery pain came by way

of coughing, laughing or hiccupping. Some patients took sadistic joy in telling jokes—with laughter and groans following. Patients could leave the hospital anytime they weren't required for treatment. Bertie and Dorothy scheduled morning care, which left them the rest of the day plus weekends to explore.

Together, sharing expenses with friends they had met in the hospital, they visited the Jesse James Home Museum and the Truman Library. At the Buick Assembly Plant in Kansas City, a shocking sight greeted them: thousands of doors and fenders, in different colors, swung under the ceiling to match bodies and hoods of the same color on lines approaching from opposite directions on the floor. Ceiling-hung lines curled in a tight maze, and the man accountable for green door meeting green body held the most important job in the plant. One misplaced color brought the entire plant to a screeching halt.

Who says hospital stays are bad? Mother and daughter had a blast. After their release, Dorothy took the bus home, and Bertie drove home to welcomed news.

Earl's best friend Bob worked at the airlines and needed a place to live. Earl, back from Alabama, told Bertie, "If you want to rent out my room, I'll sleep in the attic again." Bertie liked Bob and jumped at the opportunity to earn extra traveling money. He lived, but only slept, at Bertie's home five years. He and Earl loved to explore Montana.

From the day Earl learned to drive, he became obsessed. Like a bloodhound on a scent trail, he spent every spare moment driving somewhere—anywhere. He knew every street, lane, and dirt road in the city and surrounding area. He thought nothing of driving miles to go somewhere, often with no goal in mind but to turn around and drive home again.

One time, Dorothy and George were on their way

home after visiting in their RV. They pulled into the rest stop at Wolf Creek Canyon to admire the spectacular view. They were drinking in the awesome sight when they heard a car screech to a stop. It was Earl.

"What on earth are you doing here?" Dorothy asked.

"You forgot something and I thought you might need it." The item he drove 110 miles to return—a fork.

Spur of the moment trips were common for Earl. In 1959, he found himself with eight days off work at the Anaconda Smelter. He asked Bertie if she wanted to visit Dorothy and George in Bossier City, Louisiana.

"That would be great, but eight days won't be enough time."

"Yes, it will. I'll ask Bob to go with us and we can drive straight through without stopping."

Bertie started packing. They took her Karmann Ghia for good gas mileage. Dorothy had no idea they were coming. The trio almost drove across the entire country for a three-day visit.

CHAPTER 39

The next year, Bertie and the ever-faithful Sylvester drove to Bossier City again. Dorothy took a few days off work and they did some sightseeing in New Orleans and the Cajun countryside, leaving Sylvester behind. Dorothy took special joy in showing her mother Belle Helene, the Civil War ruin from Life magazine that had started her travel hobby twenty-five years earlier.

Dorothy called Bertie when she got home. She answered breathless with excitement. She had just received the most phenomenal thrill of her calling career. It happened at the Five-State Square Dance Festival held in Billings, the biggest one ever held. Callers came from surrounding states and Canada.

When Bertie entered the hall, energy oozed from every pore. Looking around, she saw only male callers, which wasn't surprising. Later, she saw a female caller arrive, the first she'd ever seen. She introduced herself and they chatted, comparing similar career difficulties.

Full of confidence, wearing her new skirt that had taken hours to encrust with swirls of gold sequins, Bertie awaited her turn to call. Dancers and spectators jammed the hall. When introduced, she received polite applause like the other callers. Stepping up to the microphone, she broke loose with a popular patter call. As the last words left her mouth, a thundering roar erupted in the auditorium. Stunned, she didn't realize for a few seconds what was happening. The crowd was on its feet—cheering and giving her a standing ovation. Tears of joy flowed down her cheeks. That response didn't endear her to the male callers and some looked annoyed. No other caller received that honor the entire evening. Bertie basked in sweet, pure vindication and felt the honor justified, in some small way, for the many years the male callers had ignored her and brushed her talent aside.

Bertie was again finding it more difficult to make ends meet, but she refused to dip into her travel fund. Dorothy tucked a five-dollar bill in her weekly letter, but it probably went straight to her travel fund. Bertie wanted work.

Again, she failed at several interviews. It was the same old story: no high school diploma or job experience. Near the end of possibilities, she obtained an interview at Duval's Department Store. Mrs. Duval asked the now familiar questions. She wasn't impressed.

Bertie's stomach churned. As Mrs. Duval ended the interview, Bertie blurted, "Let me work a week free; then you can decide if you want to hire me."

Mrs. Duval stared at her, openmouthed. "No one has ever approached me with that proposal before. It's certainly fair. We'll try it."

Bertie took a deep breath, and said, "You won't be sorry."

She worked only three days gift-wrapping packages before Mrs. Duval said, "You're hired." But at the end of the week: "Do you always work this way?"

Bertie's knees trembled. *Is she going to fire me?* "What do you mean?"

"I can't believe how fast you work," Mrs. Duval replied. The next day she let another employee go because Bertie did the work of two people. Like her work as a domestic, she'd become a hazard to other workers for the second time.

Later, Bertie's boss discovered none of the packages she mailed ever had claims for broken items. That wasn't true of the other clerks. From then on Bertie became the mail clerk. She preferred wrapping the beautiful packages; it wasn't her decision to make. She worked at the store eighteen years part-time and full-time during June and December. During all those years, only two claims were filed for broken items, and she mailed many fragile purchases.

Bertie's house once again needed painting. She couldn't afford it. Dorothy said, "I'll come paint the house. It'll be easy; it's only one story." Dorothy boarded the train in 1961. When she arrived, she returned to her old haunt, the roller rink, for an evening's fun before starting work. Gliding around the rink, a wheel rolled across the floor in front of her. *Oh no! Some poor soul has had it.* A nanosecond later she hit the deck—it was *her* wheel.

At the doctor's office, Dorothy learned she'd cracked her elbow's radial head. If she moved the arm too much, it wouldn't heal and would require surgery. "Well, you can't paint the house now," Bertie said. Dorothy had inherited her mother's stubbornness and insisted she could paint the house with one arm in a sling. Bertie couldn't dissuade her daughter, so she helped every way she could, including shouting instructions from the ground when Dorothy ran into a wasp's nest in the peak of the roof. No one ever saw a one-armed painter come down a ladder so fast.

Bertie had dreamed of attending a World's Fair for years, but it didn't seem possible until New York City hosted the event in 1964. She checked her travel fund. If she was frugal and shared expenses, the trip was possible. She dialed Dorothy. Was she interested? Of course she was, and Bertie made the arrangements through Triple A.

Bertie landed in Jersey City two hours before Dorothy, waving and smiling when her daughter stepped into view. The pair settled in the National Hotel on the corner of Seventh Avenue and Forty Second Street. When they entered the room, they were delighted to find a combination stove, sink, and refrigerator all housed in one small unit, but they only ate breakfast and late-night snacks in their room.

Their first sight of the incredible fair Unisphere glistening in the sunshine astonished them. The twelve-story fair symbol fashioned as a world map on stainless steel bands rested in a pool with rings of water spouting around it.

Every popular pavilion had two- to four-hour waiting lines. Like the crowing rooster, they arose at dawn to eat, shower, and catch the subway in order to arrive at the entrance before the fair opened. Then, every night they planned which exhibit to rush to when the gate opened the next day, thus avoiding the long lines. Using this method, they visited their favorite exhibits twice, never waiting in line.

They were tourists extraordinaire and determined to see everything. For fourteen days—gate open to gate closed—they trekked from exhibit to exhibit seeing all 150. Six were closed.

Most pavilions were created for exotic beauty like the

271

Tower of Light; some were fanciful, designed to look like waves; others hovered in their allotted space. The General Cigar exhibit blew twelve-foot smoke rings from a giant cigar, and the Royal Tire's exhibit was an eighty-foot, tire-shaped Ferris wheel offering spectacular views. The Bank of America's Money Tree sprouted more than a million dollars in international currencies—a wire cage encased the tree.

The International Plaza contained twenty-six kiosks that wafted enticing aromas on the breeze, becoming their favorite eatery. Their taste buds tingled in delight with flavors from around the world: Danish crepes, Irish coffee, Dutch spicy beef, Korean kimchee, and tandoori chicken from India that was so tasty they ate it every day. Eating so many delicacies during the day meant they often weren't hungry for dinner. Then another kiosk morsel provided the evening meal with a snack of fruit, milk, and cookies later in their room.

As blister piled on top of blister, Dorothy abandoned shoes in favor of thong sandals. Bertie suffered blisters rather than wear thongs. The fair offered many free street shows: fire dancers, carillon bell concerts, a motorcycle troop demonstrating maneuvering skills, and many strolling musicians and singers.

Both agreed the New York City pavilion was their favorite. The one million dollar exhibit had taken three years to build and claimed to represent every edifice in the city in miniature—they circled it three times. Beside the eleven reflecting pools and nine spectacular fountains, 3,500 benches scattered throughout the fairgrounds. They never found one—unoccupied.

After two weeks of restaurant food, Bertie craved fresh fruit. Their hotel was in the once-stylish theater district, but now was dotted with strip joints and tattoo parlors accounting for the cheaper room rate Bertie had sought. The hotel lay on the edge of a sleazy neighborhood that became seedier when they ventured onto Ninth Avenue, the only close place to buy fresh fruit.

At a sidewalk stand, Bertie picked up a grapefruit to inspect it. A pasty-faced man with an enormous potbelly and grimy tank top burst half out a battered green door, bellowing: "Hey! No squeeza da fruit." Bertie recoiled dropping the grapefruit. He was so rude she wanted to go elsewhere but knew there was no competition nearby. He knew it too.

Ready to take a bite out of the Big Apple's other sights, Bertie and Dorothy set out for the Statue of Liberty. They were awestruck standing at the Lady's feet and like others wanted to go to the top. Climbing the torch wasn't allowed because that section was too weak, and halfway up, Dorothy was wishing people weren't allowed to scale the body either. At times, she didn't think she would make it, but Bertie breezed right along behind her. Once anyone starts the climb, they must climb the 300 plus steps to the top. The spiral staircase was so narrow it was impossible to squeeze past anyone behind them. When they reached the top, Dorothy thought the agony was worth it—almost. On their return, they learned tourists often had suffered heat exhaustion, breathing problems, panic attacks, claustrophobia, and vertigo climbing those stairs.

Radio City Music Hall is the largest indoor theater in the world with 6,000 seats. Built in 1932, it was a must see on their list because of its national treasure in their opinion, the Rockettes. They sat through *The Unsinkable Molly Brown* twice, in order to see the celebrated Rockettes a second time. It was the most rest they had during the entire three weeks.

CHAPTER 40

Once back in Montana, Bertie and Sylvester made several small trips statewide, but nothing elaborate for the next four years. Her lifelong dream was to visit Hawaii, and at sixty-two, she felt she should do it soon. She called Dorothy; did she want to go? She did. George didn't.

Their escapade began in March 1968 when Bertie flew to Mesa, Arizona, to visit her sisters Mamie and Ella. Meanwhile, Dorothy and George drove to Tucson to visit with his parents. They picked up Bertie and departed for Pasadena for a quick visit with George's brother Bob. The next day, Bob, who was familiar with the terrifying Interstate System, drove everyone to the Los Angeles airport.

Bertie and Dorothy had seen few Interstates in their travels as yet, and near downtown Los Angeles, their eyes widened in shock as The Stack loomed into view, the world's first four-level cloverleaf interchange.

At the airport, Bertie and Dorothy boarded the plane for Honolulu. George stayed with his parents. In those days, flying was an enjoyable experience, and oversea travelers were treated with a bonus—champagne. Bertie and Dorothy sat next to the steward's station in back. When he finished pouring for the passengers, the bottle wasn't empty and he offered them a second glass. Dorothy didn't like flying and felt edgy flying over the ocean—two glasses of champagne helped ease her anxiety.

When they landed, no young ladies in hula-skirts put leis around their neck as depicted in the movies. Only resort hotel guests received that honor, but they didn't care—they were in Hawaii. During the taxi ride to their hotel, they gawked and craned their necks like tennis spectators. Bertie had reserved a motel two blocks from Waikiki Beach. The room had a kitchenette but they only ate breakfast there. First on their agenda was the International Market Place. Buying three muumuus each "Hawaiian-ized" them. The muumuu, a gaudily colored gown that flows from the bust, has no waistline. A fabric shop drew Bertie's attention and she couldn't decide between six exotic patterns. She bought them all and made muumuus at home the next twenty years.

Bertie always figured on one big splurge per trip, but for Hawaii she had reckoned on at least two, a small compact rental car being the first. Honolulu's traffic wasn't yet hazardous, but Dorothy did the driving because time was precious and Bertie drove slower. Their rental also afforded them the opportunity to picnic for lunch and sometimes dinner, saving money.

The second planned splurge was a luau at the Diamond Head Hotel, where at last someone draped sweet-smelling leis of baby orchids around their necks. Several twenty-foot tablecloths lay on the grass; fresh fruit decorated the center of the table from end to end with guests sitting on woven ground mats. When the waiters peeled back the banana leaves from the pit-roasted pork, a delightful aroma filled the air—it not only smelled delicious, it tasted divine. Poi, they agreed, must be an acquired taste. After dinner, hula skirt dancers swayed to strumming ukuleles. It was their only expensive dinner. Mostly they picnicked or ate at out of the way Oriental restaurants visited by local Asians; at one, English didn't exist. They ordered pointing to the menu. Their surprise meal was tasty, but the only eating utensils were chopsticks. Little food made their mouths. Eventually, the waitress saw their problem and brought forks.

Everything in Hawaii was beautiful, a joy to behold—everything except the USS Arizona Memorial in Pearl Harbor. The ship is still commissioned and flies the U.S. flag. After twenty-seven years, oil still oozes from its hull. Knowing 1,102 lost souls still slept in the deep under their feet brought tears to their eyes as it does most visitors. After the war, the government tried twice to raise the ship, and twice the divers died from poisonous gases. It seemed an omen and the government chose to memorialize those ill-fated lost souls where they lay.

Nu'uanu Pali, near Honolulu, holds the record as the windiest place in the world. Two 3,000 foot cliffs flank the beautiful site. Lightweight objects thrown off the cliff come right back to the thrower. Reading that statistic didn't prepare Bertie and Dorothy for the tornadic blast that greeted them. The moment they stepped out of the car, their muumuus wrapped around their necks. Pictures were impossible—they couldn't let go of their dresses. In seconds, Bertie had enough and returned to the car with Dorothy following. Both were annoyed at not getting pictures but enjoyed the view for a few minutes. Then, Dorothy said, "Look, Mom, everyone has left—there's not a soul in sight. If no one is here to see, there is no need to hold my muumuu down." She got out. Wrestling with her muumuu, she snapped time-consuming pictures for both she and Bertie.

When she turned to get in the car, three men stood right behind her grinding away with movie cameras zoomed directly at her panty-clad butt. As if that wasn't bad enough, a tour bus full of sailors from Pearl Harbor had also pulled in and all the shutter-happy sailors were outside making Dorothy an international film star. The wind was so deafening she hadn't heard the noisy bus pull into the parking lot. Mortified, she ran to the car to find Bertie doubled over in laughter. Who says fame takes years?

They drove every road on the Oahu map except two requiring four-wheel drive. Daytime temperatures hovered around eighty degrees, and every afternoon a light shower sent people scurrying for shelter. Minutes later, the sun came out and everyone returned to their activities as enchanting rainbows appeared, presenting colorful arches for shutterbugs.

At Maui, the Valley Island, a rental car awaited them at the airport as it did each island thereafter. They were overjoyed to find a ten-mile highway that required backtracking—the scenic drive had dozens of waterfalls, many too small to be named. None were too small for them. Dorothy had inherited her mother's obsession for waterfalls. The drive, however, would have challenged a mountain goat. A steep, narrow road confronted Dorothy, who kept her hand on the horn as she rounded tree lined, hairpin after hairpin turn. They stopped every few yards to take a picture which was lucky. On the return trip, "someone up there" turned the spigot off—most of the falls were gone, not to return until afternoon showers replenished the mountain runoff.

Later, they stumbled across an unnamed waterfall at the bottom of a deep hollow. Lush tropical ferns surrounded the charming cataract and the fragrant aroma of white ginger floated on the breeze. At the bottom of the falls, a cloud reflecting pool beckoned one for a swim. Bertie said, "Oh, it would make a nicer picture if someone was in it."

Dorothy took the not-so-subtle hint. Tossing off her muumuu, she began the steep hike downward, clad in the leopard print bikini she wore under her muumuu every day for such occasions. After a difficult descent, she posed seductively by the pool long enough for Bertie to take pictures. Beginning the tough trek back, Dorothy saw Bertie, who seemed frantic, waving her arms and shouting. The water's roar was deafening and Dorothy couldn't hear Bertie. Dorothy's heart raced—something must be wrong—and she scrambled up the bank as fast as she could. Puffing like a steam engine, at the top she learned nothing was wrong. Bertie was yelling, "Go back. Go back." She pointed to a man who had appeared and was trying to set up his tripod and telephoto lens to get a shot of Dorothy. She may have missed another chance at international filmdom, but she wasn't making that steep climb again.

Kauai, the Garden Island, brought an unplanned splurge: an hour long, forty dollar helicopter tour of the Nā Pali Cliffs. The cost badly dented their travel kitty, but they considered the price worth it for an once-in-a-lifetime experience; the only way to see the spectacular valley was by helicopter. No roads existed. The sheer high coastal cliffs, one after the other, were formed by lava flowing into the sea. In between many crags lay a tiny, white sandy beach—if you had a boat to get there.

The flight included Waialeale, an extinct volcano that ties the world record for the wettest spot on earth with 400 to 600 inches of rain per year. One side of the volcano had collapsed years ago, and trade winds forced through the opening cause the enormous rainfall. Yet, fifteen miles away lay a desert and an alkali swamp. Their chopper descended *into* the volcanic cone where dense fog filled the crater as it did ninety-five percent of the time. They saw nothing but haze. Moments later their prayers were answered, the fog lifted as if by magic.

Before them lay a wondrous sight—waterfalls *surrounded* them. Bertie and Dorothy gasped, pointing and clicking away on their cameras. Their tourist brochure listed one thousand waterfalls. They weren't counting—they were gawking. Leaving the crater, the sight of their first round rainbow—the mirage seen from the air—enchanted them even if they couldn't capture it all in their lenses.

Molokai, the Friendly Island, was dotted with small farms and only three modest hotels. Triple A listed only two attractions. However, the tourist bureau informed them that it had rained for two days and they should not attempt to see the waterfall on the eastern end of the island unless they drove a four-wheel-drive vehicle. Their Datsun didn't qualify. The clerk said, "You might—and it's very speculative—make the scenic western end of the island that overlooks the Leprosy Colony." Bertie and Dorothy were determined not to leave the island without seeing something. They drove west. Halfway up the mountain they became stuck in deep mire. Dorothy tried to find something to give them traction. Nothing worked. "You wait here," she said, "and I'll hike back to that farm where we saw those men using a tractor."

The two men were still in the field when she asked for assistance. They answered her—she didn't know what they said. They didn't speak English. Her muddy feet must have given them a clue because after a good deal of sign language they appeared ready to help. Piling onto the tractor, they headed up the hill. After driving only a few yards, they encountered Bertie sailing down the mountain in the car she'd freed herself. Embarrassed, Dorothy tried to thank the men. She didn't know "thank you" in sign language.

Appalled at leaving the island without seeing a single site, Dorothy flagged down the next vehicle. "Do you know any place that rents four-wheel-drive vehicles?" she asked the young man.

"No, I don't think there are any."

She told him their tale of woe. "That's a shame," he said. "I have a four-wheel drive and I'd take you, but I don't have money for gas. The pineapple factory where I work is on strike."

Bertie asked, "Is that the only reason you can't go?"

"Yes," he said, his eyebrow cocked.

"Would you take us if we buy the gas?"

"I'd be glad to, but there's still a problem. My vehicle is a two-seater and the engine is between the seats."

"Don't worry," Bertie said, "we'll manage." They followed him back to town, parked their Datsun, filled his vehicle with gas and away they went. Dorothy shared the seat with Bertie, but was uncomfortable. She spent the rest of the time bouncing on the engine box.

The Kalaupapa Leprosy Settlement lay in a beautiful valley between a pair of 2,000 foot cliffs. The settlement was accessible only by boat, air, or switchback horse trail. The valley, frosted with puffy-white clouds, and the Pacific Ocean stretching into infinity provided a vision of awesome beauty for their photo album. On their way back, their new friend turned onto a narrow dirt road. "Now I'll show you something not listed in the brochures."

Driving through a tropical forest they arrived at their destination. Their friend told them the legend: "A Hawaiian prince took two young maidens to the rock overnight. One of the young ladies became pregnant, but he swore he had nothing to do with it. Since everyone knew a prince wouldn't lie, the people blamed it on the rock." One look at the rock towering over them, and they had a graphic mental idea how the legend started. Phallic rock was so realistic it looked carved, but wasn't.

Back in town, they thanked their guide, and went to lunch. When they finished eating, he stood talking to some men outside the restaurant. "I don't have anything to do the rest of the day," he said. "Would you like to see the waterfall on the other end of the island?"

Bertie hesitated. "I don't think we have time before the plane leaves."

"Oh, we can make it."

Dorothy said, "Come on, Mom, he says we can make it," and they were off. Dorothy saw no reason for concern; it was a good road until they passed through the huge Pu'u O Hoku cattle ranch. Then the road disappeared, becoming a mere trail where jeeps ran over the grass, flattening it—the boulders and chuckholes remained. Driving fast was essential and Dorothy recoiled off the engine housing like a yo-yo. Worst of all, they were too pressed for time and saw Moa'ula Falls only from the far end of the valley. Two minutes later, they jumped in the jeep and drove like maniacs to get back in time for their flight. When they returned, Dorothy's *derrière* smarted like she'd been spanked. The risk takers filled their new friend's gas tank again, and Bertie tipped him five dollars from their kitty fund. His face broke into a wide smile and he thanked them again and again.

Back in their hotel, frenzied packing and a wild dash got them to the airport in time for their flight to Hawaii, the Orchid Isle. The Hawaii Volcanoes National Park, one of the world's most active volcanic areas, was their main goal. They drove up late that afternoon for a daylight view as well as the impressive night sight. Both Mauna Loa and Kilauea are active and they stared at the red lava gushing through the cracks at the bottom of the crater, an awesome spectacle.

The night before their flight home, Dorothy awoke in the wee hours of the morning shivering uncontrollably. Bertie piled on blankets and coats to no avail. She didn't have a fever and Bertie was at a loss. Dorothy's Saint Vitus Dance boogied on. Bertie was ready to call a doctor, when she remembered something. "I know what's wrong with you—it's your nerves." Dorothy's teeth chattered like a playful squirrel, and she felt her mother had lost her mind. Then Bertie reminded her of the dreadful event that had happened on their way back to the hotel.

An afternoon shower had left the world glistening in the sun-filled sky. Driving a country road, Dorothy topped a hill to see six or seven canines in the middle of the lane. The dogs scattered in all directions. Doing her best to miss them, she was mentally congratulating herself when she heard a sickening thud. Anguished screams pierced the quiet countryside. Jumping out of the car they found a small yellow dog lying on the road. Heartsick, Dorothy raced to the nearest farmhouse to ask someone to put the creature out of its misery. The man of the house was at work as they were at the other houses. She tried to borrow a gun to do the deed herself. No one had a gun. Dorothy stood by the still howling dog, tears filled her eyes. Suddenly, the mongrel rose up on his front legs and began dragging itself down the road. Unable to ease the animal's suffering, Dorothy, a devoted critter lover, was an emotional wreck. They could do nothing but drive back to the hotel. Dorothy couldn't believe her nerves caused the horrible shaking, but in the morning she felt fine. Mother was right.

Their hotel had an early morning checkout. Not wanting to pay another day only to bathe and change clothes for their evening flight, they departed. They revisited a gorgeous waterfall and late in the afternoon, they stumbled across an empty beach. Ambling down the coastline, they could tuck in one last memory of their glorious vacation. Gentle waves caressed the shore as the sun hung low in the sky, streaked clouds promising a spectacular sunset.

A park and bus station across the street had restrooms with hot water; benches and tables were scattered throughout the park with a row of vending machines by the bandstand. It was the perfect place to wash, relax, and eat the last of their picnic supplies in thoughtful solitude with one last magnificent view. Spreading out their feast, they watched the orange orb sink lower in the sky. Muted orange and pink clouds painted a bright Monet sunset.

A few bites into their buffet, a grubby Oriental man arrived with a cup of coffee. Soon another and then another joined them. They had stumbled into Hobo Haven, and before they knew it, seven scruffy bums were buying hot coffee before ambling over to the nice dry bandstand for the night. Two of those "bums" made a hasty retreat.

CHAPTER 41

Arriving in Los Angeles, George, his brother, and sister-in-law picked them up. It had been a fantastic escapade—the family reunions an added bonus. Bertie was home only long enough to unpack and see to the mail. Two weeks later, Charlotte and George suggested Bertie accompany them to Alaska, a state still on her goal list. She agreed. Her ruptured travel fund held barely enough to pay for half the gas and food. Because of her over-powering guilt complex, she always worried people would think she took advantage of those she traveled with. The opposite was true. Even with Dorothy, she insisted on paying half of the gas and always squeezed ahead at the cash register to buy the largest portion of groceries. In general she paid more than her share.

Seeing Charlotte's new coach, Bertie couldn't believe the improvements made since her and Art's Cree Coach. It was quite roomy, but she didn't know something fishy was going on. Charlotte and George were ardent fishermen and had neglected to mention fishing was the purpose of their trip. Bertie saw only the scenery driving from one fishing spot to the next, but she loved it and didn't regret going. Now she could strike Alaska off her list.

Bertie's house-painting tradition lived on. This time it was George, who had retired from the Air Force. He drove to Montana and Dorothy flew up later. When she arrived, the house was painted with no wasps in attendance. They devoted a few days to enjoy family and revisiting sights in and around Great Falls—and one not of this world.

Science wasn't in the realm of Bertie's interests, but she made an exception on July 20, 1969. The family gathered around the television for the historic event. During her sixty-three years, Bertie had welcomed the birth of television and jet airplanes, but never in her wildest imagination did she believe she would see a man walk on the moon. That was Buck Rogers stuff. Bertie and the entire world watched Neil Armstrong step onto the moon and utter the immortal "That's one small step for a man, one giant leap for mankind."

Before George and Dorothy started home, her cousin Cliff asked George if he wanted to work the harvest at a huge ranch east of Great Falls. Cliff had hired on, but they needed more wheat haulers. Dorothy and George did some fast calculating. He could earn enough to pay for her flight home and still make a nice profit. George became a temporary farmer.

Happy to have his company, Bertie packed lunches for George the night before because his alarm went off at 4:30 a.m. She was a night person, often not getting to bed until 1:00 a.m. and she wasn't about to get up three hours later. Bertie made lunches containing sandwiches, pickles, salad, fruit, puddings, fried chicken, or homemade cookies. The other hired hands were always jealous—and George wasn't into sharing.

Temporary farmer pay was excellent, but George

labored from 6 a.m. to 9 p.m., seven days a week. Returning to Bertie's at night, his body—hair root to toenail—was layered with thick black grime that ringed the bathtub almost requiring Brillo to clean.

Unfortunately, Dorothy and George's financial planning hit a fatal snag. Her name was Camille. Before he finished the harvest, Mother Nature whipped up Hurricane Camille, a Category 5 storm, headed for Fort Walton Beach. A worried George headed home but the storm changed directions and went to Mississippi. The horrendous storm missed their home for which they were forever grateful—but by not completing the job, "farmer George" lost money.

Bertie had wanted to sell her house for years but felt guilty putting Earl out of his home. He was thirty-four-years old and other than paying for half the food, he wasn't much help around the house. She couldn't keep up with the yard and finally sold the house in 1970. Ready to move on to the next chapter of her life, she wondered what destiny chose to bestow on her next. She hoped fate would be kinder than the years of financial difficulties she'd suffered after Arlo's and Art's deaths.

Bertie found the Summit Apartments, two blocks from the Senior Citizens Club. The apartment had a lot of storage areas that she needed because she hoarded anything interesting, sentimentally or pretty. The house had a lovely shaded backyard. In the alley by the garbage cans grew a hollyhock. A seed, perhaps dropped by a passing bird, had given birth to the lonely plant that struggled for existence in the gravel. She knew she would be happy there when the landlord gave her permission to plant a garden. For the first time since 1927, she became a renter.

Taking the first load of boxes to her new home, Bertie

carried a two-pound coffee can with holes she'd punched in the bottom with an ice pick. Filling the can with water, she set it down beside the alley hollyhock, continuing the practice until winter killed the flower.

Once settled, Bertie discovered a fascinating new hobby perfect for her dormant artistic urge, Christmas ornaments made from kits. The craft store samples were attractive, but looked skimpy. She knew she could make prettier ones—without a kit. She knew they would sell and she could earn some travel money. Bertie bought supplies at the craft shop, and her imagination blossomed, ricocheting in all directions. She saw something different when she looked at empty toilet paper rolls and styrofoam cups—she visualized pretty tree ornaments.

Bertie's breakfast nook became a workshop. Her dining table was now a workbench. It held a tiny vice, several pairs of scissors and tweezers, toothpicks, and other assorted surgical-like tools for gluing, holding, and drying. Everywhere the eye fell, multiple dozens of tiny jars; miniature chests with drawers, small boxes, and a large sideboard were crammed with supplies. Even without labels, she knew the location of every bead. From the large, round pull-down lampshade, appendages of styrofoam, and glitter always hung in various stages of drying.

She ate her meals on a card table in the kitchen.

Each year, Bertie designed new ornaments embellishing them with glitter, foil, ribbons, beads, pearls, rickrack, or braid. Half a styrofoam cup with a Christmas card background created scenes with miniatures figures, animals, and an inch-high, handmade, decorated Christmas tree. Under the miniature tree, she arranged minuscule hand-wrapped packages of foil and ribbon—some one-quarter inch long.

She couldn't buy a crèche or straw for the nativity

scene, so she made it. Her entrenched perfectionism required constant checking and redoing a single misplaced sequin. Each and every ornament was exquisitely detailed and perfect in every way. Once again, she found a way to earn extra money; this time doing something she loved as much as dancing. She sold the magnificent ornaments for far less than they were worth.

Dorothy said, "You need to charge more, Mom."

"No one would pay the cost if I considered my labor." She was right. Although she needed money, she made the decorations as much for the joy of creating them and she never regretted the twenty-five cents an hour she earned.

Always thinking of her family, she first made six ornaments for each sibling as a gift. That amounted to thirty-six ornaments—a loss to her of 250 dollars. She kept the originals for a pattern and her tree later held more than fifty unique ornaments.

The demand was so great she couldn't make them fast enough. One year she took requests. To fill the orders, she worked every night for weeks until 2:00 or 3:00 a.m., making 926 dollars. That was a lot of ornaments since they sold for six to eight dollars each. The overwork sapped her strength; it took a long time to get back to her energetic self. She never again took orders. Two stores offered to buy her decorations, but it took twenty hours to make one and she couldn't produce them fast enough.

Bertie never did anything half-heartedly and her life was now consumed with making these unique treasures— only dancing or traveling could pry her away. She became so devoted to this endeavor that she resented being interrupted. But she did welcome a special kind of interruption—a new man in her life.

His name was Harry Craig. Ironically, the circumstance of their meeting was an exact repetition of how she met

Art. As floor manager she saw him standing in the door and not dancing. She later introduced herself and asked him to dance for ladies choice. Like Art, Harry danced only with her that night. He was a smooth dancer with superb posture and had won prizes for his dancing. They began dating, and won several dance contests. Once they were approached to teach in Spokane and put on exhibitions. Teaching was the last thing Bertie wanted at this point of her life. She—at long last—enjoyed an excellent dance partner and she intended to dance, dance, and then dance some more.

A quiet, stocky man, Harry wore black plastic-framed glasses. Born in Scotland, he possessed a picture of himself in full Scottish regalia, sporran, kilts and all. He was a widower with no children. As a major, he fought in World Wars I and II. He was a gifted raconteur, often regaling people with tales of those terrible days.

He proposed twice, but Bertie didn't want to marry again. "I enjoy the relationship just as it is."

Dorothy later asked, "Why don't you marry him? You enjoy each other's company."

"I'm afraid he'd be too demanding as a husband."

Harry kept insisting they marry. "I'm all alone in the world; I need somebody in my life."

She didn't want to marry him. She didn't want to lose him. He kept pleading and at last Bertie said, "Why don't we marry ourselves."

"That would be fine as long as you're faithful and don't date anyone else." Together they placed their hands on the Bible and promised to "take care of each other in sickness and in health." They said all the proper words; but didn't get a license to make it official. If they had married legally and he died first, her Social Security check would have doubled. She didn't want the legal tie, and she no longer needed to sacrifice herself for her children. Their agreement suited her fine.

She insisted each keep their own apartment, but they always told everyone they were married. If Harry was ill, Bertie stayed at his house until he was well. He never needed to reciprocate because her incredible health was still intact. He paid half of the food bill, but she did all the work. He was from the old school and never lifted a finger to help, but she was satisfied—he was a good dancer. They always ate dinner together, sometimes at his place, but most often at her apartment because it was handier for her. Best of all, they danced every place they could find.

The pairing was much the same as her other two marriages; they shared few common interests, but she was elated the one they did have was dancing. That was enough for her. Harry didn't like traveling and they made only a few short trips in Montana. He never objected to her visiting Dorothy or taking trips by herself, and he always asked if she needed money. If she said, no, he gave her some anyway. She handed it back after the trip because she believed accepting his money was taking advantage of him.

Bertie remained faithful, but twice she caught Harry at another lady's house, and she felt sure he was two-timing her. She'd no conclusive evidence but was so angry that the next time he came over she shrieked, "Get out! Get out—it's over. Good-bye and good riddance." He ran out the door because Bertie seemed ready to explode. The next day he came back acting as if nothing unusual had happened; he never brought up the subject. Now calmer, she forgave him. Later, she learned from his friends he was often unfaithful to his first wife.

CHAPTER 42

Dorothy and George were living in Florida by 1972. He had retired from the Air Force, but she still worked. Tiring of their dollhouse trailer, he wanted a real home, so in June they bought a house in Shalimar, Florida. The next February, Bertie and Sylvester were on their way. Bertie picked that month to get out of the cold and snow. The day after she arrived in Florida, it snowed. Everyone laughed, but in reality the weather was beautiful and the smidgen of snow lay on the ground only two hours.

Always the perfectionist, Bertie couldn't resist telling Dorothy she didn't like the eclectic arrangement of paintings and fans on her bedroom wall when she took the grand tour. Dorothy, away from her mother's influence for many years, had managed to become more independent. She didn't change the arrangement—she would have when she was young. But she did make one compromise. A devoted Michelangelo fan, Dorothy had a beautiful two-foot replica of *David* in the bathroom. She remembered her mother once saying, "Nudes make me physically sick." Dorothy felt her mother exaggerated, but rather than make her ill, she wrapped *David* in a towel and banished him to the closet floor during her mother's visits. Perhaps Dorothy hadn't gained as much independence as she thought. Poor *David* came *out of the closet* many times before it became popular to do so.

For the first time, there were no sightseeing trips because Bertie pitched in to work on the new house, making curtains, pillows, and more. It was a fun but busy vacation for Bertie.

After exploring Montana with Art, Bertie had set new traveling goals. Rafting down the Colorado River topped her bucket list. It had some of the most dangerous rapids in the world. In 1973, she decided to go—she was sixty-five. The tour furnished everything except passengers. Tourists needed to be in good physical condition, and be able to swim. Bertie not only couldn't swim, she was afraid of the water. The company had an age limit of fifty-five for obvious reasons. When they told Bertie, she smiled. "Oh, how lucky, I'm just fifty-five." They didn't ask for proof; Bertie never looked or acted her age, so the ten-year fib was believable.

Each thirty-three-foot yellow raft carried fourteen passengers and five crew members. The square dance caller was in good company: a doctor, nurse, movie producer, lawyer, accountant, and two airline stewardesses. Mae West life jackets were mandatory and no one needed to ask Bertie twice to put her jacket on. Underway, the rafts rampaged through narrow gorges, some with 3,000 foot cliffs. In the Royal Gorge, Bertie came face-to-face with the horrifying Pipeline, Sledgehammer, and Grateful Dead, where fourteen voices harmonized in piercing screams.

Bertie, the only woman in a dress, looked forward to evening camps to dry out and stop her pounding heart. After dinner around the campfire, the navigators told stories, played guitar, and the group lifted their voices in song. Bertie, who loved the evening ritual, decided to reveal her age since nothing could be done about it then. No one believed her until she produced her driver's license.

Afterward, during an interview for a newspaper article, Bertie said, "It was sure no leisurely pleasure trip. I really needed to concentrate and hang on hard when we hit those rapids. I loved it, but I would *never* do it again— it was terrifying. There were times I looked up to heaven and knew I was going to die." The trip was not for the timid or those with weak stomachs. Dorothy was thankful she hadn't been invited—she might have been dumb enough to go.

Bertie's feet were itching to travel and she visited Triple A and signed on for a bus tour to Washington DC and New York City in 1973. Harry gave her some money and asked her to place a wreath on the tomb of the Unknown Soldier for him. He also wrote a letter for her to carry along.

Bertie bought the wreath, but when she wanted to put it on the tomb, the guard wouldn't let her, saying, "Only military personnel are allowed to approach the grave." She was heartsick; it meant so much to Harry. Bertie had a stubborn streak, and she asked to speak to the guard's supervisor. He only repeated the strict edict. Bertie pushed the letter across his desk. "Just read the letter," she demanded.

He opened the letter. "On my behalf this wreath is placed in honor of thousands of men who served as I did until that memorable day of Nov 11, 1918. Thousands still lie in cemeteries in France, but some of us were fortunate to be spared and to return home, not to forget, but to carry on in some small way the torch of freedom for those who gallantly defended our country and gave their lives. Signed: Major Harry Craig."

The officer was so impressed with the note he told the guard, "Instruct her how to approach the tomb and accompany her to the grave." He gave her the letter back. "No civilian has ever been allowed to place flowers on the grave before." Bertie knees quivered. Dozens of people would be watching. Strict, traditional protocol governed the procedure and the guard spent several minutes coaching her with precise instructions how to approach and retreat from the tomb. She felt so honored she was almost in tears before the emotional ceremony started; they flowed freely as she stepped away from the tomb. An accommodating tourist took pictures of the momentous occasion for her—another treasured memory to relive in her old age.

Back in Montana, Bertie began thinking of where to go next. Someone decided for her. Dorothy had passed the rental store on Eglin AFB where a pop-up camping trailer caught her eye. Intrigued, she stopped. The pop-up contained only two double bunk beds but she and George had everything else needed. Dorothy was still attempting to reach her goal of traveling in all fifty states and those left were New England and on the way there. The pop-up sounded ideal. Dorothy dialed Bertie. "Would you like to tour New England, Mom?"

"When do we leave?" Most of the states Bertie lacked for her goal were also in New England and she was excited. She flew to Florida in September 1974, and two days later the happy campers set off with George behind the wheel of their GMC pickup pulling the pop-up trailer. Riding was a bit cramped for three, but they felt it a small price to pay for such adventure.

Historic Williamsburg, Virginia and Mystic Seaport, Connecticut, an authentic old whaling town with a whaling ship, enchanted them. In Newport, Rhode Island, they were fascinated to learn that most multi-millionaires had lived only three months a year in their Victorian summer homes that cost twenty million or more in 1890 dollars. When new residents arrived, each attempted to "out-shine" his neighbor. These excessive displays of wealth stretched two miles along a scenic ocean cliff walk. They visited Marble House and the Breakers before driving on to Cape Cod.

The Adirondack and Catskill Mountains provided return trip scenery. Outvoted by Bertie and Dorothy, George drove the entire 496-mile Blue Ridge Parkway with its constant mountaintop curves. When it came to majority-rule, George never stood a chance—he was always a minority of one.

Back home, Dorothy wondered if the dealer would have rented them the trailer had he known they'd wear off 5,893 miles of tire rubber. The trip was the first of its kind and set a precedent.

Bertie rode back to Florida to spend Christmas with Dorothy and George. That year, their tree, with dozens of Bertie's ornaments, was surrounded by beautifully wrapped presents, some bows with real miniature pinecones, and tiny Christmas bells. Bertie enjoyed spending the holiday with Dorothy and George, but she missed the many Christmas dances and activities at home. It was the only Christmas she ever spent with them.

Traveling with the pop-up tent trailer was such fun that Dorothy and George decide to utilize it again to tour the opposite corner of the country. Their target was the fabulous northwest coast. Dorothy called Bertie. "Do you want to visit Oregon and Washington?"

"How long do I have to get ready?"

Dorothy and George drove north and picked up Bertie the summer of 1977. Cascade National Park contains the only rainforest in the contiguous forty-eight states, and they were surprised at the intoxicating, damp, woodsy aroma that permeated the rainforest like the deepest Amazonian jungle. At Neah Bay, they couldn't drive farther north without a dunking, so they turned south.

Shi Shi Beach was noted for amazing natural arches and caves to explore at low tide. It wasn't low tide, but Dorothy hoped it might be possible to see a portion of the arches. The so-called three-mile-forest road required four-wheel drive, so the adventurers grabbed their hiking staffs. Their only objection to hiking was the deep puddles of pure thick-oozing mud every ten to twelve feet. In some places the mire couldn't be avoided; shoes came off and were retrieved by muddy hands. Dorothy felt sure someone would fall in the slimy goo and be encased head to toe in mud. She sang out, "The first one who falls must stay down until we get a picture." She repeated the command so often Bertie swore Dorothy was disappointed when no one fell.

At the halfway point they could see the arches were all under water; there was no need to proceed. Unfortunately for photography, the hike out also didn't produce a picture of a sitting mud pile.

From Neah Bay, the carefree wanderers drove south on U.S. Highway 101 through Oregon, detouring from the coast to visit Bertie's nephew Walter in Salem. The next morning, they followed Walter and his family driving to Silver Falls State Park, noted for five waterfalls. Alas, it was raining. Only Bertie, Dorothy, and Walter didn't mind getting wet hiking to two of the falls while the others sensibly remained in the car. After saying good-bye to their relatives, the ramblers drove around Crater Lake and headed to the giant Sequoias. Bertie had seen the redwoods before, but she always enjoyed seeing any pretty attraction again.

The 2,000-year-old General Sherman sequoia, the tallest tree in the world at the time, stood 275 feet high. Feeling like microscopic nothings at the base of the gigantic tree, they all craned their necks skyward to see the top that almost disappeared in the clouds. Bertie knew what to expect, but Dorothy stood in complete awe—never feeling so insignificant.

The travelers then *sampled* their way through Napa Valley wine country before heading to more spectacular scenery in Colorado. Then, out of time, they headed home with Bertie electing to ride back to Florida to see the scenery on the way before flying home. This time the roving gypsies wore 8,180 miles of tire rubber off the pop-up camper. The following year, the camper was no longer available. Dorothy couldn't help but wonder if their 14,073 miles of wear and tear on the same pop-up in two years caused the retirement.

Before Bertie flew home, the trio rented a flat-bottom canoe for a slow drift down the Blackwater River in the state park of the same name. No one had canoe experience, but the river flowed smooth with no rapids. This was a cake walk for Bertie after the Colorado River; any anxiety came only from her water phobia. When they became hot, a swoop of the hand brought a cooling spray of water. All day Bertie had drawn stares, constant comments and chuckles from others on the river. She didn't care; she laughed and tossed a witty remark back. Because Bertie had suffered heat exhaustion as a youngster, she was careful about getting overheated. The item that caused such laughter: a small, red and white striped umbrella mounted on tiny metal stilts. The stilts attached to an elastic band that fit around her head creating a hat that shaded only her head.

CHAPTER 43

Bertie returned home to work at the pari-mutuels. After thirty-four years, she was the oldest employee in years of service at the State Fair. The hustle and bustle didn't seem as exciting anymore, and she still seethed at being overlooked for the cashier's position. She resigned in 1977. A month later, she received an invitation to attend a recognition banquet in appreciation of the pari-mutuel's successful year. "Department superintendents will be recognized and awards will be presented to some very special guests."

Arriving at the dinner, Bertie was stunned to be seated at the head table with its huge floral arrangement—she was the 'very special guest.' Following the awards ceremony, the manager presented her with the obligatory, engraved gold watch and a gold pass entitling her to lifetime free fair admission.

Then the fair manager took Bertie's arm and told her to come with him. He led a puzzled Bertie outside to the large stage where the evening grandstand program was in progress. He guided her onto the stage, and she stood in shock not knowing what was happening. Using the microphone, the manager made a speech about her years of faithful service. It was an impressive talk because she received a standing ovation from a crowd of thousands. Overwhelmed, with tears glistening on her cheeks, she was as thrilled with her "second standing ovation" as she was her first.

The *Great Falls Tribune* interviewed her and ran an article with pictures. In the article, Bertie said: "I make a little money, and then take another trip." By that time, she'd completed twenty-seven big trips and was planning the next—whenever she saved enough money in her vacation fund.

Dorothy and Bertie called each other once or twice every week and during one conversation Dorothy mentioned the pop-up trailer they had rented was no longer available. "It's a shame. We planned to use it again." Nothing more was said.

A week later, Dorothy received a call from Bertie, her voice an excited pitch. After a quick hello, she exclaimed, "I bought a tent and three camping mattresses. I've plenty of blankets and you have everything else we need."

Dorothy laughed at the *subtle* hint. She and George headed for Great Falls in August 1978 where an eager Bertie awaited their arrival. Dorothy's allowed five-week vacation always sounded ample, but never was. Changing camps every night proved to be labor intensive. They discovered their work schedule by accident. The first night making camp, Dorothy whined how she detested making beds. Bertie said "I don't mind that. I hate the cooking." From then on each camper had a 'duty,' after putting up the tent and gathering firewood. George built the campfire, Bertie made beds, and Dorothy prepared a quick dinner—opening cans.

None of the gypsy wanderers liked Ma and Pa

campgrounds. They preferred scenic state parks where they could build a campfire. They liked to stop early to gather firewood, before other campers depleted the scarce supply. Bertie always said, "I'll buy some." Dorothy thought scouting for wood was half the fun; she seemed to have a "nose for wood," always finding some.

Columbia River Gorge in the Cascade Range was famous for its numerous volcanoes, all thankfully asleep at the time. The north side of the canyon wall was Washington State and the south, Oregon. The gorge, an eighty mile geological wonder, featured seventy-seven waterfalls and they marveled at the magnificent 622 foot Multnomah Falls and four others viewed from the highway. The cement bridges were sheathed in living moss due to frequent rains and heavy mist.

Oneonta Falls was a scary place for Bertie. Unlike the other falls seen from the road, this one was in a narrow gorge. George—on waterfall overload—elected to wait while Dorothy and Bertie hiked in. After a short distance, they needed to ford the river. Dorothy wore shorts but Bertie, as always, was in a dress. The shallow crossing gave them no problems, but later the trail crossed the river again and was thigh high.

"You won't be able to cross, Mom. Do you want to wait here or go back?

"I'm not quitting now."

"But you'll get your dress wet."

"No, I won't." Bertie hoisted her dress and pulled the back hem forward through her legs, tucking it in her belt to form what looked like very short, tight harem pants. She received some amused smiles, but her system worked. Then, within a mere fifty feet of the fall, a high sheer rock wall blocked their view. The water was too deep to wade around the outcrop, even with harem pants.

They couldn't see the fall, but the water's roar was

deafening. Dorothy wasn't about to give in. Previous hikers had placed pinions in the sheer wall, but the only place for a foot was a two inch wide ledge. Dorothy said if others made it, she could too. Bertie begged her not to try.

Dorothy laughed and tried to lighten the mood. "The worst that could happen is that I'd have to swim out and freeze my butt in this icy water." Bertie wasn't amused. Dorothy handed her mother the camera in case she took a dunking. Slowly she crept across the wall face, leaning in toward the rock. Once around, she called to Bertie to swing the camera back and forth by the strap until she caught it. Taking pictures for both of them, she started back. Inching across hadn't been too difficult, but returning was a different story. Unable to find secure footing, a slow churning began to knot her stomach. Three young men waiting to come over the same precarious route she now blocked called out directions for foot placement. With her heart thumping, she made it back dry. Bertie wasn't—she was sobbing.

Rocky Mountain National Park advertised several waterfalls. The so-called road to one was steep and full of boulders and potholes. George scowled. "I am *not* driving the RV up that road, waterfall or not."

Undaunted, Bertie and Dorothy grabbed their hiking staffs. Dorothy was short-winded; her lungs hadn't developed fully because of her deformed spine, and she was puffing after only a few yards. She playfully stuck out her thumb.

Bertie's eyes widened. "What are you doing?"

"It should be safe to hitch a ride with some family driving to the falls," and a minute later, a couple offered them a ride. Gray hair probably helped.

Hiking back, they used their staves. A number of them littered the ground at most trailheads where people discarded them when leaving. They'd found one so perfect for them that Dorothy kept both with their camping equipment, ready for the next trip. Those staves saw more country than most tourists, but weren't needed at their next destination.

At Dinosaur National Park the bones were left where they were discovered instead of being assembled. The building was erected around the bones.

In Pueblo, Colorado, Bertie boarded a bus for Great Falls while Dorothy and George continued home to plan their next adventure.

Dorothy flew to Great Falls in 1979 and she and Bertie made a ghost town excursion around Montana to see Gallatin City, Frontier City, and Virginia City where Bertie doubled over with laughter when she saw a two-story outhouse; she insisted on investigating the oddity to see *how* it operated. She circled around it and deciding one wall was offset. They also visited Rimini, Art's childhood home, and spent time in Helena.

Being a cautious driver, Bertie never had an accident in her life—until Helena. She was driving and when Dorothy saw the road they wanted she blurted, "That's it, turn." The sudden directions flustered Bertie and she turned. She wasn't in the turn lane.

The accident was only a minor fender bender and there were no injuries, but Bertie felt heartsick. She loved setting goals and had wanted to say she never had an accident in her life. Now her goal was ruined. That upset her as much as the accident. Waiting for repairs, Bertie felt antsy. She retrieved a thin box from the car. Inside were the tweezers and materials to make the minuscule gift packages for her tree ornaments. She set to work. Dorothy couldn't believe it. Wrapping one-fourth inch packages was relaxing? It was for Bertie. She never had another car accident and drove into her nineties until her eyesight failed.

At seventy-five, Bertie read a brochure for a snowmobile tour in Yellowstone National Park. Her interest erupted like Old Faithful. Geysers and bubbling cauldrons steaming in the frozen air amid glistening snow would make gorgeous pictures. Remembering those tinkling-bell sleigh rides and the clippety-clop of horse hooves zooming over the crystal snow as she'd done in her youth, she signed on. But her tour was not in a snowmobile; she rode in a snow coach that held thirteen people. Unable to get a window seat, she couldn't take the pictures she wanted. Afterward, she was angry with herself for not investigating the particulars closer. That was the only trip she ever made that didn't thrill her because she allowed her bitter disappointment to outweigh any joy of the event. She liked revisiting beautiful places, but never again the park in winter.

Bertie and the ever-faithful Sylvester once again crossed the country in 1982 to visit her daughter. Bertie and Dorothy were both experiencing waterfall withdrawals and decided to dedicate a trip seeking out their obsession. Dorothy's travel hobby put more information of that sort at her fingertips than Triple A. She suggested they loop around Kentucky, Tennessee, and North Carolina where there were many waterfalls; the glorious October color would be an added bonus. Everyone hoped the weather wouldn't be too cold for camping. Sylvester didn't care—he rested snug and warm back in Florida.

Arriving in Tennessee long after dark, the trio was unable to find firewood and went to bed under pounds of blankets. George built a roaring fire in the morning and surprised Bertie and Dorothy, waking them with steaming mugs of java. Coffee in bed—in a tent—that was living.

George had built the fire, but he was unshaven. His shaving cream was frozen.

Any camping trip with Bertie required marshmallow roasting. On her first encampment with Dorothy and George, she'd unpacked long metal spikes. "Look, I bought roasting sticks." They became permanent camping gear. In the evenings, tall pine sentries guarded their secluded campsite. Crackling red and orange flames soared skyward as blue smoke lingered in the treetops. The aroma of roasted marshmallows and woodsy smoke wafted in the air as coffee royals bestowed a warm glow to their insides.

The rolling bluegrass of Kentucky enchanted the trio; miles of black fences seemed to be replacing the decades old traditional and picturesque white fences around horse barns and fields. They visited one of the many racing stables. The "Sport of Kings" seemed an accurate adage because the current owners had remodeled the expensive colonial home and stayed in it only one night in two years, according to a gossipy employee. Much to Dorothy's dismay, they learned horses that didn't win were relegated to the slaughterhouse. There was a horse cemetery and one horse rated a place of honor right in front of the home. The stone was simply marked Ribot, a horse undefeated in his lifetime.

Near Stanton, Kentucky, the trio stumbled across Natural Bridge State Park that somehow had eluded Dorothy's personal travel books and she insisted on seeing the huge arch.

"We don't have time," Bertie said, "it's too late in the day to hike a mile."

Unable to stay over, Dorothy said, "I'll go and you wait here."

Bertie snatched her hiking staff. "C'mon, we'll have to hurry."

The sun was almost down and George hiked with Bertie as Dorothy rushed ahead to discover people were allowed on top of the spectacular bridge, a rarity. She climbed to the top and took pictures for herself and Bertie who arrived in time to start back down. Almost dark on the moonless night, the trail was hazardous with many rocks. Worst of all were the small, shadowy tree roots running across the path. The descent was ultra-slow. George called out, "Watch out for the root," with Dorothy echoing the information to Bertie who always brought up the rear, setting her own pace. The caution calls were helpful, but by repeating them constantly, it tickled their funny-bones, and they giggled all the way back, singing out "rocks" and "roots."

Back in Shalimar, Bertie and Dorothy told everyone about the thirty-five gorgeous waterfalls they'd seen. When anyone asked George if he enjoyed the falls, he replied, "I'm only the chauffeur." George was as agreeable as Sylvester and drove them anywhere they wanted to go—as long as they stopped for *his* coffee breaks. He usually accompanied them hiking, but if a museum, boat trip, garden or such was the goal, he often preferred to wait for them.

CHAPTER 44

Bertie never wanted to travel outside the U.S.A., but when Dorothy invited her to accompany them to Scandinavia in 1983, it was a different story—Norway advertised hundreds of waterfalls. Strangely, this time Harry didn't want her to go. He whined, "You'll be gone five whole weeks." She'd already made many five-week trips with his blessing, so his complaint bewildered her.

"This is a chance of a lifetime. I'm going." She got her passport.

A few days before departure, Harry told Bertie, "I don't feel well."

"Do you want me to make you a doctor appointment?"

"No, I'm not really sick, I just don't feel good."

Every time Bertie mentioned the trip, Harry wasn't feeling well, but still refused to go to the doctor. Dorothy told Bertie if he wasn't ill, she should go. In the end, her guilt complex wouldn't let her abandon him if he was ill. When the day arrived that it was too late to make the trip, Harry felt fine again.

Bertie was furious. She never forgave him; especially when Dorothy's magnificent postcards arrived. She regretted the lost trip the rest of her life. In her nineties, she told Dorothy, "It was the second biggest mistake of my life."

At seventy-seven, Bertie was still devoted to making ornaments when Dorothy and George spent the 1983 holidays with her. Bertie complained, "I've done so many designs, I can't think of a new one for next year."

That evening they went to a Christmas party at the Senior Citizens Club where wine was served in little plastic glasses. When Dorothy helped clear the dishes after dinner, she held aloft one of those glasses. "Could you make an ornament from this?"

Bertie's eyes brightened. "That's it."

Dorothy hurried to collect the rest of the glasses before they were thrown out. The first plastic domed ornament off Bertie's assembly line went to Dorothy.

The next year, a dreadful incident left Bertie panic stricken. Thieves broke into her apartment and robbed her. Fortunately, she wasn't home, but the substantial cash she kept in her apartment was. She hid it, earmarked for different funds, in various places of her desk. The police felt it an inside job because the robber smashed the door, went to her desk, grabbed all the money from different hiding places and fled taking nothing else. The police did lift fingerprints but the culprit didn't yet have a record. Her nerves were shattered for weeks. Relatives and tenants had been the only people inside her apartment and she couldn't understand how any of them would betray her that way. Later, she felt she knew who the thief was. Earl's stepson and a friend had visited her a week before the robbery. For some reason she'd gone to the desk for change—they saw her hidden stashes. The timing was right, and she was sure one of them made a return trip to *visit* her money.

307

Bertie flew to visit Dorothy and George in 1985. The three of them spent five days seeing Busch Gardens and Disney World. Mother and daughter again rode the little boats through Disney's *"It's a Small World"* twice as they had at the New York City World's Fair twenty-eight years earlier. Once was never enough—they couldn't get that damn song out of their heads.

Busch Gardens with its beautiful flower beds and vast rolling lawns enchanted them, and they loved the new suspended monorail that carried them high above the animals in their natural habitat. They didn't utilize their customary campfire and marshmallow ritual—the motels would not have appreciated it.

Dorothy called Bertie a few months after she got home. "We bought an RV." She could almost hear Bertie gasp. The pre-owned twenty-three foot motor home slept three. Dorothy and George always enjoyed taking Bertie when they traveled because she was such fun and game for anything. Now, everyone waited for Dorothy's coming retirement.

But Bertie retired first. She quit calling professionally at age eighty. Two weeks later, the Senior Citizens Club asked her to call for them once a week. She couldn't resist; thus her retirement ended almost before it began.

Aging never troubled Bertie. At eighty, she looked sixty and her wrinkles didn't bother her. Her dark hair had so little gray, she was often accused of dying it, but she never did. She'd shrunk a few inches and developed an osteoporosis hump but it didn't cause her pain. She fell several times, but never broke bones. Still active, she danced often, loved living alone, spent hours in her craft shop, took no medicine, and was still blessed with flawless health. She told Dorothy, "I'm enjoying my senior years far more than I ever dreamed possible. I never believed I could have so much fun in old age." But those joyous times were about to end.

Bertie's sister, Charlotte, moved to town. Widowed in 1986, she seemed to believe Bertie should take care of her, and "Little Mother" couldn't say no. Charlotte was lonely and demanded much of her sister. She didn't drive and expected Bertie to drive her anywhere she wanted to go. She had macular degeneration and was a hypochondriac and expected Bertie to drive her to doctors and wait to drive her home. At first she was glad to help, but the demands grew so great she began to resent the hours away from her craftwork.

Taking Charlotte to the eye doctor once, she told the doctor she also had macular degeneration. He checked her eyes and said, "No, you don't." Bertie knew better—she recognized the same symptoms she'd read in the literature given to her to care for Charlotte. She got the disease three years later and all four sisters would also go blind. Bertie badly needed knee replacements. Dorothy tried to convince her to have the surgery, but Bertie refused because of the six-month recuperation for each knee. "I don't want to waste that much time. I treat it myself with ultrasound and it helps." It didn't. But her knees were the least of her problems—she couldn't say no to Charlotte. She looked forward to the coming getaway.

Dorothy and George made two short trips in their RV to experience the home on wheels lifestyle. Then ready for adventure in Alaska, Dorothy's last goal was in sight. Bertie had seen only the states prime fishing streams with Charlotte and her husband, and she was eager to go again.

In the spring of 1987, Dorothy and George arrived in Great Falls to pick up Bertie. At Prince Rupert, British Columbia, they took the ferry through the Southwest

Passage, the 500 mile archipelago with a thousand plus islands. The islands—covered in old-growth temperate rainforests—were beautiful and they stayed one day each at Ketchikan, Petersburg, and Wrangell. Originally, they planned to take the ferry to Skagway, but debarked in Haines after studying the map. They had showered aboard the ferry, but afterward, cleanliness became a problem. The RV had a shower, but with a six-gallon hot water tank, dumping stations few and far between, three people couldn't use it. Dirty clothes were another pressing urgency and while stopped at a laundromat, they discovered that coin laundries also had, for a price, hot showers. From then on, they looked and found laundromats everywhere. In between cities, it was back to spit baths.

Road conditions in Alaska and Canada depended on the phase of highway construction. Most roads were in some stage of disrepair due to frost heaves and repairs could be done only in summer. Roads with boulders required dropping speed to a galloping three miles per hour. RVs that roared over those roads at a speed of sixty wondered why their cabinets broke loose from the walls. Others told equally horrible tales, like their floor flooding. Many travelers carried extra spare tires for those lonely stretches of road. Rather than sacrifice precious space to tires, Dorothy and George gambled. He drove ultra-slow over any construction—most of Alaska and Canada.

Delighted to find that overnight stops were legal anywhere they could park eight feet off the highway, they stopped whenever tired. The Forest Service didn't have outhouses at campgrounds so travelers were no better off using them. The trio accepted the hospitality of a gravel pit one night; and later, another RV joined them.

In Valdez, they watched the heart-wrenching film of

the 1964 earthquake carnage. The 9.2 quake had registered as the largest tremor ever in North America, and the second largest in the world. The tremendous jolts raised the land east of Kodiak thirty feet and dropped the Portage area eight feet. Now it looked pretty.

Denali National Park was a thrill, but disappointing in that they saw few animals, the only bear a block away. The scenery, however, was worth the tail-jarring, 100-mile bus ride to Mount McKinley. No private cars were allowed, but the bus let people off and picked them up anywhere along the route. Clouds covered the majestic mountaintop ninety-five percent of the time. They saw the peak—not from the bus ride, but from their campground late that day. They didn't see many animals; however, millions of the *state bird*—mosquitoes—clouded the sky.

Bertie and Dorothy took a boat tour on the Kenai Fjords and saw otter, mountain goats, and birds. Standing at the rail, a whale flapped its huge tail right under Dorothy's nose, startling her into a loud shriek that in turn made everyone else scream. They never saw another whale.

The famous signposts at Watson Lake, Yukon, captivated Dorothy. A homesick GI working on the Alcan Highway had posted the first sign in 1932. Soon, other GIs added signs and tourists continued the trend, creating a mock forest. More than 100 wood poles graced the skyline. Each twenty-foot post was filled with signs from all over the country. Some were "borrowed" highway signs; others were hand carved, painted, and brought from home. Hammer, nails, ladder, and posts were furnished by The Chamber of Commerce, but unprepared tourists were left to their own devices in finding sign-making material. The imagination shown by spur-of-the-moment sign posters was fascinating: a rock on the ground from Grant Stone, names painted on antlers, foil plates, a cowboy hat, kettles, lids, and a toilet seat from Flushing, New York. New posts were added as needed. Signs were never removed unless they become unreadable or fell off.

Dorothy said, "We cannot leave without putting up a sign from Shalimar." But what to make it from that would not fade, rust, or break in the wicked Alaskan weather? A few seconds of thought and a lightbulb moment beamed. Dorothy said, "Let's go to the hardware store." There, she bought a small piece of aluminum sheeting. An hour's worth of nail pounding produced a sign with nail-hole letters that would remain readable forever. Back home, they told everyone planning an Alaska trip to take a sign with them—discarded highway junk was scarce.

Not wanting to retrace their ferry trip, the trio faced a decision. Should they take the Alaska-Canada Highway or the new Cassiar Highway home? Everyone they asked said the road *they took* was the worst. One man filling his gas tank was so disgusted with the horrendous Cassiar that he was returning home over the same terrible road he'd just traveled without even reaching Alaska, his destination. Others told equally horrible tales about the Alcan, and construction crews were working both highways. Some people felt the Cassiar might be a bit prettier, but it had the added hazard of logging trucks breaking windshields.

After a family pow-wow, the trio determined if both roads were equally bad, they would take the slightly prettier way. To avoid a broken windshield they drove only after 5:00 p.m. when the logging trucks quit for the day, but that meant they didn't see much of the slightly prettier scenery.

Most people believe a person can't drive to Alaska's Southwest Passage. This is not true. Just north of Prince Rupert, British Columbia, Highway 37 branches off to Steward and then Hyder, Alaska, without so much as a fence or crossing guard at the border. Neither country believed it matters—once you drive to tiny Hyder, you can drive nowhere else but back to Canada.

Back in Montana, Dorothy and George were relieved their RV made the seventy-eight day trip without a broken windshield or ruined tire. Bertie beamed. "I sure saw a lot more of Alaska than I did on my first trip." That was always true of any return trip she made with Dorothy and George.

After the Alaska trip, Bertie made many trips in the RV with Dorothy and George whenever their route included pretty scenery. She boarded a bus, train, or plane to meet them somewhere on their way. At the end of the vacation, she went home the same way.

CHAPTER 45

Still a kid at heart when it came to Christmas, Bertie went all out decorating her apartment. The village she started in 1928 ballooned and grew every year until she had more than two dozen little houses. From the first year she began a new tradition: "adding at least one new thing every year." It might be only a tiny clay bird, but one thing was added. Styles changed over the years, and the stores didn't have anything she could use. That didn't deter her—she made things: leafless trees, two-seater outhouses and a cardboard sleigh. She created miniature decorated Christmas trees with ornaments for the church and town square. The village covered a fourth of her living room floor, and she put it up every year until age ninety-nine, needing assistance only the last few years.

The *Great Falls Tribune* ran an article with pictures about her village in 1964. Again in December 1986, the entire front page of the Parade section was devoted to her hobby. The village would later grace the Havre paper in 2003, and again in Florida at Dorothy's home in 2011. Bertie's name and face was no stranger to *Tribune* readers as there were many other articles about her calling, talking about the early days of square dancing, showing off a homemade square dance costume, and two of her assistant cashier duties at the pari-mutuels.

Dorothy and George decided to meander in Michigan, known for its many waterfalls. Bertie took the train to Kalamazoo in 1987. Dorothy and George arrived two days early because they didn't want to risk breaking down somewhere and Bertie arriving before them. They passed time at an RV sales lot and did some daydreaming. They loved an Escaper RV, but their old RV suited them fine.

Elkhart, Indiana, was the RV manufacturing center of the country with several factories headquartered there. At the Sport Coach plant they took a tour and then paid to have a newly invented air-leak test done on their RV even though George had re-caulked the seams before the trip. The report was appalling. They only thought their RV survived Alaska's hellish roads unscathed. The test confirmed the walls were pulling away from the roof and would need extensive repair sometime in the future.

Their thoughts turned to the Escaper they liked. When Bertie arrived they returned to look at it again. Bertie agreed it would suit their purposes beautifully—it slept three. They held a pow-wow and concluded it was time to trade. With the decision made, they were crestfallen to learn the loan paperwork would take five days. The dealer saw their anxiety and suggested they tour in their old RV and return in five days. They did.

When they returned, Bertie helped transfer everything to the new RV and to shop for new accessories. Dorothy bought a Michigan grid map because it listed the state's waterfalls, all 200. Routes were somewhat planned around falls, but they mostly rambled wherever their curiosity took them. Driving out of the way to see one fall, Bertie roared with laughter when she saw the seventy-five-foot wide fall that was a mere fifteen inches high.

Hiking out from Minnehaha Falls in Minneapolis, their usual pattern was in progress: George leading, Dorothy sandwiched in the middle and Bertie in the rear, setting her own pace. George, a big tease, called back to Bertie. "C'mon Poke-a-han-tus—let's get moving," putting strong emphasis on the "poke."

Bertie laughed. "I'll get there eventually."

A short time later, George, smug with his little joke, said, "Minnehaha isn't doing much better than Poke-a-han-tus."

The biggest laugh came moments later when Dorothy sang out "Poke-a-han-tus and Minnehaha are right behind you, Chief Shitting Bull."

When Mikie, their Pomeranian, joined the family, he too received an Indian sobriquet and became "Little Fuzz in the Butt." They had fun using the names when traveling, except Dorothy. A couple they met on an earlier camping trip had given her a more appropriate one. Dorothy had highlighted a road atlas with every route she and George had driven since the day they married thirty-five years earlier. The couple was so impressed with her map and the stories of their hikes to waterfalls that they named her, "Falling Water Walks the Earth Mapping Woman."

The explorers zigzagged around Michigan and decided to return south by way of Wisconsin. At the Wisconsin Dells, Dorothy and Bertie took a scenic boat tour that left in the cool morning hours. Soon, the heat of the day and sun's reflection began overwhelming Bertie. Landing two hours later, they rushed to an RV park to get her into air conditioning, planning to continue the trip afterward. The next day Bertie wanted to go home and boarded a flight two days later.

Back in Florida, Dorothy received a pleasant surprise. The couple who gave Dorothy her Indian name wrote to the *Northwest Florida Daily News* telling them about the adventurous Wilsons. The newspaper called and a reporter interviewed Falling Water Walks the Earth Mapping Woman for an article and picture. Since birth, marriage, and death notices were the only time Dorothy ever expected her name to be in the newspaper, she was delighted with the article and sent one to Bertie, saying, "Andy Warhol *was* right—I got my fifteen minutes of fame."

Charlotte, who was nearly blind from macular degeneration, was also diagnosed with Alzheimer's. No medication existed, and the always demanding, self-centered Charlotte became unbearable. Bertie kept reminding herself, "It isn't her fault—she's sick."

In addition to driving Charlotte everywhere, Bertie visited her often because her sister had become afraid to be alone. She spent hours on the phone trying to comfort her sister who called six or seven times a day. She also spent hours at her apartment trying to ease Charlotte's fright. It became a daily routine. Dorothy suggested she get caller ID and not answer the phone if it was Charlotte.

Bertie's replied, "But it might *really* be important that time."

One frosty February night in 1989, Harry, in his mid-nineties, died sitting in his easy chair. Bertie found him the next morning looking so peaceful she thought he was asleep.

Bertie always felt like Harry's wife, so in her heart she was now a widow for the third time.

Already an experienced grieving widow, she was again devastated. But this time, she didn't suffer the heavy burden of guilt she did with both Arlo and Art. Now the cemeteries held three graves for her to decorate on Memorial Day. In her grief, she remembered earlier events—the two Indian women had been right—she did have three husbands.

Harry was buried in the Veterans' Memorial at Highland Cemetery. After the graveside service, Bertie went to view the headstone. She stepped back in utter shock. The government had made a terrible mistake. The tombstone read "Corporal Harry Craig." Everyone in town knew Harry served in two wars as a major; he'd told people stories about it for years. Harry's niece was there, but she made no comment. Bertie didn't want to cause her more grief, so she didn't say anything. Later, when his niece visited, she asked about the error. The niece said as far as she knew he was a corporal. Then Bertie remembered a photograph Harry had shown her of him in uniform. When she asked why he wore corporal stripes, he replied, "The picture was taken before I made major."

Was Harry a braggart who liked to embellish his war years or did the government make a mistake? It seemed extraordinary to have served in two world wars and never been more than a corporal. His niece didn't appear interested in resolving the intriguing mystery—so forevermore, there lies Corporal Harry Craig.

After Harry's death, Bertie turned down many chances to date. Friends kept suggesting she marry again. Her reply: "I've killed off enough men. If I don't date anyone, I won't be *pressured* into a relationship." Now she was responsible only for herself, able to do what she wanted when she wanted and she'd not enjoyed that option since her single days in Great Falls. Going to dances alone was fun, and she always received many invitations to dance. Due to her knee pain, she couldn't dance all night, but she still enjoyed life.

In the spring of 1989, Bertie declined to wander around Missouri with Dorothy and George. While the state was pretty, it didn't have mountains or waterfalls. Dorothy called her worrying mother to check in every few days when traveling. A week into their trip, Bertie became highly nervous—those damned psychic *feelings* were haunting her again. The *feelings* had become fewer in her senior years, but this episode was potent. She knew something was wrong. She didn't know what. Too upset to work on her ornaments, she almost wore a path in the carpet from pacing. When Dorothy finally called, Bertie didn't even say "hello," she blurted, "What happened? I know something is wrong." George had suffered a heart attack. Dorothy had waited until she knew he would survive before calling. She didn't want to worry Bertie. Unfortunately, Dorothy's consideration caused her mother many days of anxiety.

In 1989, Montana celebrated its centennial with a gigantic sixty-mile cattle drive from Roundup to Billings with 2,800 cattle and more than 200 covered wagons. Three thousand modern-day cowboys and cowgirls, from age five to 102, joined the drive including astronaut Jim Adamson, television magnet Ted Turner, and Bertie's Brother Floyd. Events lasted for weeks.

Bertie was overjoyed to be selected Grand Marshall for the city's festival ball. Glowing with pride, she promenaded in front of the procession wearing her Grand Marshall, white-satin banner, emblazoned across her chest in glittering blue.

Following the big parade, Courtnages from all over attended a reunion hosted by Chris and Kay. They had mailed invitations to any known Courtnage, sixty-nine in all. Sixty-seven came from eleven states. The *Tribune* ran an article and Dorothy wrote the story for the *Fort Benton River Press*. Someone gave her a picture of her great grandfather, John, the only Courtnage to immigrate to the U.S.A. Bertie won a prize as the oldest attendee and Dorothy for traveling the most miles for the event.

Soon after the reunion, the Courtnages suffered the loss of two family members, Grace and Harold. Bertie took the death of any Courtnage as mournfully as she would her family, but she felt a keen loss with Grace's passing because she'd saved Earl's life when he swallowed a toy jack. Bertie now had a fifty-three-year-old son only because of Grace and God.

CHAPTER 46

Bertie made many fishing trips with both her children when they were young; but as a teenager, Dorothy quit going. Later, she was working when Earl traveled with their parents in the Cree Coach. When Dorothy retired and Bertie traveled with her, Earl was working so Bertie and her children never enjoyed a vacation together. That changed in 1990 when Bertie enjoyed her first adventure with both her children.

Dorothy and George drove their RV to Page, Arizona, to meet Bertie and Earl. Lake Powell was one of the most scenic and colorful lakes in the world, as well as one of the most controversial, because hundreds of multicolored box canyons and gorges favored by hikers disappeared forever when it was built thirty years earlier. They rented a houseboat for a fun-filled week. The evening before departure, Earl, Dorothy, and George drove to the marina to look around. There was only one kind of wood on the lake—nonexistent. Evening campfires were a must, and Dorothy seethed at the exorbitant price the marina charged for firewood.

Driving back to the RV and Bertie, Dorothy, who was

in the backseat shrieked, "Stop!"

Earl spiked the brakes. "What's the matter?"

"I saw a two by four."

"What?" both males howled. "You scared us to death for a board."

"Well," she purred, "We can take it along for firewood."

Hearts beating normally again, they snatched the board and then searched for other wood, finding a healthy supply around the lake.

The next morning, the eager boaters were at the marina early to take full advantage of the day. Watching them load their enormous pile of firewood, the wood attendant looked miffed—he saw dollar signs floating past him. With cheerful anticipation, the foursome motored into the deep blue water amid glorious red, orange, and pink canyons aglow in the morning sun.

Earl owned a boat, so Captain Earl did the piloting when navigating the pinpoint-tight fjords and Captain George relieved him on open water. Bertie kept her Mae West life preserver nearby. The boat slept six so with only four aboard it felt quite roomy. Bertie and Dorothy prepared quick, easy meals in the tiny galley so as not to miss anything. Each night, they beached the houseboat and made a campfire, so the wood lasted only three days. Dorothy and Earl went on a wood scouting party that everyone felt would be fruitless. Even Dorothy, who rarely failed to find wood, doubted a successful search since there wasn't as much as a toothpick in sight. She scrambled up a high dune to look around. At the top she called for Earl to come help carry the flotsam she found, part of an old building that flooded when the dam was completed.

Perfect weather blessed the trip, but they were disappointed they saw only a minute section of the huge lake. Afterward, Earl drove back to Montana, and Bertie went with Dorothy and George to tour Zion and Bryce State Parks. She'd already seen them, but was eager to see the colorful honeycomb pinnacles again. And Arches National Park was unique no matter how many times you saw it because they were still discovering new arches every year. Dorothy wanted to hike a particular one-way, two mile trail and suggested Bertie wait in the RV. She, of course, refused to stay behind. She did well and George and Dorothy only needed to push her up one rock face. All along the trail everyone they met stopped her. "You're doing great," and "I hope I can do that good when I'm your age." Then they were shocked to learn she was eighty-four.

Bertie always wore a pair of her brother-in-law's old tennis shoes. No amount of coaxing could convince her to buy proper hiking boots. "These are comfortable," she said. They were not a proper fit and around the three-mile mark she had blisters and began hobbling. For the first time she said, "I don't think I can make it." They stopped often to rest, but that didn't help her tormented feet; the last mile was turtle-paced slow. If she had known the outcome in advance, she would have gone anyway—that was just how "I want to see it" stubborn Bertie was.

Bertie hadn't seen a doctor in years, but due to her age, she decided to have a checkup. She went to a partially retired doctor and thought him most unusual. He spent most of the time asking about her lifestyle. When she prepared to leave, he made her another appointment.

"Why? I feel fine."

"I'm studying you." He often asked her to come in to talk to him without charge—and spoiling her for future doctors.

When he retired, Bertie had difficulty finding another

doctor who "would talk to her." At last, she selected a doctor at the Great Falls Clinic. She went to her first appointment with some trepidation. The doctor sat reviewing her ultra-thin medical record lying in front of him. He smiled. "You are some kind of miracle woman. You're never sick." Then his voice raised two octaves. "What? You had smallpox?"

"I definitely had the pox, but it's possible I might have told someone the wrong kind." Her parents' blended gene pool had produced one healthy family, but none as amazing as Bertie. With her incredible health she might have survived smallpox, but it's doubtful because all the members of her family wouldn't have been so lucky—it's a highly contagious disease.

Bertie had called square dances at the Senior Citizens for five years before she retired once again in 1991, ending her career the way it began—volunteering. She filled in as a substitute caller occasionally, but came down with a flu-like illness that settled in her vocal cords and she lost a bit of her fabulous calling voice. She'd thrilled dancers with her husky *allemande left* for seventy years; but now she refused to call with anything less than her usual deep booming voice and she retired completely—if you don't count the spontaneous times she burst forth in the privacy of her own living room when listening to records.

As Bertie's traveling pace slowed, she spent numerous evenings "armchair traveling" looking at thousands of her slides. Her memory soared like the bald eagles over Grand Canyon. She relished revisiting Hawaii's spectacular waterfalls and the New York City World Fair. Reliving these trips, she often laughed or dabbed a happy tear.

Bertie's nephew Walter wanted her to attend his

Oregon wedding in 1991, but at eighty-five she decided against driving, even with Sylvester. She wouldn't have missed the wedding for anything; she and her sister, Mamie, took the bus. When they arrived, Bertie thought the house needed floral decorations. She hitched a ride to town, bought some crepe paper, and made a beautiful floral centerpiece. The bride and groom loved her contribution.

Back home again, Bertie needed to solve a serious problem. As usual, she found her cherished garden a helpful place for solemn thought. The sun winked in and out of billowing clouds providing a bit of shade as she worked. A fusillade of excuses ricocheted through her mind. She knew what her decision must be. She did not want to do it. Wearily, she climbed the back stairway to her second floor apartment putting her gloves and dirty shoes in the red Belgium cast-iron pot by the door. Walking inside, pink, blue, and green shafts of light danced about her kitchen as sun glinted off the crystal prisms hanging in the window. The room, alive with cheery color, contrasted the deep blackness she felt in her heart.

Once she'd made the decision not to drive to Oregon, she knew her days of long-distance driving were over. Resigned, she went to the closet and brought out a black plastic bag and laid it on the kitchen table. She untied the sack and withdrew Sylvester. His shiny black button eyes were fixed on her—did he wonder if another exciting trip lay on the horizon.

Bertie stared at him remembering what a faithful traveling companion he'd been. Gazing fondly at his face, vivid memories of their trips together flooded her mind. Whether lying in the car floor at night or hanging on a peg at Dorothy's house, he was always content just to be with her. Slowly she began to dismantle him splashing his face with tears. When only the head was left, she kissed him tenderly and pulled the stuffing from the pillowcase throwing it in the trash. Sylvester was dead! At least she did not have to bury the fourth man in her life.

Losing Sylvester didn't mean the end of traveling. One location famous for waterfalls still remained on Bertie's "to-see" list, and she *happened* to mention it to Dorothy. Her mother's recommendation was good enough for Dorothy, and she and George drove north while an excited Bertie boarded the train for La Crosse, Wisconsin. Bertie preferred train travel to flying because she could see the countryside. She intended to splurge—after all she was eighty-seven—and she booked a roomette. Delighted with the good food and comfortable sleeping arrangement, she wished she could have afforded these accommodations earlier. Afraid she might miss something, she never read, napped, or went to the lounge car; she sat at her window captivated by the passing panorama whether it was pretty scenery or cattle in a pasture. She was in high spirits because the North Shore was the last big waterfall area on her "wish list." The days were cheery and exciting. At night with nothing to look at, each clack of the train wheels reverberated with memories—Ar—lo, Ar—lo, Ar—lo.

Waterfall lovers are not disappointed by Minnesota's North Shore, Duluth to the Ontario border. Along the route the land drops 300 feet. Waterfalls plunge into Lake Superior every fifteen or twenty miles. Each one was a state park; some days they drove only twenty miles. The drive was a great choice to leave until later in life, because Bertie could see the falls without hiking.

At the Canadian border, Navigator Dorothy, found two falls on the map in Canada. "We might as well see them before turning west—we're so close."

"We can't," George said, "we've got a gun, and you

can't take a gun into Canada."

"Oh, there must be a way."

"I am not hiding a gun," George bellowed.

"I didn't mean that. There must be another way; surely other people who want to cross the border have guns too."

Questioning a local, she located a business that held guns for people until their return. Problem solved, they were off.

The first fall wasn't special and seemed farther than the map legend showed. Dorothy began to regret the added miles, but later, everyone was glad they didn't turn back. Kakabeka Falls near Thunder Bay was awesome. The wide, 120-foot-high falls subsisted of hundreds of tiny falls all making one dramatic, giant waterfall. At the end of the trip, Bertie once again boarded the train at St. Cloud and returned to Montana.

Back home, she resumed working on her designer ornaments. She still went to the Senior Citizen dances and enjoyed herself, but one knee was becoming quite painful and she usually danced only two or three times. Then she went home to dream about the next RV travel adventure—*that* she could still do.

Dorothy and George drove to Great Falls in 1994 *en route* to Spokane for a reunion of her school girlfriends, two of whom she'd known since first grade. Planning to tour the Black Hills in South Dakota on the way, Dorothy invited Bertie to join them. She began packing. They were to meet in Rapid City. Mother Nature decided otherwise. A vicious late storm closed all the roads. Dorothy called Bertie. "Don't unpack; we'll go somewhere else." They altered their route, but at Yellowstone National Park the falling snow was blinding. Dorothy asked the entrance ranger. "Can we get through?"

"Yes, but do not stop!" That was scary, and they

didn't stop anywhere except when a buffalo blocked the road. The beast was driven off by seven-pound, Killer-Mikie's vicious bark at the window.

Once in Great Falls, Dorothy suggested Bertie accompany them to Spokane. "You can join the reunion and then we can tour northern Idaho and points south; you can take the bus back home wherever you want." Bertie had known all the ladies as children, and she enjoyed the day.

Driving north in Idaho, they saw the world's largest log home and some beautiful waterfalls, but as they headed south Bertie began to feel ill. Someone at the reunion suffered a cold, and she believed she caught the bug. She wanted to go home. Dorothy and George wanted to drive her back, but she insisted they put her on the bus as planned. Bertie boarded the bus in Missoula, still claiming it was only a cold.

Dorothy called the next day and learned Bertie had the flu. She was so ill she needed help off the bus and into a taxi. Dorothy wanted to go back because they were still in Montana, but Bertie said, "No, I'll be fine; keep going." Worried, Dorothy talked to a nurse about seniors with the flu and called her mother again. Bertie actually *promised* to follow the nurse's advice completely, but the only reason she *promised* was to keep Dorothy from returning. It was the only time Dorothy remembered Bertie making a vow of any kind.

Dorothy knew Bertie's friend upstairs would bring her food, and she knew her mother always took good care of herself when ill. They drove on reluctantly and checked on her twice daily by phone. Four days later, she was better.

CHAPTER 47

Dorothy and George drove to Montana in 1995 to collect Bertie and mosey around Washington State. It was a seventy-mile trip. At 1:00 p.m. near Lincoln, Montana, two deer jumped out of a ditch and bolted onto the highway right in front of the RV. George left fifty-five feet of skid marks before striking the doe. Somehow, the animal became wedged in the wheel well and was pulling the RV off the road. The deer flopped around with each tire revolution. George pulled at the wheel, but could not keep the vehicle on the highway. He shouted, "Hang on, we're going over." Terrified, they held on for what felt like minutes, but was only seconds. Incredibly, twenty-five feet of soft dirt and dead grass on the bank brought them to a stop still upright, but waggling like a metronome. "Mom," George yelled, "are you okay?" Bertie sat behind Dorothy, and all the dishes in the cabinet across from her had flown out and hit her in the head. Ghostly pale and shaking, she was unhurt.

Now, the ashen family sat rigid, too terrified to move in the wobbling RV. If the weight was removed from the driver's side, they feared the vehicle would roll over. If

Dorothy got out, the vehicle might roll on top of her. Agonizing seconds passed—they had to do something. Finally, George slowly eased out the driver's side—they were still upright. Then Dorothy crept out the driver's door, and Bertie inched her way up front as everyone held their breath. Unbelievably, she too made it out with the RV wobbling but still upright.

Dorothy flagged down the next vehicle. The man drove her into Lincoln to get a tow truck and then took her back. He took pictures and stayed to comfort Bertie and Dorothy who were visibly shaken. When the tow truck driver arrived, he refused to move the RV until the police saw it. He said it was against the law. "No other vehicle is involved. The RV won't stay upright long enough for the police to get here," Dorothy wailed. He still refused. Every time a vehicle passed, they all prayed as the RV tottered with each windblast. The two front tires were cocked sideways and Dorothy told the driver, "Please call for another tow truck to keep the vehicle from rolling over once you start pulling it back onto the road."

"Don't worry," the driver said, "it'll be fine." The shaken trio waited an agonizing hour, then two, and then three for the police, who were in Helena sixty-five-miles away.

When the policeman arrived, he merely glanced at the vehicle, and in seconds the tow truck driver started to work. Everyone held their breath as the driver slowly began towing. *After* he pulled the RV back onto the road, the driver wiped his forehead. "I never believed I could do it—I thought sure it would go over." Dorothy had to be restrained.

Anxiety still plagued Bertie, and Dorothy said, "Never mind, Mom, when we get the vehicle repaired, we'll leave again." What Dorothy thought would take only days turned into weeks. Because the refrigerator was not level for hours of waiting and towing, it was ruined. The replacement didn't arrive for three weeks. Dorothy and George had been gone five weeks and they couldn't extend. They went home.

CHAPTER 48

The Clawiter farm still held many old family items, and Max wanted to start a museum. In the late 1980s he had put 40,000 dollars in escrow to create one. Advertising for donations in the local paper, he received a gratifying response. Volunteers worked tirelessly to create the Big Sandy Historical Museum housed in the old railway depot. Max donated enough items to have a Clawiter room in one of the best museums of rural life in the state. The family's potbelly stove, toy hay wagon, cream separator, carpet sweeper, sausage maker, cobbler's sewing machine, and much more found a new home. Among the treasures was the lower half of Dorothy's ill-fated organ. Visiting the first time, tears rolled down Bertie's face when she recognized the remnants of her childhood.

In the 1990s, large corporations began buying the small farms around Big Sandy. Each farm sold took the purchasing power of another family from the town's economy. By the early 2000s, the population dwindled to about 500, as it had been when Max Sr. first laid eyes on what would become the Clawiter farm. Business establishments were closing, and there were over forty houses for sale. The town, like many farming communities, was dying.

Five years later, Max Jr. wanted to retire. He didn't have children, so like others he sold to a conglomerate, the only ones buying acreage. Max Sr. could never have imagined what would become of his 1912, 160 acre relinquishment. He later bought a quarter of a section, and when her mother died, Della inherited 500 dollars and bought a quarter of a section. Max Jr. bought more land during the war years and traded bordering property at least twice. The acreage fluctuated but the eventual sale encompassed more than 3,000 acres.

Although her childhood was unhappy, Bertie still felt sad when the old home place sold. Images of poverty and drudgery inundated her memory, but still she felt proud of her contribution that gave birth to the farm. It wasn't a dynasty, but it was the family home for eighty-two years. Working the land brought forth birth, life, and death for the Clawiters. Sun, rains, joys, sorrow, all blossomed for nearly a century. But they didn't own the land. They, like the Indians, believed they were only caretakers of the soil; now it passed to another custodian for birth, life and death, and on into eternity.

Years of caring for Charlotte took their toll. Dorothy began recognizing signs of depression when she called Bertie. She was horrified one day when Bertie barked, "I want to die! Some days I don't do anything but sit in this damn chair and rock all day. I might as well be dead."

Dorothy begged her mother to go to the doctor for medication. "Promise me you'll go."

Bertie said, "Yes, I'll go—but you know I never make promises." She never went. The pattern continued. Then it changed. Shivers radiated down Dorothy's spine like electric shocks when Bertie spat out, "I'm going to kill myself. Life isn't worth living." Dorothy and George left for Montana.

To restore Bertie's peace of mind, Dorothy and Earl hired a companion for Charlotte. The young woman worked from 10:00 a.m. until 7:00 p.m. Charlotte was content. But as dependable as sunset, at 7:05 each evening, Charlotte called crying and asking Bertie to come over. Floyd wouldn't help—he considered his sister a nuisance and wanted to put her in a nursing home. Bertie couldn't bear that because Charlotte cared for her apartment and herself, didn't wander and still recognized everybody. She was only terrified of being alone.

Bouncy and vivacious Bertie became an emotional wreck. Her stress grew and expanded to clinical depression. "Little Mother" couldn't turn her back on her sister. Dorothy continued to urge Bertie to see a doctor for medication. Her answer: "I've never taken medicine in my life, and I'm not starting now." She became so disturbed that Dorothy and Earl feared the worst. Something must be done. But what? The solution was surprising—a change of scenery.

When the Anaconda Smelter closed a few years earlier and Earl lost his job, he moved to Havre. It now provided the solution for Bertie's Charlotte problem. Earl took Charlotte to live with him in 1996. But seventeen months later when they were walking in the mall, she suddenly started screaming. "Somebody help me. I don't know this man; he's kidnapping me." She shrieked and clawed at Earl trying to get away. The police arrived and Earl had to explain the embarrassing situation. He realized he could no longer care for her and Charlotte was moved to Missouri Manor in Great Falls. He'd kept her away from Bertie and out of the nursing home for a year-and-a-half.

Charlotte didn't recognize Bertie, but she still visited

often. She wanted the staff to know Charlotte's family checked on her. When Charlotte died in 1998, Bertie took it hard and told Dorothy, "I should have done more for her."

Bertie didn't tell Dorothy for many years, but during that appalling decade of caring for Charlotte, Bertie *did* reach the breaking point. She had made up her mind life was not worth living. Taking a heavy blanket from the closet, she folded it in thirds and laid it in the center of the living room floor so the blood wouldn't ruin the landlord's carpet. Unfolding the paper on a new razor blade, she stared at the shiny blade cradled in her hand. The glistening blade seemed to beckon—I am the answer. She centered herself on the blanket, took the blade, and located a vein for the fatal cut. The doorbell rang. Furious at being interrupted, she bolted up and flung open the door.

Arlo's brother Chris said, "I came by to see how you're doing."

Bertie stared at him wild-eyed and then burst into tears. Through gasping sobs she told him her plan.

Chris paled. "You can't do that, Bertie. God put you in this world for a purpose, and He is the one who will decide when it's time to go." He reminded her of all the nice things she'd done for everyone. "You need to stick around, other people might need you." He talked to her a long time, and at last she agreed not to attempt the desperate deed again.

Bertie later told Dorothy, "The man upstairs must have sent Chris because if he hadn't arrived at that exact moment, I would be gone."

Dorothy shuddered. Bertie was capable of the deed because of her strong will. She had spent a decade caring for her sister, ruining her own life in the process.

CHAPTER 49

May 25, 1996 was Bertie's ninetieth birthday party, an occasion that Dorothy worked on for six months. The Methodist Church provided the hall. Ninety pink, purple, blue, and white balloons with extra-long dangling ribbons floated on the high ceiling, because according to Bertie, a party wasn't a party without balloons. Her 1927 wedding dress flanked by two square dance dresses decorated one wall with greeting cards hanging from streamers on both sides. A freestanding picture frame depicted a smiling Bertie at twenty and another at ninety.

Arlo had died fifty-six years earlier, but his family still treasured Bertie. Twelve Courtnages pitched in to make refreshments, chauffeur guests, and pick up balloons and last minute ice cream; they shot video and provided background music. Lorraine Clawiter managed the guestbook. Bertie arrived wearing a bright dress of pink, white, and yellow swirls. No longer the sylph that stepped off the train seventy-seven years ago, she nevertheless had aged well. With little gray in her hair, young-looking hands and a healthy complexion with few wrinkles, she looked twenty years younger.

Earl presented her a red and pink carnation corsage, and before a surprised Bertie knew what was happening, Dorothy spun her around and pinned a long, felt tab with straight pins on the back of her dress. Bertie, thinking something was wrong with her garment, sputtered, "What's the matter?" Turning a still confused Bertie back around, Dorothy pinned a dollar bill on the front of her costume. Then all the guests swooped in, surrounding her with hugs, good wishes and pinning bills on her dress sheathed to the waist. Bertie always cried when happy, and tears streamed down her cheeks.

Dorothy's monologue began: "We are here to honor Albertine Roseline Clawiter Courtnage Moore. With a handle like that it's no wonder she is known simply as Bertie." George and Bertie's nephew spoke about their love and devotion. Earl, who was never able to express his love in words, stood at the podium and became too emotional to complete his composed speech. He left the dais halfway through.

Bertie was euphoric to see old friends she hadn't seen in years. Recollections and memories rippled through her mind like ocean swells as she flooded tissue after tissue.

Dorothy presented her mother a memory book of pictures and notes from friends and family; she would keep it on her bureau for three years. The cake came out in a blaze of glory with ninety candles. As guests ate, Bertie rose and made an impromptu speech. Still not needing a microphone, she thanked everyone for coming to help her celebrate and told them, "I never thought I'd live for ninety years, but here I am." Later, her brother Floyd played his guitar and mouth organ so ninety-five guests could dance—the harmonica holder was a gift from Bertie when he was young. Bertie and a friend were the first ones on the dance floor.

After the party, everyone swarmed around Bertie and

Dorothy, saying, "This was the best birthday party I've ever attended." Dorothy found that hilarious because Bertie, who knew about the party in advance, was uneasy knowing Dorothy had never planned anything like it before. Worried, Bertie kept saying, "You'll have to have games or something or people will only eat and go home." It was difficult for an expert organizer to let go.

After the party, Bertie felt weary. Days of anxiety about Dorothy being able to put the event together had unnerved her. But she loved her party and wanted to relive every moment when she went home. She sat in the Lazy Boy and closed her eyes, as images floated past. It was a fabulous day, but what's more, she realized what a wonderful life she'd lived. She smiled thinking of the rash promise she'd made herself as she pulled out of the Big Sandy railway station seventy-years earlier. Promising to lead a better life than the one she left behind had been an immature vow, but damned if she didn't think she'd accomplished that. She'd become a professional square dance caller against all odds, and she reached her goal of traveling in all fifty states. Her love life was a little rocky in that she couldn't keep a man long, but she "felt blessed to have found three such incredible men, each special in their own way. Arlo was the love of my life; I learned to enjoy traveling with Art, and had the most fun with Harry, dancing." Bertie felt like she'd lived well, but the shocking surprise at her party brought her the most sought—most satisfying moment of her life!

She'd been overjoyed to see so many of her old-time dancers whom she hadn't seen in years. Then she had blinked and looked again—male callers. The men had all closed ranks and turned their backs on her when she attempted to join them as a young woman. All had refused assistance of any kind and hampered her progress for years. Now they were celebrating her. Her emotions rode a roller coaster, and the sudden plunge was more than she could bear—her stomach did an *allemande* left.

Then a late arrival, a male caller Bertie had known for years, came over and hugged her. "We all hated to see you retire—you hooked me the first time I heard you." For a nanosecond, Bertie looked puzzled. Then her eyes widened. All the male callers hadn't disliked her. Some had admired her. It was all she'd ever wanted. The male callers had accepted her years ago, but none of them said anything to her nor displayed their acceptance—she never felt it in her heart. Bertie had waited a lifetime for this acknowledgement. Now, at long last, she felt accepted by her male peers and she allowed herself to revel in their tribute. As the men came up to congratulate her, she hugged each one and drenched their lapels with salty tears.

EPILOGUE

At ninety-five, Bertie still drove her beloved Karmann Ghia—without Sylvester—but her macular degeneration was worsening, both knees were bone-on-bone, all her fingers were curled with no feeling in the tips, her nervous condition had worsened so much that her stomach visibly shook when she became upset, and she had signs of dementia.

Bertie had lived at her much loved Summit apartment for thirty-one years, but she was forced out when a new owner told her Dorothy and George couldn't visit with Mikietoo, their Pomeranian that Bertie loved.

Dorothy and Earl knew Bertie needed more help. Moving her and the huge number of things she wanted to take with her across the country to Florida was impossible, so Bertie moved to Havre to live in Earl's duplex. Going through the mountain of memorabilia she had saved—some from grade school—had Bertie in tears and the three-week task was monumentally difficult for her. The actual move required a furniture van and three trips with a fully loaded pickup, Astro van and Karmann Ghia. The entire process was a six-week effort.

Dorothy visited three times a year but there were no trips. Bertie enjoyed reliving her life over and over with Dorothy, and the old "guilts" resurfaced every time: She couldn't get Arlo's begging words, "not to put him in the hospital" out of her mind; she still worried she might have blinded the man who tried to rape her; and the most common guilt, how her life would have been different if she had gone to Portland. When Dorothy pointed out that she and Earl wouldn't exist if she'd gone instead of marrying Arlo, Bertie thought a moment. "That's right. But it was still my biggest mistake." And a *new* story surprised Dorothy when Bertie said she was not afraid of dying. "I've always *known* I'd have an easy death." Her *feelings* had informed her of the event when she was young. In her nineties, as her gray cells had slowly withered and died, the *feelings* faded away like morning mist. She was delighted.

She still enjoyed life playing cards, going to the Eagles nightclub with Earl, and having a neighbor who drove her to the stores, but slowly dementia began to rob her of life's joy. Her incredible internal health was still intact with blood pressure of 128 over 70 and she took no daily medication until she was ninety-five and her dementia worsened. She never conquered her mental demons because she didn't recognize them as such or didn't know why she had them. She'd bent over backward all her life to get along with everyone because "I never want anyone to dislike me."

At ninety-nine, Bertie wanted to "ride the train *one more time*." Dorothy was visiting and she bought three tickets for Columbia Falls, where the route followed the border of Glacier Park—a two day adventure. It was only the second time she'd traveled with both her adult children.

Three months shy of 100, Dorothy and Earl were

forced to place Bertie in Cambridge Court, nursing home, formerly the Deaconess Hospital, the same building she'd given birth to her two children and where her two husbands died. Bertie was happy—she'd returned to the "big city" of her youth—her beloved Great Falls to spend the remaining years of her remarkable life. Her hundredth birthday party was small because she'd outlived six of her younger seven siblings and most of her friends.

Her indomitable light had paled as slowly as the descending sands in the proverbial hourglass, dimming and blinking out on January 15, 2009. The Lord called her home at dawn on a crisp, sunny Montana day. She had graced the earth and those lives she touched for one hundred two years, seven months, and eighteen days.

It wasn't long enough.

Feedback is essential for Indie Authors such as myself. If you've enjoyed ONE LIFE - ONE CENTURY, please leave me a review on Amazon. However, if you bought this book from the author, you must state that fact in the review or Amazon will not post it because they didn't sell the item. I would appreciate hearing from you.

ABOUT THE AUTHOR

Born in Great Falls, Montana, Dorothy Courtnage Wilson developed a passion for writing at an early age. Twenty-five years later, she married a service man stationed at

Malmstrom Air Force Base. A gypsy's life commenced as the happy couple relocated from Montana to California, Texas, Georgia, Louisiana, and Florida where she retired from the Civil Service. Her husband was never stationed abroad, so now she travels extensively.

Her interest in writing began at school with a love for poetry, which soon developed into self-pleasure writing: short stories, a novella, and a biography. Dorothy's second book THE GREEN TUNNEL is her first published work. It received such high praise that she is now publishing her first book, ONE LIFE - ONE CENTURY before starting the sequel to THE GREEN TUNNEL.

Made in the USA
Lexington, KY
23 September 2019